Troubleshooting Your Multimedia PC

John Montgomery

Addison-Wesley Publishing Company

Reading, Massachusetts • Menlo Park, California • New York

Don Mills, Ontario • Wokingham, England • Amsterdam

Bonn • Sydney • Singapore • Tokyo • Madrid • San Juan

Paris • Seoul • Milan • Mexico City • Taipei

Library of Congress Cataloging-in-Publication Data

Montgomery, John (John I.), 1967–
        Troubleshooting your multimedia PC / John Montgomery.
            p.   cm.
        Includes index.
        ISBN 0-201-48347-5
        1. Multimedia systems.   I. Title.
    QA76.575.M66   1995
    006.6—dc20   95-1577
                                                                              CIP

Sponsoring Editor: Kathleen Tibbetts
Technical Editor: Scott Naylor
Project Manager: John Fuller
Production Coordinator: Ellen Savett
Cover design: The Visual Group
Set in 11-point New Century Schoolbook by Vicki L. Hochstedler

1 2 3 4 5 6 7 8 9 -MA- 9998979695
First printing, April 1995

Addison-Wesley books are available for bulk purchases by corporations, institutions, and other organizations. For more information please contact the Corporate, Government, and Special Sales Department at (800) 238-9682.

Contents

Acknowledgments

In creating, the only hard thing's to begin;
A grass-blade's no easier to make than an oak.

—JAMES RUSSELL LOWELL, *A Fable
for Critics,* 1848

When people give advice on what to write, they usually say,
"Write about what you know." The more I write, the more I
realize that I don't know very much. So it's only with the
help of many friends that this book sits before you.

It is without doubt that I cast my first thanks to **Kathleen
Tibbetts,** my editor. By now, she must be in the prefaces
and acknowledgments of a thousand books. That's an amaz-
ing accomplishment. I have no idea how she can be so sure
that someone can write a book when that person is so completely unsure.

This book truly wouldn't be possible without the help of
Marnee Clement at Media Vision, **Benita Kenn** from
Creative Labs, and **Andrea Sausedo** from Reveal. They
loaned me hardware, software, and the ear of their technical support staffs when necessary. Also to be commended for
an opportune loan of some really interesting video capture
hardware is **Bob Hatton** from Fast Electronics. Thanks to
all of you. I also must thank **Denise Klapperich** from Dell
Computer and **Bob Margolis** from Intelligent Systems.
Everything in this book was tested on computers from these
two vendors.

Speaking of testing, **Scott Naylor** performed the technical
edit on this book. That's a fancy way of saying he caught all
my errors. At least, I hope he did. Also, **Matt Lake** and

Wendy Taylor from *PC Computing* magazine provided some insight into the multimedia market.

Woody Leonhard, master of the odd, got me into writing books, so you and I have him to bla— uh, thank for this. Buy his (and Barry Simon's) books, *CD-MOM* and *PC-MOM*. They're a hoot.

All the photography in this book was done by **Amy Johnson**, so a big THANKS goes to her, especially since she had her own book to write at the time.

Oh, and who could forget **Mom** and **Dad**? Certainly not I.

Introduction

There's a sucker born every minute.

—P. T. BARNUM

Thank goodness we got here in time. You were about to return that multimedia upgrade kit, weren't you? Thought so. Well, don't do it quite yet. First of all, it's a hassle. I mean, if you bought it at some kind of computer store you're going to have to drive/walk/bicycle/trudge over there, explain that you couldn't get it to work to some teenage clerk who will probably treat you like you're a lower life form because you couldn't install it, then fork over your credit card so they can credit it. Or you bought it from some kind of telephone order company and you're wondering not when but if they'll pick up the phone when you call and exactly what kind of welcome they'll give you when you say no, you don't want to buy something but return something.

Have no fear. We all go through the same tribulations. But always remember this:

My mantra

IT'S NOT YOUR FAULT

In fact, sit down in your living room with a cup of hot chocolate right now. Make yourself comfortable, close your eyes, and relax. Then start to chant quietly, "It's not my fault, it's not my fault." And so on. Soon a sense of peace will come over you. If that doesn't work, try shifting the blame explicitly.

There is a hoard of technical information that will support shifting the blame. For example: If adding a multimedia kit to your PC were supposed to be easy, then why do PC manufacturers lock up those cases with half a dozen screws? If it's supposed to be easy, why do none of the components that are inside your PC have instructions on them? If it's supposed to be so easy, why was the manual obviously translated from the Aramaic version of the Urdu translation of the original Greek pidgin? Tell me *that* if you can.

Plug and Play

So, as you can clearly see, it's *not* your fault that this multimedia upgrade kit won't install. It's the fault of the entire PC industry. Fortunately, some of the big guys are making moves to fix these problems by introducing a technology called Plug and Play (PnP), thereby bringing the PC roughly to the state that the Macintosh was in ten years ago. PnP will make most of this book obsolete because it makes all the tough stuff (installing all that hardware) easy. You just plug the components into your computer, and the computer and operating system together figure out how to configure everything so that it will work. We should be seeing fully PnP PCs starting sometime in 1995—after Microsoft ships Windows 95 (its next version of the Windows operating system).

But for now, you have a plain, old PC running plain, old software and you have a plain, old desire to break it into kindling. Don't. I've tried, and all that plastic doesn't burn very well. (Although you do get some pretty flames, the fumes will probably kill you.) This book will lead you through the steps for installing any sound card and any CD-ROM drive that I've come across (and that's a *lot* of different hardware). Here's how I plan to do it.

Breakdown of the Book

C'est magnifique, mais ce n'est pas la guerre.[1]

—PIERRE JEAN FRANÇOIS JOSEPH
BOSQUET, 1854

How It Works

Chapter 1 discusses how a PC works. If you're like me, you don't really care *how* it works. You just want it to work, period. Well, this is one case where I'm going to beg you not to skip to the "how to" chapters. First of all, this chapter introduces a lot of terms that you're going to need to know in

---

1. It is magnificent, but it is not war.

order to read the rest of the book. Second (and more importantly), it's kind of interesting. PCs are actually pretty fascinating when you ignore the times that they don't work. In this chapter, you'll learn what a bus is, what an interrupt is, and how your PC uses interrupts and memory to talk to its components. In fact, I'll bet that if you read this and only this chapter you'll know enough to sit down and figure out how to get your multimedia upgrade kit installed. Granted, I won't bet very much, but . . .

In Chapter 2, it's time to install some complete multimedia upgrade kits. If you don't want to try figuring out how to install your multimedia upgrade just by reading the first chapter, then you're in good company. I'd rather go for the quick hit than the lengthy discourse any day. So this chapter will discuss some of the general principles of installing new hardware into your system, then give detailed instructions for installing some of the more popular kits.

Multimedia Upgrade Kits

Chapter 3 assumes you already have one of the components of a multimedia upgrade, so we'll look at installing the others. Got a sound card? We'll help you connect a CD-ROM drive. Got a CD-ROM drive? Here's how to get that sound card installed.

Multimedia Components

Chapter 4 explains how to create and play all sorts of sounds and how to take advantage of some of the software that came with your sound card. It also (and more importantly) includes a hit list of some of the software you should rush out and buy for your newly multimediaed PC.

Making Music

Chapter 5 is the Q&A—common problems and solutions. If you've got most of your upgrade working and have just a few questions about why gizmo A won't talk to thingamabob B, then this is the place (although you may have to know some more concrete terminology).

Q&A

Chapter 6 explains how to optimize the performance of your computer so that your resource-hungry multimedia applications have no problem going full blast.

Faster, Pussycat!

Appendices

Finally come a few appendices. Appendix A contains the technical support phone numbers of the vendors of some of the major multimedia upgrade kits. Appendix B covers the specifications of virtually every multimedia kit available—consider it a kind of buyers guide. Appendix C is for everybody who forgot the high school physics classes about how sound works. Appendix D explains how Plug and Play works, and Appendix E tells you what I'd look for in a new multimedia PC.

Assumptions

> Bring us together again.
>
> —RICHARD MILHOUS NIXON, 1968

I will say that I'm making a couple of assumptions about you, your toolbox, and your computer.

Patience

First, I'm assuming that you have a bit of patience. Fiddling around with your PC's innards the first few times is frightening: just like the first few times you relight your furnace's pilot light and you don't know if you're going to be basking in the warm glow of success or hurrying to the hospital to see if they can reattach your eyebrows. Consequently, opening and playing with a PC can make you tense and irritable (kind of like when you have too much coffee and too little sleep). So have a bit of patience.

A screwdriver

Next you should have a small toolbox. Very small. All you'll really need are your hands and a Phillips screwdriver (to open your PC's enclosure). You may not even need the screwdriver since many of today's enclosures are "screwless" and are designed to be opened by hand. IBM Value-Point, for example, has a screwless case.

Your PC

Finally, I'm assuming that you have an IBM PC compatible that has at least one floppy drive, a hard drive, and a 16-bit industry standard architecture (ISA) bus. Yes, I'm throwing around new terminology—16-bit ISA to be exact (I assume you know what a floppy drive is and what a hard drive is).

If you don't know what kind of bus is in your computer (or don't know what a bus is) don't worry: you probably have a 16-bit ISA bus. How do I know? I don't. I'm playing the odds: Nearly every PC sold in the last five years has a 16-bit ISA bus. Before that came 8-bit ISA, which has shorter slots (much, much shorter).

It can have another additional bus—VESA-Local bus or PCI bus are good candidates—but I'm not going to deal with Micro Channel Architecture (MCA) buses (found in IBM's PS/2s), nor will I take the time to fiddle around with an enhanced industry standard architecture (EISA) bus computer. These last two buses have some advantages over ISA, but they're (1) very different from anything else, and (2) a fraction of a percent of all the PC buses out there.

Next I assume that you're running DOS and probably Windows 3.1^{2} (or Windows for Workgroups 3.11). I'm not going to deal with OS/2, nor with Windows NT, and certainly not with any kind of UNIX. Those are for others, braver than I, to detail.

DOS and Windows

Finally, and most important, I'm assuming that your computer works just fine *without* the multimedia kit installed. In other words, it boots when you turn it on, loads DOS and Windows just fine, and runs all your favorite applications. If your PC doesn't work *before* you start installing new stuff, you can't very well expect it to work right *after* you install it, can you? No, I thought not. If your PC is behaving oddly, get it fixed: call a friend who knows something about computers, buy a book, call technical support, but *don't try to install new software or hardware*. You'll just drive yourself insane.

It all works.

And now, on with the show.

---

2. Windows is a registered trademark of Microsoft Corporation (as are, it seems, most of the words in common usage today). But I just thought I'd let you know.

1
Parts Is Parts—
How It Works

The absurd is the essential concept and the first truth.

—ALBERT CAMUS, *Le Mythe de Sisyphe*, 1942

This is all John Scully's fault. Yeah. When he was at Apple and Apple was busy pumping out Macintoshes, he coined the term **multimedia.** He then proceeded to spend an awful lot of time *not* defining it. He left it vague. That's a great marketing ploy when you think about it: introduce a term, don't define it, then whatever your company does is assumed to be that term.

All of which leaves us with multimedia still undefined. Well, I'm going to go out on a limb here and say that multimedia is whatever you get when a computer does something unexpected yet intentional. So a crash isn't multimedia (unexpected but unintentional), but an electronic symphony is.

Okay, so maybe I'm joking a little bit. The original idea behind multimedia was that a **digital** computer could do traditionally **analog** things (like play music or show a movie). But this is a completely ludicrous concept: anytime a PC (IBM compatible or not) does anything, it's digital. That's the nature of the beast. If a computer's playing music, that music has been digitized. If you're watching a movie on a computer screen, it's an all-digital cast. Now that I've completely destroyed the entire precept of this book, let's figure out what I'm going to spend the next two hundred pages writing about.

What's a Multimedium?

Computers are really good at a lot of things, like number crunching and word processing. They can sort, collate, spindle, mutilate, and maim data much faster than any human. (Although the IRS gives a computer a run for its money.) The traditional way to talk to a computer (not going back to the dark ages of punch cards and paper tape) is through a keyboard. The computer talks back through its screen. These two devices are really good at showing characters and numbers.

The history of computers balances increases in power with increases in the size and complexity of applications.

As computers got faster and computer screens got better at displaying graphics, people began to make computers that interacted with people using a graphical environment that is allegedly "more intuitive" (which usually means people can learn it faster). In a move to make things yet more intuitive, somebody decided that computers should give us aural feedback as well as visual, so some elementary sound production capabilities were built into computers like Apple's Macintosh. The IBM PC didn't follow suit, but several third parties like Creative Labs in California figured that this might not be such a bad idea, so they created sound cards for the PC. Now computers could play tunes.

Sound is the heart of multimedia. The rest of the stuff is really just a refinement of existing PC components—video, for example, really just uses your hard disk and your monitor. And sound.

Anyway, the continuing effort to make computers and software easier to use led to "application bloat." The software we use today takes up huge amounts of disk space. A simple word processor can take up 20MB once it and all its extras are installed. Multimedia files (sound and video clips) are especially bad disk space hogs. This wasn't so much a problem for hard disks, which now come in sizes over 9 gigabytes (GB) (Seagate, thank you very much), but it is for floppies, which have never gotten much bigger than the 1.44MB of yesteryear. Enter the CD-ROM. This single flashy plastic-and-metal sandwich can store 650MB of uncompressed data. And it's faster to access than a floppy disk. And it's cheap—the actual medium costs about a quarter. So vendors started to distribute applications on CD-ROMs. In particular, multimedia application vendors (mostly games) used CD-ROMs. (Imagine playing Virgin Games' *The Seventh Guest* on floppies—it takes up about 1GB.)

So CD-ROM drives became the body of multimedia. The rest of multimedia—video capture, voice processing, and all that sort of stuff—is still in its infancy. Mostly that's because nobody has found a really compelling use for it. But someone will, probably pretty soon.

Now that you know what multimedia is, let's take a look at how it works.

Open Saysme

When you crack the case on your PC, you're going to be staring into a morass of circuit boards, chips, wires, and various other accoutrements. But it's like dealing with an animal: if you show no fear, you will be its master. You are about to do battle with an implacable foe—one who won't rest until it is either victor or vanquished. So gird your courage. Onward. Once more onto the breech, and all that stuff.

Open your PC. Before you do this, turn it off (monitor and the main unit) and unplug it. Why unplug it? Mainly as a precaution: you don't want to be fiddling around inside this box with a screwdriver and suddenly tap the power switch by accident. That would be most . . . unpleasant. At the very least, you could damage the computer. At the worst, you'd wind up in the hospital.

These are excruciatingly detailed instructions for how to open your computer. Skip 'em if you want.

Anyway, now that it's unplugged, pull it out from the wall and look at the back. Your owner's manual should provide instructions for opening the enclosure. What? You say you don't have an owner's manual? Join the club: I haven't had one for any computer I've owned. Or rather, I've had them but have always thrown them out. That's one of my mottoes: "Manuals?! We don't need no stinkin' manuals! Ptui." That's right, I actually say, "ptui." Except that when I say it, it comes out more like "patooey."

Anyway, let's get this case open. When you look at the back, you should see a whole bunch of screws. If your PC is like mine (a Dell Dimension XPS 466V), five of them (usually) hold the enclosure onto the rest of the computer.[1] Other PCs use different systems for holding the back on: the IBM ValuePoint, for example, has a single clasp on the front of the enclosure; the Compaq DeskPro uses three or four screws that can't be worked with a normal Phillips screwdriver (you'll need a flathead or Torx screwdriver).

Regardless, some of these screws will allow you to remove the enclosure. Others will loosen key internal components. Clearly, you want to loosen the ones that will remove the enclosure while leaving those that loosen key internal components alone. This is a good practice. How to get there is something of a different matter. Here are some hints for locating the screws that will probably remove your case (I'm saying "probably" to hedge my bets, but I've *never* seen a system with screws that breaks these rules):

- They will probably be on the perimeter, not in the center.
- They will probably be on the sides and top, but not on the bottom.
- If the enclosure overlaps the back, they will be seated on the enclosure, not the case.

Face the back of your computer right now. Look for one screw in the upper-left corner and one in the upper-right corner. Those are the corner screws, and you can remove

---

1. Truth be told, I'm in and out of my computer so often that I only use one screw to hold my case onto my computer. I used to not even use one, but one day the weight of the monitor caused the case to slide off in a most noisy fashion.

them. Now look for one in the center of the top of the back, probably about a quarter inch from the very top. You can take that one out. That's three for five. Now look at the lower-left and lower-right corners. See those screws? Remove them. Now set them someplace where you'll be able to find them later (I've lost a hardware store full of screws from the backs of computers).

Now separate the enclosure from the rest of the computer. Usually you can do this by pulling the enclosure about one inch toward the back and lifting up. On some systems (such as the Austin Power System 60 across the room), you slide the enclosure about one inch forward, then lift up. On still other systems (such as my Dell), you have to slide the enclosure backwards until it's completely free of the guts of the computer.

Just to completely undermine everything I've written, I've seen enclosures that adhere to none of these rules. One such comes from Acer: it's a tower case (it stands vertically) and you open a few clever latches, then crack the case in half from front to back. Never seen anything else like it, and, since the hinges are pretty flimsy, I doubt anybody will be emulating it soon, but it's one of the most clever ideas I've seen.

Components—For Beginners Only

Your case is open. Great. Now what? Okay, let's look at some of the components. Take a look at the photo of the innards of my PC shown in Figure 1.1.

The CPU

In the bottom-right corner of Figure 1.1 sits my computer's central processing unit (CPU). This is the central point of any PC, and it's the part that drives the rest. You can think of it as a kind of mouth. Other parts feed it, and it eats and makes the rest of the system run.

Figure 1.1 A pretty standard desktop model PC

In this system, the CPU is an Intel 80486 DX2/66; my other systems have Intel Pentium processors running at a variety of clock speeds. The clock speed of a CPU is a measure of how fast a CPU can eat the food that other components supply it. For example, a 66 megahertz (MHz) processor chews about 66,000,000 times every second. That's pretty fast— about as fast as I eat when confronted by cheesecake. There are CPUs on the market today that "chew" at rates in excess of 300MHz (the Digital Alpha AXP, for example)—except they aren't being built into any IBM compatibles because . . . well, because they aren't compatible.[2]

---

2. There are also Intel-compatible CPUs made by Advanced Micro Devices (AMD), Cyrix, and IBM. Although compatible, they have different designs. That means you can't judge a processor's performance by its clock speed alone anymore. I don't know what measure of performance is going to emerge, but megahertz won't be it.

The RAM

Feeding the CPU's voracious appetite is primarily the purview of the random access memory (RAM). RAM is composed of chips, each of which can hold upwards of 256K. (Each byte is about one character, so 256K is 256×1024 or 262,144 characters, or about 52,429 five-letter words—about nine times as many as are in this chapter.) With most modern systems, each of these chips will hold at least 1MB of data (that's four times as much as 256K, or about two chapters).

RAM is incredibly fast—the CPU can pull data out of it about once every 80 nanoseconds (every 0.0008 seconds, or about 1,250 times a second). At that rate, you can see that, despite its speed, the RAM is feeding the CPU more slowly than the CPU can eat. This condition, where one component in a PC is so much slower than another, is called a **bottleneck**. In the case of this bottleneck, since the CPU frequently doesn't eat as fast as it can (for reasons I won't get into here), things work out for the most part. With faster CPUs, however, faster RAM can make a difference, and many RAM vendors are working toward fixing the problem.

Anyway, a "typical" PC has 4MB of RAM (the one I'm working on here at 16MB, and the one next to it has 32MB). With the CPU's appetite, that's not enough—the CPU will quickly use all the data and instructions in RAM and need more. That's what the hard disk is for—to feed the RAM. Hard disks these days are measured in hundreds of megabytes.[3] The one in my PC is even bigger: it's over 2,000MB, or 2GB. A friend down the hall from me at work has a 9GB drive from a company called Seagate.

The Hard Drive

So what's a hard drive? Well, if you have your PC open, look for a (usually) black box that has two cables coming out of it—one wide and flat, the other composed of four multicolored wires. That's probably your hard drive. If you cut it

---

3. Although 4MB may sound like a lot of RAM, it's not enough to run Windows 3.1 very well. Install 8MB and you'll see better performance. Install 16MB and you've found Windows' sweet spot. You can also install interesting operating systems such as IBM's OS/2 Warp and Microsoft's Windows NT Workstation. If, that is, you're a masochist like me.

open (don't try this at home, unless you feel like buying another), you'd see why it's called a hard drive: There are several platters inside that are made from aluminum (or
ceramic or glass in some very advanced drives) then sprayed
with a thin coat of magnetic alloy. They spin very quickly
(3,600 rpm and up) and very small data-reading devices
called read/write heads move over them to pick data off.

Hard drives are good for storing large amounts of data, but
they're not nearly as fast as RAM—it takes 10 milliseconds
(ms) to access data on even a fast hard drive. Compare that
to the 80 nanoseconds it takes to get data out of RAM, and
you can see why RAM sits between the hard drive and the
CPU: it can feed the CPU faster.

The Bus

Now we've covered the basic food chain: from disk to RAM
to CPU. So what's everything else for? What are bus slots,
for example? Well, they're a computer's way of adding extras. For example, look at the back of your monitor. There
are two cables running down its back: one plugs into the
wall, the other into a D-shaped connector on the back of
your PC. Well, if you look inside your PC to see what's connected to the D-shaped connector, you'll see a **card**.
Specifically, you'll see your graphics accelerator (the fancy
term for what we used to call a video card). It's the component that enables your PC to show you what it's doing.
That's an example of an extra (although you'd think that a
video card is so ubiquitous that computer makers would
build them onto the basic unit). There are five major buses,
and I describe them next.

Industry Standard Architecture (ISA): There are several kinds of buses in use today. ISA bus is the most widely
used because it's the original. Open up an old IBM PC-AT
and you'll see an 8-bit ISA bus, capable of a throughput of
about 0.625MB/second. In later computers you'll see a 16-
bit ISA bus (which can do about 2MB/second). That is dog-
gone slow. But there are so many cards available for ISA

bus, and most of them have such light throughput requirements, that ISA is just fine. Except for video, but we'll get to that in a second.

Enhanced Industry Standard Architecture (EISA):
Some kinds of computers, called **servers** because many users connect to them at once, place demands on a bus that ISA can't handle. For them, there's EISA, which rhymes with *LEEsa*. Basically, if you take ISA, make it 32-bits wide (maximum throughput about 33MB/second), add a technology that enables you to plug in cards without configuring them, you'll get a kind of EISA. But you probably don't have EISA because it's not used in very many desktop machines. Why? Because there aren't very many good peripherals for it, and it's very expensive. But at least you can plug ISA cards into EISA slots and have them work. That's more than you can say for the next item.

Micro Channel Architecture (MCA): This is IBM's attempt to screw up an already confusing industry. The only widely used (to use the term loosely) computer ever to use MCA was IBM's PS/2. MCA is also 32-bits wide, like EISA, but it's not compatible with all those wonderful ISA cards out there, and it's expensive to produce. In its favor, it has the same capability as EISA: you can just plug in cards and (with a little software configuration) they work—no DIP switches or jumpers. (We'll get to those in a minute.) Oh, did I mention that MCA is dying? Yup, I think IBM is making what is rumored to be its last MCA model as I write this book. Don't buy one if you can avoid it.

Back to that video throughput problem I was talking about earlier. Even the 33MB/second that EISA offers isn't enough to display all those neat graphics that Microsoft Windows, IBM's OS/2 Warp, and other graphical user environments use. For them, there are two relatively new buses: VESA-Local bus and PCI.

Video Electronics Standards Association (VESA):
Pronounced to rhyme with "MasterCard," VESA is a group

of vendors dedicated to creating a very fast bus to plug very fast graphics cards into. They did. The VESA-Local bus (or VL-bus for short) is basically directly connected to the CPU's own internal bus (which it uses to talk among its various components—cache memory, floating-point unit, arithmetic logic unit, and so on), so it's called a local bus (because it's local to the CPU—get it?). This bus can pump data through at a whopping 132MB/second. Since it is connected directly to the CPU's own bus, it runs at whatever speed the CPU's external clock is running at. In a 25MHz 486DX, it runs at 25MHz; in a 33MHz 486DX, it runs at 33MHz. In a 66MHz 486DX/2, it runs at . . . 33MHz.[4] The VL-bus slots themselves are actually ISA slots with a twist: an extra slot thing that sits at the end of the regular ISA slot, making the slot about four inches longer. The system in Figure 1.1 has a VL-bus.

Peripheral Component Interconnect (PCI): The other superfast bus is called PCI. It's the brainchild of Intel (the same guys who designed the CPUs that are standard in today's PCs). It also runs at 132MB/second, but that's about where the similarity ends. It's not a local bus, for example: there's a bus interface unit that takes care of talking between the CPU and the bus slots. It's also got the same capability as EISA and MCA: plug hardware into it and don't worry about DIP switches and jumpers and all that—the bus is self-configuring. The PCI bus is standard equipment in PCs equipped with an Intel Pentium CPU, and it was in fact designed to overcome a limitation of the VL-bus. See, the VL-bus is tied to the 486 architecture because it's hooked up into the CPU directly, without an interface unit. In order to work with a Pentium, the system creator will have to add an interface unit. It's an added hassle and kind of negates VL-bus's strongest advantage. Basically, as the 486 dies, so will VL-bus.

---

4. We're talking about the *external* clock: a DX/2 CPU may run at 66MHz *inside,* but *outside,* it's talking to all its parts at 33MHz. Clock-doubling like this is a way to get the CPU running faster without requiring a major overhaul of the rest of the PC.

So those are the major buses into which you can plug your peripherals. But once you've plugged them in, what happens? Let's get back to basics and see.

How PCs Talk to Their Parts

Three acronyms are the bane of PC users: IRQ, DMA, and base memory address. Okay, so the last one isn't an acronym. Whatever. These are the communication channels that peripherals use to talk to CPUs and CPUs use to talk back. It works like this:

You're sitting at your keyboard, typing. How do all those characters appear on the screen? Well, the CPU has to process them. How does it do that? Each time you press a key, the keyboard controller sends an interrupt request (IRQ) to the CPU that says, "Stop whatever you're doing and print this letter." Since the CPU can process many thousands of interrupts each second, you don't need to worry that you're going to stress your CPU by typing. But other components are vying for attention, too. Like when you move your mouse—that generates IRQs. And when your modem sends data back to your PC—that generates IRQs. And when your printer has some kind of status message— more IRQs.

IRQ stands for "Interrupt ReQuest"—it's how a PC's components get the CPU's attention.

As if that weren't enough, each device must have its own IRQ line. That's right, it's like having kids: if you don't give each one its own phone, you'll have an awful mess. Well, a CPU only has one line capable of processing interrupts. So the creators of modern PCs use programmable interrupt controllers (PICs) to create lots of separate interrupt lines to the CPU. Each PIC can support eight interrupts. Most modern systems connect two to each other to generate fourteen interrupts (it takes one channel on each PIC to talk to the other PIC). So your whole PC can only have fourteen peripherals. If this sounds like a kludge, it is.

But wait, it gets worse: Some of those IRQs are already taken. Table 1.1 shows what I mean.

Table 1.1 The IRQ Heartbreak

IRQ	What uses it
0	System timer
1	Keyboard
2	Connection from PIC #1 to PIC #2
3	COM2; this is your PC's second communications port (look for a smallish D-shaped connector on the back of your PC). You may have a mouse connected to it.
4	COM1; why somebody put COM2 before COM1 eludes me.
5	LPT2; this is your PC's second printer port.
6	Floppy disk drive
7	LPT1; reversed again
8	Real-time clock
9	Connection from PIC #2 to PIC #1
10	Usually unused
11	Usually unused
12	Usually unused, unless you have a bus mouse (or PS/2-style mouse)
13	Usually unused
14	Hard disk
15	Usually unused

So let's look again. Seems you can have IRQs 10, 11, 13, and 15. And maybe 12 if you don't have a bus mouse. Oh, and maybe 5 if you don't have two printer ports. Gee, lucky you. If you're like me, you have the following in your PC: a SCSI host adapter, a network card, a sound card, and a graphics accelerator. So you go from six to two free IRQs. Now let's add an internal modem and a video capture card. No IRQs. Yikes.

When you go to add new boards, you have to install them at unused IRQs. If you don't, at best, the peripheral won't work. At worst, your system won't boot until you take the card out and resolve the IRQ conflict.

There are some tools that can help you figure out what your IRQs are. One that comes with MS-DOS (and isn't very good) is Microsoft System Diagnostics (MSD). Type MSD at the DOS prompt (but not from Windows) and then type Q. MSD will try to figure out what components are using what IRQs. Usually it doesn't do a very hot job. You may have better luck with a third-party utility such as CheckIt Pro Analyst or Symantec/Central Point's PC Tools. Then again, you might not.

DMA

Anyway, to get the CPU's attention, a peripheral sends an interrupt request, which the CPU then services (that's the technical term), usually returning a signal and possibly data to the thing that requested the interrupt. Frequently, a card (like a SCSI card) will ask the CPU for some piece of data. The CPU will stick that data into RAM and tell the card, "OK, I got the data you want, now ask me for it again and I'll give it to you." As you can imagine, that's not very efficient. So from the people who brought you IRQs comes direct memory access (DMA). With DMA, the CPU responds by saying, "OK, look at this location in memory and get it yourself." This is a lot faster.

But it introduces the potential for conflict. Again. See, when you install a card that can use DMA (and not all can, or even need it) you have to tell the card where its special section of memory is going to be. And (you guessed) it can't overlap with any other card's DMA channel. There are eight DMA channels, two of which are already taken (number 2 by the floppy disk controller and number 4 by the DMA chips).

Rarely is there actually a DMA conflict because not that many boards use DMA. And those that do usually come with a default setting that's "safe"—in other words, all SCSI host adapters will come with the same DMA by default, and all sound cards that use DMA will come with a different DMA by default.

Base Memory

The last of the nasty three are base memory addresses, sometimes called I/O ports or port addresses. Remember when I was talking about how the CPU responds to IRQs? Well, it can't respond down the IRQ line—that's kind of a one-way communication channel. Instead, it sets up a port—a kind of virtual conduit—between itself and the peripheral so that they can exchange data directly. Well, as with everything else, there are a limited number of ports, and they look something like what appears in Table 1.2 (they're usually written in hexadecimal notation, which is kind of like counting from one to ten if you have sixteen fingers—and the last six fingers are numbered A through F).

Table 1.2 Common Base Memory Addresses

Port	Usually used for
0200	Sound cards
0278	LPT2
02E8	COM4 (if you have one, which you probably don't)
02F8	COM2
0330	SCSI host adapter
0378	LPT1
03B0	Video cards (which use through 03CF)
03E8	COM3 (which you probably don't have)
03F0	Floppy drives
03F8	COM1

You can try to use MSD to figure out what your port addresses are, but you won't have much luck; it's about as accurate at this as it is at IRQs. But at least it's free.

The Software

What we've been talking about so far is how the hardware talks to itself. If it were anybody else, talking to itself would be considered grounds for psychoanalysis. Since it's hardware, it's grounds for a book. Anyway, once we've got the hardware all squared away, there's yet another layer. Think of your computer as looking like what appears in Figure 1.2.

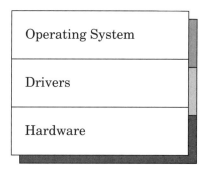

Figure 1.2 Hardware layers

So you drive the operating system, with either mouse clicks or keyboard strokes (or whatever). The operating system, in turn, uses these things called drivers—little programs that know how to talk to the hardware, which sits at the bottom and does all the dirty work.

Some drivers, like the ones for talking to your floppy drive and your IDE hard disk and your keyboard, are built-in software. On a PC, that kind of built-in software is the Basic Input/Output System (BIOS); it's pronounced to rhyme with "BUY-ohs," except the "s" is an "s" sound, not a "z." Anyway, when you turn your computer on, this built-in software runs and enables the operating system to talk to some standard hardware. But lots of hardware (like a sound card) is not considered standard, so it's not built into the BIOS. For that you need extra software drivers.

MS-DOS loads these drivers as it boots. It knows to check two files, called CONFIG.SYS and AUTOEXEC.BAT, for all the extras it's supposed to do as it boots. In these files, you (or a clever installation program) puts the software that tells the operating system (MS-DOS) how to talk to the new hardware.

Microsoft Windows also has some files that it checks as it's loading. The two most common are WIN.INI and SYSTEM.INI. They contain the driver information that Windows looks for. Why can't Windows know enough to check to see what MS-DOS is doing? Well, I could cite the technical reasons, but basically the DOS and Windows are kludged together as it is. Expecting that degree of interoperability would be like expecting Rush Limbaugh and Howard Stern to work together to throw a party for Bill Clinton.

Your Multimedia Hardware

Unlike the Macintosh, the IBM PC was never designed to be a multimedia box. The most popular operating system (DOS) doesn't even have sound support built in (I don't count the beeps the speaker can make; I mean real sound). So in order to make your PC sing, you'll need to add some hardware. Specifically, you'll need at the very least a sound card and a CD-ROM drive. The sound card enables your PC to make pretty music; the CD-ROM drive is the storage element you're going to need because multimedia files are so darn big. A typical word processing document is a few kilobytes; a typical multimedia file (like a video clip) is many, many megabytes. Here are some of the components, what they do, and how they work.

Sound Card

A typical sound card does two main things: it takes sounds from some kind of input (usually a microphone or keyboard) and dumps it into your computer. More commonly, it takes sounds stored on your computer and plays them, usually through a pair of fairly cheap speakers.[5]

How does a sound card store sounds on your hard disk? There are two basic ways: it can actually digitize a sound and record it as a series of zeroes and ones (binary code), or it can use a shorthand called Musical Instrument Digital Interface (MIDI).

The generic term for digitizing a sound is "digital audio," or sound wave storage. It works like this: you connect a micro-

---

5. I would be remiss if I didn't point out that you can get better speakers or even run your sound card through your stereo. Bose makes some very powerful and good-sounding powered speakers, as does Altec (powered speakers don't need an amplifier). To connect a sound card to a stereo, all you need is a cable with an ⅛-inch stereo plug on one end and two RCA plugs on the other. Plug it into the audio-out port of your sound card and the auxiliary port of your stereo.

phone to your sound card's microphone port. A membrane in that microphone vibrates as you talk (for example). The microphone transfers that **analog** signal to your sound card, where an analog-to-digital converter (ADC) **samples** the sound. Sampling is the technical term for taking snapshots of a sound. In the case of most modern sound cards, the sample uses 16 bits to store information such as the sound's frequency (pitch) and amplitude (volume). Eight-bit samples, common on low-quality sound cards, sound noticeably less realistic than 16-bit samples. How often the sound card can sample is determined by this ADC; in good sound cards it will be 44.1 kilohertz (kHz).

Digital audio files tend to have filenames that end in .WAV. These files take up much more space on your hard disk than the MIDI files (a 16-bit by 44.1kHz sample can take up 0.18MB on your hard disk in a second), but the sound quality is generally much better than MIDI.

MIDI is a kind of sound synthesis and, at its worst, is tinny and completely unbelievable. MIDI's key benefit comes if you want to record your own music. If your sound card has a MIDI input, you can connect an electronic keyboard to it and record and mix music right on your PC.

When you go to play back a MIDI file, your sound card uses one of two methods to generate sounds: FM synthesis or wave table synthesis. FM synthesis is the inferior of the two; it stores a bunch of "operators" (basically bits of sine wave) in a chip on the board. When you go to play back, say, a clarinet sound, the FM synthesis module says, "Oh, boy, a clarinet—here's a sine wave that sounds like a clarinet." And it plays its sine wave. Unfortunately, clarinets don't generate simple sine waves—they generate very complex sine waves. That's where wave table synthesis comes in. Rather than storing bits of artificial sine wave, this type of synthesis relies on a bunch of stored samples of musical instrument sounds. When you go to play that clarinet sound, the wave table is able to look up the clarinet sound it has stored and then transpose it to whatever pitch you specify. Although better than FM synthesis, wave table synthesis still isn't perfect. But neither is life. Turtle Beach makes by far the best-sounding sound cards on the market. They're also among the most expensive. Most of the newer sound cards are moving to wave table synthesis, but it's something you should still ask for when you're buying your sound card. MIDI filenames generally end in .MID.

Along with your sound card should come a microphone and speakers. Generally these extras will be very low quality (although some companies, like Reveal, are bundling higher-quality parts in their kits).

Sound cards have other functions, too. For example, many have a port into which you can plug a joystick. And most have a connector for the next component we're going to talk about: CD-ROM drives.

CD-ROM Drive

If you've ever played a CD on your stereo, you're familiar with the shiny round disks. Audio CDs like those you play in a stereo lay down their information a little differently from CD-ROMs that you use with a computer (although most computers can read music from an audio CD).

CD-ROM drives are actually pretty interesting in themselves. As you probably know, they work by bouncing a laser off that shiny disk. The disk itself is actually grooved like a record (although the grooves are much closer together). In those grooves are tiny pits and flat surfaces, or plateaus. When the laser bounces off a pit, its reflection is diffused, but when it bounces off a plateau, the reflection is very clear. So clear that a diode can sense the reflected pulses and translate them into digital ones and zeroes—the same ones and zeroes your computer uses to think.

CD-ROM drives used to come in only one speed: slow. They could pull data off a CD-ROM at about 150K/second, roughly fifty times slower than a hard disk. Newer drives spin CDs two, three, four, or even six times as fast as the original drives, resulting in transfer rates of 300K/second (double-speed or double-spin), 450K/second (triple-speed or triple-spin), 600K/second (quad-speed or quad-spin), or 900K/second. Right now, you can get a double-speed CD-ROM drive for about the same price as a single-speed. The triple and quad-speed drives are coming down in price quickly, so some time soon expect them to become the norm.

Unfortunately, none of these newer drives has significantly improved a CD-ROM drive's speed at finding data on a disk—what's called **seek time** in technical parlance. CD-ROM drives still take about ten times longer than a hard drive to find data, so you'll probably notice that your CD-ROMs don't run as fast as your hard disk.

Once you know how fast you want your CD-ROM drive, you'll probably get a choice of **interfaces** to choose from. Interface is the technical term for both the wire that connects the CD-ROM drive to the computer and for the types of electrical signals that get passed over that wire. There are three main interface types: Small Computer Systems Interface (SCSI), Integrated Drive Electronics (IDE), and the ever-present "other"—usually a proprietary interface type. When selecting a CD-ROM drive (or a multimedia kit with a CD-ROM drive), you want to make sure that its interface is "open"—not proprietary. When you have a CD-ROM drive with a standard interface, you can replace it with commonly available parts without worrying about compatibility. That's why "open" is good.

SCSI: Right now, if you purchase a CD-ROM drive alone it will probably have a SCSI (pronounced *scuzzy)* or SCSI-2 interface. SCSI-2 is a standard electrical system to connect all sorts of computer peripherals—disk drives, tape drives, and scanners—to your PC. This electrical system comes in many shapes and forms. Sometimes the connectors are a flat, ribbon cable with fifty wires and a kind of nasty-looking connector on the end; such systems are usually used inside your computer. Sometimes, the connector has a large D-shaped connector that clips on.

The SCSI "bus" (the technical term for the wire that connects all the SCSI devices together) can talk to eight devices. One of these devices is always the SCSI host adapter, which is a bunch of chips that translate between your computer's internal bus (ISA, for example) to SCSI. That leaves seven. These are numbered 1–7. Before you plug a device into the SCSI bus, you must make sure that its SCSI ID is unique. You must also make sure that the last device in the SCSI chain is terminated. Termination is an electrical engineering term that's a bit hard to explain. Think of it like this: if you don't plug up the end of the SCSI hose, all the data will come flying out the open end. Or something.

If you buy your CD-ROM drive in a kit, you're not going to have to worry about any of the intricacies of SCSI because the kit will (presumably) take care of everything for you. Most likely, it will give you a hobbled SCSI interface on the sound card capable of supporting only one device. This is fine: the goal is to be able to keep your CD-ROM drive if you switch sound cards or to purchase a new CD-ROM drive for your existing sound card without having to worry about compatibility problems.

IDE: Integrated Drive Electronics and a more recent version called Enhanced IDE or E-IDE have some advantages over SCSI. While maintaining similar performance, they don't require you to think about device IDs or about termination. You plug your CD-ROM drive into your E-IDE controller and off you go.

The main problem with IDE is that, although a standard when you're connecting hard drives to your computer, it's not a standard when it comes to CD-ROM drives. So your sound card will probably implement a proprietary IDE-alike interface that's little better than having a completely proprietary interface. Fortunately, E-IDE *does* include support for CD-ROM drives. Unfortunately, it's still in its infancy.

Proprietary: Many kits use proprietary interfaces. Some purport to be SCSI but don't support seven devices, nor do

they require termination. These interfaces, although sometimes similar to SCSI, aren't.

Multifunction Modem

Another component you may get for your multimedia PC is
a multifunction modem. At minimum, multifunction
modems incorporate facsimile and frequently add the capability to handle (recognize and generate) voice. There are
both internal and external multifunction modems. If you get
an external one, it will probably connect to one of your serial
ports. If you get an internal one, you're going to be dealing
with IRQs and DMAs and all that good stuff.

Graphics Accelerator

You may not think that your PC's graphics accelerator is
multimedia, but it is. At the very least, your graphics accelerator is going to be responsible for displaying the images
from your multimedia software on the screen (and it really
bites when Sam 'n Max hit the screen out of synch[6]).
Increasingly, high-performance graphics accelerators include some technology to decode compressed video.[7]

Why compress video? Because it takes up a whole heck of a
lot of room. Here's how it works. You capture video just like
you capture sound: you take snapshots of what's going on.
These snapshots, called frames, can occur anywhere from
thirty times a second down to one or two times a second. At
thirty frames per second, video is perfectly smooth—television quality smooth. At fifteen frames per second, there will
be some odd lapses where somebody's mouth is closed yet
they're speaking. And so on.

Each frame occupies a bit of hard disk space. How much depends on how big the image is, how sharp you're making it,
how many colors you're capturing and so on. A single frame
can be several megabytes (but usually isn't). Now capture

---

6. In case you're wondering, *Sam 'n Max Hit the Road* is a supercool game by
LucasArts.

7. Some, such as Sigma Design's ReelMagic, provide high-resolution, full-motion
video on your PC—SuperVHS quality. They're neat, but right now pretty expensive and not very useful (they lack a large base of software).

fifteen or thirty of these a second and you see why things get big.

So you compress. Video compression is usually "lossy"—some information is discarded to save space. You may remove some of the crispness around the edges of objects, for example. In addition, video compression is pretty smart; it can look at each frame and determine what changed and store only that data. That way, if you have a sequence with a person talking to you in front of a set, unchanging background, the video compression will save only the talking person and throw away all but the first frame of the background. (That's not strictly accurate—actually, the software checks in periodically, updating the background along with the rest of the picture.)

There are two kinds of compression: the kind that needs special hardware to be decompressed and the kind that doesn't. As you can imagine, the former is generally higher-quality than the latter. Some of the standards for compression may have familiar names. MPEG, for example, is widely used, as is Motion JPEG. Both of these have been around for a while. More recent is Intel's Indeo compression technology, which doesn't require special hardware. Indeo is one of the several compression types supported by Microsoft Video for Windows, Microsoft's umbrella term for a bunch of video standards. The last of the PC video compression types is Apple Computer's QuickTime, which is extremely popular in games.

Video Capture Card

At the other end of the spectrum from video cards are video capture cards. These connect to a VCR, television receiver, or video recorder and store video directly onto your computer. Creative Labs' VideoBlaster is one such board. Fast Electronic's MovieMachine Pro is another. I'm not going to go into much detail on these because they're pretty rare. Cool toys, though.

The End

You've now taken a very brisk tour of a multimedia PC.
What should you take away? Mainly that you're going to be
dealing with IRQs, DMAs, and base memory addresses as
you install your new sound card and CD-ROM drive. Brace
yourself.

2
Installing a Multimedia Kit

The significant problems we have cannot be solved at
the same level of thinking with which we created them.

—Albert Einstein

When I was a kid, I'd occasionally badger my parents into
buying me a model of some kind—a model battleship, model
car, model airplane, supermodel Cindy Crawford, something
like that. I wanted what every kid wanted: to have a life-
size version just like what was pictured on the box. I still
believed in truth in advertising at that point in my life.
Anyway, I'd get the kit home, break out the glue, and open
the box only to be confronted by a bunch of gray plastic
blobs all stuck together. Needless to say, I didn't complete
the assembly of many kits, let alone actually paint one. To
this day, disappointment looms large whenever I see a
model battleship box.

Fortunately, I discovered multimedia kits. You can do interesting things with them and they're easy to assemble.
Really. How could installing a multimedia kit be hard? After
all, it's just a green board, and it pretty obviously slides into
a slot inside the computer. What's so hard about that?
Nothing. Absolutely nothing. In fact, this whole chapter is
dedicated to showing just how easy it is. The only catches in
installing that card are easy to watch for, once you know
what they are. If you spend a few minutes with this chapter, you'll save hours of aggravation when you install.

This chapter is very long and has many parts. There's an overview of the whole installation process, then a series of sections for installing specific cards, followed by general instructions for any card. The chapter will deal with installing three specific cards: a Creative Labs Sound Blaster 16 kit, a Reveal Sound FX Wave32 kit, and a Media Vision Pro Audio Spectrum 16 kit. If your kit isn't listed, flip to the section entitled "Installing a Generic Kit." Although it won't show you where to move jumpers as the first three sections do, it will supplement your manual (some of them are lacking, to put it politely) by explaining in simple terms what's going on.

An Overview

The basic process for installing a multimedia upgrade kit in any PC is as follows:

1. Check for free resources. This is where you make sure you have bus slots, drive bays, power cords, IRQs, DMAs, and base memory addresses.
2. Configure your card. Make your card conform to your free IRQs, DMAs, and base memory by moving jumpers.
3. Install the card.
4. Install the CD-ROM drive.
5. Boot your computer.
6. Configure the card and CD-ROM software.
7. Enjoy the fruit of your labor.

The key to an effortless installation lies in Steps 1 and 2. Remember to plan ahead.

Of course, it never works out this easily, but you can see that it's a pretty simple process. True, there's a learning curve: my first multimedia kit took about an hour to install, if you don't include time I took to hurl particularly choice invective at the card, computer, and world at large. (I've cut down on caffeine and mellowed a bit since.) While researching for this book, I got to the point where I could install a multimedia upgrade kit I'd never seen before into a computer that I'd just met in about ten minutes.

The First Steps for Any Card

No matter what kind of card you have, you need to run through the following nine steps.

Step 1: Determine that your PC meets your kit's requirements.

Before you open your kit or unscrew your case, check to make sure you have the following:

✓ ISA bus
✓ 386 or better CPU
✓ VGA monitor and video card
✓ 5MB free hard disk space
✓ DOS 3 or later
✓ Windows 3.1 or later

This step is really kind of perfunctory because most PCs today meet every kit's requirements, but just in case, you'd better check.

Most multimedia kits will install into any IBM-compatible with an ISA bus (also called an AT bus) and a 386 or better (for example, a 486 or Pentium) processor. You'd better have at least a VGA monitor and video adapter (although some kits still support the old EGA standard) and about 5MB of free disk space on your hard disk (you *do* have a hard disk, don't you?) for the drivers and other software the kit will need to install. Oh, and you'll probably want at least DOS version 3 or later (version 6.22 is current as I write this paragraph). Finally, if you expect to do any work in Microsoft Windows you should have Windows 3.1 or later—I've never seen a kit that supports previous versions.

Step 2: Determine free IRQs, DMAs, and base memory addresses.

Check for the following:

✓ Free IRQs

✓ Free DMAs

✓ Free base memory addresses

This step is kind of tricky. There's no really easy way to 100 percent guarantee that you'll get it right if you do it from software. Microsoft includes with MS-DOS 5 and later a utility called Microsoft System Diagnostics (MSD). As you can see in Figure 2.1, it's not very helpful.

```
 File  Utilities  Help
╔══════════════════════════════ IRQ Status ══════════════════════════════╗
║  IRQ  Address    Description      Detected                Handled By    ║
║  ───  ───────    ───────────      ────────                ──────────    ║
║   0   09A8:04B7  Timer Click      Yes                     SNAP.EXE      ║
║   1   C95E:1923  Keyboard         Yes                     Block Device  ║
║   2   0430:0057  Second 8259A     Yes                     Default Handlers ║
║   3   0430:006F  COM2: COM4:      COM2:                   Default Handlers ║
║   4   D543:0096  COM1: COM3:      COM1: COM3: PS/2 StyMOUSE.EXE          ║
║   5   0430:009F  LPT2:            No                      Default Handlers ║
║   6   0430:00B7  Floppy Disk      Yes                     Default Handlers ║
║   7   0070:06F4  LPT1:            Yes                     System Area     ║
║   8   0430:0052  Real-Time Clock  Yes                     Default Handlers ║
║   9   F000:EC2D  Redirected IRQ2  Yes                     BIOS            ║
║  10   0430:00CF  (Reserved)                               Default Handlers ║
║  11   0430:00E7  (Reserved)                               Default Handlers ║
║  12   0430:00FF  (Reserved)                               Default Handlers ║
║  13   F000:EC36  Math Coprocessor Yes                     BIOS            ║
║  14   0430:0117  Fixed Disk       Yes                     Default Handlers ║
║  15   0430:012F  (Reserved)                               Default Handlers ║
║                                   OK                                     ║
╚═════════════════════════════════════════════════════════════════════════╝
IRQ Status: Displays current usage of hardware interrupts.
```

Figure 2.1 MSD stinks at determining free IRQs, DMAs, and base memory addresses, but it's free.

MSD will probably give you a vague indication of what kind of IRQs, DMAs, and so on you have. Make that *very* vague. The odds are pretty good that you're going to have to wait until your system is open before you can really make sure that you have this information right. For example, look at IRQ 5 in Figure 2.1. MSD says it's free, but there's a sound card installed there. Hmmm.

Fortunately, most card manufacturers don't allow you to set cards to IRQs and DMAs that they know will already be taken. Which ones will be taken? Try the information in Tables 2.1 and 2.2 and see if it helps.

Table 2.1 The IRQ Heartbreak

IRQ	What Uses It
0	System timer
1	Keyboard
2	Connection from PIC #1 to PIC #2
3	COM2; your PC's second communications port (look for a smallish D-shaped connector on the back of your PC). You may have a mouse connected to it.
4	COM1; why somebody put COM2 before COM1 eludes me.
5	LPT2; your PC's second printer port
6	Floppy disk drive
7	LPT1; reversed again
8	Real-time clock
9	Connection from PIC #2 to PIC #1
10	Usually unused
11	Usually unused
12	Usually unused, unless you have a bus mouse (or PS/2-style mouse)
13	Usually unused
14	Hard disk
15	Usually unused

Table 2.2 Common Base Memory Addresses

Port	Usually Used For
0200	Sound cards
0278	LPT2
02E8	COM4 (if you have one, which you probably don't)
02F8	COM2
0330	SCSI host adapter
0378	LPT1
03B0	Video cards (which use through 03CF)

Table 2.2 Common Base Memory Addresses (continued)

Port	Usually Used For
03E8	COM3 (which you probably don't have)
03F0	Floppy drives
03F8	COMI

Nonetheless, write down the free resource information MSD provides on a Post-it note. You'll need it in just a minute.

If you're really at a loss for the configuration information of the cards in your computer, there are several programs that can maybe help a little more. At work, I use one called PC Tools for Windows from Central Point Software (see Figure 2.2). There's also one called SysInfo, and another called CheckIt Pro Analyst. Truth to tell, though, PCs weren't designed with configuration-determining software in mind. There's no 100 percent sure piece of software available that will figure out every card you might have plugged into your computer. Sorry.

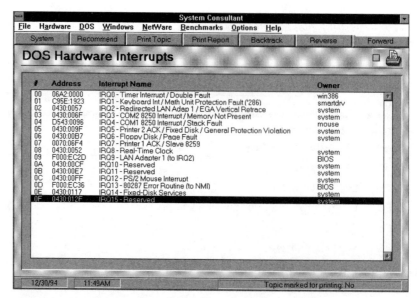

Figure 2.2 Central Point's PC Tools doesn't do a much better job.

The new Plug and Play standard (from Intel, Microsoft and Al, as in et al.) should help fix that, but that's future stuff, and you have to figure out your configuration today. Well, if MSD didn't give you a full report (how do you know? I'll tell you: it didn't) then wait a minute and I'll tell you what to do.

Step 3: Back up the important stuff.

This may sound silly. It may sound ridiculous. It may sound like a pain in the buttocks. But. And I underline that: <u>But</u>. Heck, I'll underline it, italicize it, boldface it, and put it into a different font: ***But*** you had better do it. Start by backing up four critical files: AUTOEXEC.BAT, CONFIG.SYS, WIN.INI, and SYSTEM.INI. (You should be doing this any time you change your files anyway, but do it now.) To do this, put a formatted floppy into your floppy drive (I'll assume its drive A) and run these commands:

```
C:\>COPY \CONFIG.SYS A:
C:\>COPY \AUTOEXEC.BAT A:
C:\>COPY \WINDOWS\WIN.INI A:
C:\>COPY \WINDOWS\SYSTEM.INI A:
```

Now, if you run into any problems when booting your computer, you can restore these four files (copy them from the floppy back to where they came from), and things should be fine.

Now you have to back up the software that came with your sound card. This is for when (not if, when) your distribution diskettes go south. It will happen: it always does. Try using these commands (I'm assuming you have a hard disk):

```
C:\>MD DISTRIB
C:\>MD DISTRIB\DISK1
C:\>MD DISTRIB\DISK2
```

Repeat this command once for every distribution diskette so that you have unique directories for each. Now place the first of your distribution diskettes in your floppy drive. I'm assuming you're using drive A. Now run these commands:

```
C:\>XCOPY /S A:*.* C:\DISTRIB\DISK1
```

Now put the second diskette into the drive and run the command again, but this time change the target directory to `C:\DISTRIB\DISK2`. Keep doing it until all the diskettes are backed up onto your hard drive.

Now you can create a second copy of your distribution floppies really easily: just `XCOPY` the files from the hard drive onto a bunch of new floppies. You'll need to format one new floppy for each of the distribution floppies that came with your software:

```
C:\>FORMAT A:
```

When it asks you if you want to format another, say Yes until you've formatted all the floppies you need. Now create nice, new labels for your floppies that tell you what's on them, and `XCOPY` the data off the hard disk onto the floppies:

```
C:\>XCOPY /S C:\DISTRIB\DISK1\*.* A:\
```

And keep at it until you're out of directories. You should now have a fully backed-up set of floppies. You can delete your `DISTRIB` directories now. If you have MS-DOS 6 or later, you can use this command:

```
C:\>DELTREE C:\DISTRIB
```

But if you have a previous DOS version, you're going to have to go into each directory, delete all the files, then delete the directory, like this:

```
C:\>DEL \DISTRIB\DISK1
C:\>RMDIR \DISTRIB\DISK1
```

And so on. Now you have a nice, working (one hopes) copy of your multimedia kit's distribution diskettes.

Step 4: Open your PC.

Let's make like Sherlock Holmes and crack your case. PC enclosures come in two basic types: desktop and tower. The desktop version sits comfortably on . . . well, on your desktop, usually with your monitor on top of it. The tower type of case is usually too tall for your desktop and dwarfs everything on your desk when you try to put it there.

In either case (pun intended), you're going to be dealing with some kind of fastener to remove the enclosure that covers the guts of your computer. With most cases, these fasteners are screws of some kind, thumbscrews and Phillips screws being the most common. In a very few cases, you have an advanced case design that uses some kind of screwless latch to pop open.

I'd like to say, "Read your owner's manual to see how to open your case." But, if you're like me, you no longer have your owner's manual. If you ever had one at all. Never fear: here are hints for opening both types of cases.

Screwless Case: These are usually the easier of the two to open. You'll know you have one if, somewhere on your enclosure, there's a small button that turns neither the computer nor "Turbo" on or off. Usually, the latch is located either in the upper-middle of the front (as on IBM ValuePoint) or somewhere on the back. Push the button and hold it in.

Screwy Case: Look at the back of your computer. There is probably a bunch of screws there. Look at the edges of the back. You'll probably see five or six screws that pretty clearly secure the sides of the computer to the back. Just remove these.

Now wiggle the enclosure front-to-back. That's right, stand in front of your computer, lay your hands flat on the side of the computer, and give the enclosure a good hard jerk toward you, then away from you. The case (or a panel on the case) should move in one of the two directions. Pull or push it as far in that direction as it will go, then lift it up until it's clear of the rest of the computer. You're in.

Step 5: Recheck your DMAs, IRQs, and base memory while the case is open.

Check again for the following:

✓ Free IRQs

✓ Free DMAs

✓ Free base memory addresses

Now that you're inside your computer, you'll have a really great time verifying that MSD gave you totally inaccurate information about your system's configuration. How? By looking at each of the cards in your computer and checking to see what their settings are.

Of all the boards I've plugged into computers, only Adaptec has the courtesy to assume that you're going to throw away their manual and to print what each of the jumper settings means.

This is no small task for even the most knowledgeable PC people. Most cards don't have obvious settings; instead they have jumpers with names like J0, J1, H5, and N21. They have DIP switches numbered 0–7 that have nothing to do with anything. And they *don't print what the jumpers and switches mean on the board.* Some boards don't even have jumpers or DIP switches at all—they're configured through software.

Regardless, you've got to take a look just to make sure. So first you're going to have to pull your boards out of the slots they're in. In every computer I've seen, this is done by loosening a Phillips-head screw located toward the back of the computer. Each board gets its own screw. So look at each board, and trace it to the back of your computer. When you run out of board, there will be a metal plate (the plate that's exposed through the back of the computer). It has a lip inside the computer; on top of this lip, you should see a screw. Remove it. But before you wrestle the board out of its slot, *remove any wires from its back*. Any wires that protrude out the back of your computer will hang up the board as you try to remove it.

Now pull the board out as in Figure 2.3. This isn't as easy as it seems because the boards fit very tightly into their slots. Try grasping opposite ends of the board between your

Figure 2.3 Unplug, unscrew, and wiggle.

thumbs and index fingers, then lifting first the right side, then the left side. You're wiggling the board free.

Once the board's free of the computer, check it for jumpers or DIP switches. What's a jumper? Or a DIP switch? They're two ways of accomplishing basically the same thing: closing a circuit. With jumpers, you have a small piece of metal with plastic around it that either closes the gap between two electrical poles or doesn't. A DIP switch (stands for dual in-line packaging) is basically a little light switch; flick it to 0 and it's off (or "open"), flip it to 1 and it's on (or "closed").

If you're lucky, the board you're looking at has its jumpers and/or DIP switches labeled with their function. For example, jumper J1 might be labeled IRQ 5. That means if you close the jumper (put it over the two little wires poking out of the board), you'll set the board to IRQ 5. Look at your boards and see if you can determine more information about their configuration than MSD gave you. If you have the manuals for these components, you'll find out what the jumpers and DIP switches mean by looking in there (usually in an appendix).

Both DIP switches and jumpers are very small. As you work with them (and you will work with them), you might want a small screwdriver or pair of needle-nosed pliers.

How to tell a 16-bit slot from an 8-bit slot: The 16-bit slot has two parts—two separate slots—and is longer than an 8-bit slot.

Once you're done, replace all of them. It doesn't matter which slots you slide which boards into usually: any 16-bit ISA board can go into any 16-bit ISA slot, any 8-bit ISA card can go into any ISA slot at all, any PCI board can go into any PCI slot.

There may be a catch with some VESA-Local bus slots (called VL-bus slots for short). VL-bus slots are numbered (1, 2, and so on). Some VL-bus boards (like my Adaptec AHA-2842) need to go into a particular slot—the slot that matches the number that the board is configured for. Just make sure you install your VL-bus cards back into the slots they came from and you'll have no problem.

Step 6: Verify that you have enough open bus slots.

Now that all your existing boards are back home, check to make sure you have enough bus slots for the card(s) you're about to install. Most sound cards require one 16-bit ISA slot. Sometimes, as when you have an external CD-ROM drive, your sound card may come with a second card that can go into an 8-bit ISA slot.

In any event, look in your multimedia kit and count the cards (as you would when playing poker with my mom). Then count your slots. Let's take an example. At work, I have a Compaq DeskPro 466i, which is a machine with only three 16-bit ISA slots. One of these slots goes to a SCSI host adapter for my external CD-ROM drive. A second is for my network card. The third goes to an internal fax/modem. (The DeskPro 466i has a video "card" built onto its mother-board, so I don't need a video card. It also has built-in sound capabilities, but they don't work under DOS, so . . .) Say I want to add a Sound Blaster multimedia upgrade kit. It may seem like I don't have a slot. But I do—after I remove my CD-ROM's SCSI host adapter. That's because the Sound Blaster can control a CD-ROM drive without a SCSI host adapter. So I remove the SCSI host adapter and add my Sound Blaster and hook my new CD-ROM drive up to it.

Step 7: Verify that you have an open drive bay (internal CD-ROM only).

This is kind of like the previous step. If you have an internal CD-ROM (you'll know because it'll look kind of unfinished in back) you need a half-height 5¼-inch external drive bay. ("External drive bay" means there's a hole in the case through which you slide your CD-ROM drive.) Half-height bays are about 1½ inches tall, by the way. If you don't have a free bay, see if something that occupies one of your bays can be moved to an internal bay. Ideal candidates are hard disk drives, which really don't need to be exposed at all.

Moving something to an internal bay can be a royal pain in the behind (PITA). If you're lucky, you'll just have to remove a few really small screws. If you aren't, you're going to have to deal with positioning special rails.

This is a case where having a decent mechanical aptitude is the only thing that will help. Look at the other drives and whatnot and see how they're attached, then make your CD-ROM drive ready to look like that. If your computer needs rails, for example, attach rails to the CD-ROM drive. A good kit (such as Reveal's) will include a bunch of different kinds of rails.

Step 8: Verify that you have a power cord (internal CD-ROM only).

If you have an internal CD-ROM drive, take a look at your PC's power supply (the large shiny box near the back). Make sure that there's at least one free plug coming out of it. This plug should be about one inch across and have four holes in it. If you don't have a free plug, you can't attach your internal CD-ROM ; you'll need to go to Radio Shack or a local computer store and buy a power cable splitter. Just go in and ask the person behind the counter for a Y cable that will split the cable from a PC power supply into two usable plugs.

Step 9: Install the kit.

Now for the easy part: just install the kit. But seriously, if you've done all the previous steps, actually plugging the board into your PC is going to be a breeze. Four sections remain in this chapter: "Creative Labs Kits," "Reveal Kits," "Media Vision Kits," and "Installing a Generic Kit." Skip to the section that matches your multimedia kit.

Creative Labs Kits

Creative Labs makes a few varieties of its extremely popular Sound Blaster sound card. There's the Sound Blaster Pro (an 8-bit card), the Sound Blaster 16 (16-bit), the Sound Blaster 16 with Advanced Signal Processor or Wave Processor (a Sound Blaster 16 with either better MIDI or better wave table synthesis), and the Sound Blaster AWE 32 (another significantly enhanced 16-bit card). In all, I count six kits. For three reasons, I'm going to show only how to deal with the Sound Blaster 16:

1. It's by far the most popular.
2. If you know how to install it, you know basically how to install the others.
3. We have several other sound cards to cover here.

(For Steps 1–9, please see the previous section, "The First Steps for Any Card," pages 27–38.)

Step 10: Take a guided tour of a Sound Blaster.

If all goes well, you're not going to have to change anything on your Sound Blaster, but if you do, it'll be useful to know where all the different thingamabobs are. So take a look at your Sound Blaster. It should look something like what's in Figure 2.4.

There are a few points you should take note of on the card. On the far right are all the external connectors. From top to bottom, they are line in, microphone input, the volume control, speaker output, and the joystick/MIDI adapter plug. Notice that they aren't labeled; this is one of the Sound Blaster's great shortcomings.

Figure 2.4 A typical Sound Blaster

In case your board doesn't look like this, don't panic. Creative Labs changes the designs of its boards periodically (as do all hardware designers) so that they can add new features or condense old ones into fewer chips (which makes the boards less expensive to manufacture).

Moving onto the board proper, you'll see just to the left of all those connectors toward the top of the board what's called "Pin 1." I have no idea what pin 1 does. Keep going left and down a little bit and you'll see jumpers OPSL and OPSR, which turn on and off the Sound Blaster's internal amplifier (the thing that makes music loud). Default is on. Leave it there unless you're planning to connect the Sound Blaster's line out to your home stereo, in which case you can remove them.

Now move up so that you're nearly at the top of the card, and move a bit left. You'll see a bunch of brass pins poking out of the board. These make up the connector for Sound Blaster add-ons. Don't worry about them unless you're going to install an upgrade to your card, in which case you'll get instructions with the upgrade.

Move directly up and you'll see two connectors. The one on the right is labeled "CD_IN" and the one to the left is "PC_SPK." This is board-designer-speak for "the place you plug your CD-ROM drive's audio output cable" and "the place you plug your motherboard's PC speaker," respectively. You won't use PC_SPK.

Move left and to the center of the board. You're staring at a bunch of jumpers labeled IFSD, APSD, JYEN, I0S0, and I0S1. Such creative names. IFSD and APSD aren't documented, so you'll want to leave 'em alone. JYEN controls whether the Sound Blaster's joystick controller will work (by default it will). If your PC has a joystick port built in (most don't), remove the jumper from JYEN.

I0S0 and I0S1 together control the base I/O address of the Sound Blaster. Now we're getting somewhere—you could very well wind up changing the settings of these jumpers. By default, the Sound Blaster's base I/O address is 0x220 (which you'll sometimes see printed as 220H; same thing, different notation).

Keep moving left and a little down and you'll run into another bank of jumpers. These are MSEL, DAS0, DAS1, DBS0, DBS1, IS0, and IS1. MSEL controls the base I/O address of the MIDI portion of the Sound Blaster. By default, that's 0x330 (330H). Why are there two base I/O addresses on your Sound Blaster? Because the board itself is made up of a bunch of different components, all of which have different resource requirements. There's the wave table part (the one whose base I/O address is 0x220) and the MIDI part, for example. Different subsystems on the same board.

DAS0 and DAS1 together control the DMA channel of the 8-bit part of the Sound Blaster (channel 1 by default). DBS0 and DBS1 control the DMA of the 16-bit part of the Sound Blaster (channel 5 by default). Why are there two channels? Because not all systems support 16-bit DMA (which gets better performance out of your system). IS0 and IS1 together control the IRQ of the Sound Blaster (default is 5).

Keep moving left. If your board has more jumpers at the bottom, labeled JP18 and JP19, not to mention another bank labeled JP20 through JP24, you probably also have a bank at the top-left corner labeled PAN, SON, MIT, and DISABLE. This means that you got a kit that shipped with one of three CD-ROM drives: a Panasonic (labeled possibly Panasonic, Matsushita, or Sanyo), a Sony, or a Mitsumi.

Sound Blaster CD-ROM Drive Note

Many Sound Blaster 16 kits come with one of three CD-ROM drives: a Sony, a Mitsumi, or a Panasonic/Matsushita/ Sanyo. Why? A few reasons. First, Creative Labs kits are in high demand. Creative knows it can satisfy the demand for sound cards, but they need several suppliers to satisfy the demand for CD-ROM drives. So they build logic onto their sound cards to support several different CD-ROM drives, then order CD-ROM drives from several manufacturers. Since performance on the CD-ROM drives doesn't vary dramatically, both you and Creative benefit: Creative makes a sale, and you get your kit quickly.

The down side is that not all the CD-ROM drives behave exactly the same, so installation can be made a little more difficult. On your Sound Blaster 16 you may find three connectors for CD-ROM drives, one for Sony, one for Panasonic/ Matsushita/Sanyo, and one for Mitsumi. Two of the three are the same size; the third (the Sony connector) is smaller. The Panasonic connector is at the top of the card, above the smaller Sony connector; the Mitsumi connector is on the end of the card by itself. The Sound Blaster 16 won't automatically sense which drive you have connected, so you must set the jumper in the upper-left corner of the drive to match the kind of drive you're using (PAN for Panasonic, SON for Sony, or MIT for Mitsumi).

If you have a Mitsumi drive, you may also have to worry about its IRQ, DMA, and base memory address (that's what the extra jumpers at the bottom left of the board are for). Jumpers JP18 and JP19 control its base I/O address, with the default at 0x340; jumpers JP20, JP21, and JP22 control its IRQ; and jumpers JP23 and JP24 control its DMA channel.

Step 11: Configure the Sound Blaster.

Remember that Post-it on which you were supposed to write
your free IRQs and your used DMAs and base memory addresses on way back in Step 2? Look at it, then compare it
with the Sound Blaster's default setup in Table 2.3.

Table 2.3 Sound Blaster Defaults

Thing	Setting
IRQ	5
8-bit DMA	1
16-bit DMA	5
Base memory	0x220
MIDI base memory	0x330
Mitsumi base memory	0x340
16-bit Mitsumi DMA	7
Mitsumi IRQ	11

So if you happen to have these base memory addresses,
IRQs, and DMAs free, you can just plug and go. If you don't
have a Mitsumi CD-ROM drive, ignore the bottom three
lines.

If you're wondering why the sound card takes so many resources, it's because it handles so many functions. First, it
gets its own IRQ. Simple. Next, it needs two DMA channels,
one for talking 8 bits at a time, one for 16. It also gets two
base memory addresses, one for the regular sounds, and one
for all the MIDI sounds. And the Mitsumi CD-ROM drive
control logic on the sound card needs its own IRQ, DMA,
and base memory address.

If you don't have these resources free, you're going to have
to move a few jumpers. Move them now. When you're done,
write down the final configuration of your card on a Post-it
note and attach it to your monitor.

Tables 2.4 through 2.11 show what each of the important
jumpers on your Sound Blaster do when you move them.

Table 2.4 Sound Blaster Base I/O Addresses

IOS0	IOSI	Resulting Audio Base I/O Address
On	On	0x220 (Default)
Off	On	0x240
On	Off	0x260
Off	Off	0x280

Table 2.5 MIDI Interface Base I/O Addresses

MSEL	Resulting MIDI Base I/O Address
On	0x330 (Default)
Off	0x300

Table 2.6 Sound Blaster IRQs

IS0	ISI	Resulting Audio IRQ
On	On	2
Off	On	5 (Default)
Off	On	7
Off	Off	10

Table 2.7 8-bit DMA Channels

DAS0	DASI	Resulting 8-bit Audio DMA Channel
On	On	0
Off	On	1 (Default—don't change this)
On	Off	3

Table 2.8 16-bit DMA Channels

DBS0	DBSI	Resulting 16-bit Audio DMA Channel
On	On	5 (Default)
Off	On	6
On	Off	7

Table 2.9 Mitsumi CD-ROM Base I/O Addresses

JP19	JP18	Resulting Mitsumi CD-ROM Interface Base I/O Address
On	On	0x310
On	Off	0x320
Off	On	0x340 (Default)
Off	Off	0x350

Table 2.10 Mitsumi CD-ROM IRQs

JP20	JP21	JP22	Resulting Mitsumi CD-ROM Interface IRQ
On	Off	Off	11 (Default)
Off	On	Off	10
Off	Off	On	3

Table 2.11 Mitsumi CD-ROM DMA Channels

JP24	JP23	Resulting Mitsumi CD-ROM DMA Channel
Off	On	7 (Default)
On	Off	6

A Configuration Example

Let's take an example. Let's say that your kit shipped with a Panasonic drive (which is labeled Matsushita-Kotobuki) and that none of the board's settings will work in your computer. Your Post-it note tells you that you only have the resources listed in Table 2.12 free.

Table 2.12 Just as an Example . . .

Resource	Your Free Resources
IRQ	10
Base Memory	0x280
DMA	1 and 6

What are you going to do?

First, let's reconfigure your IRQ. By default, the Sound Blaster comes at IRQ 5. Find jumpers IS0 and IS1 (kind of at the lower left of the board). You want both jumpers off the pins, so pull off the jumper on IS1 (the one on IS0 should already be off). Reattach them so they hang off one pin.

Now let's set your base memory. By default, the Sound Blaster's at 0x220. Again, you want both jumpers to be off the pins to get 0x280, so remove the jumpers from IOS1 and IOS0. Reattach them so they hang off one pin—this keeps them handy for later.

Now the DMA channels. By default, they're at 1 and 5, so you only have to change the 16-bit channel. That's a good thing because most software that supports the Sound Blaster *only* supports 8-bit DMA through channel 1. If something else is at channel 1 (which is pretty unlikely), change *it,* not the Sound Blaster. To change your 16-bit DMA channel to 6, find jumpers DBS0 and DBS1. By default, both are jumpered; remove the connector over pins DBS0 and hang it so it attaches to only one pin.

Step 12: Prepare the CD-ROM drive.

You're almost ready to plug your sound card into an open slot. There are two scenarios you could be following: internal CD-ROM drive and external CD-ROM drive. Their installations are slightly different.

If you have an internal CD-ROM drive, you should take this opportunity to attach the wires that connect the sound card to the internal CD-ROM drive. It's a lot easier to attach them before inserting the CD-ROM drive into a drive bay because you can see what you're doing and maneuver your fingers more easily.

There are two wires you'll need to attach. The first is about a foot long, two inches wide, and flat. It's called a ribbon cable. The second is also about a foot long, but it looks round—more like a regular wire. The ribbon cable carries data between the CD-ROM drive and the sound card; the other cable carries the sound from the CD-ROM drive to the sound card when you play regular audio CDs in your CD-ROM drive. All the connectors on the back of the CD-ROM drive have distinctive shapes, and the cables you have will fit into only one slot.

Attach the ribbon cable. Some, but not most, ribbon cables have on their connectors a small flange that ensures that you can't insert the cable into the slot incorrectly (unless you use a *lot* of force). It's kind of like sliding tab A into slot B. And the direction does matter. So look closely at the CD-ROM drive, specifically just above the connector where the ribbon cable goes. You should see, somewhere, a label that says "Bus." Just below that, you'll see some numbers. Look for the number 1. That 1 identifies pin 1 of the connector. Now look at the ribbon cable itself; see that one edge of it is a different color from the rest (probably red). That side of the cable should plug into the connector near the number 1. Remember: red, one. When you're connecting the cable to the sound card, you're going to attach the red side to pin 1 again.

Now attach the other wire, which carries audio sound from the CD-ROM drive to the sound card when you play audio CDs. You'll probably find its connector at the right of the CD-ROM drive labeled "Audio." Both ends are different shapes, so if the end you're using doesn't fit right, try the other end. In addition, it has little tabs on it, so it can go in only one way (right-side up). If you find you're exerting a lot of force, flip the wire over and try it the other way.

Now your wires are attached. Time to insert the drive into an open bay. Actually installing your CD-ROM drive is going to be a bit different from computer type to computer type. The basic procedure is pretty similar, but the specifics vary greatly. Here's the basic lineup:

Step 12a: Open the case (I know you already have yours open, but I'm being thorough).

Step 12b: Pop out a 5¼-inch, half-height external drive bay cover. The front of your computer probably has at least one drive bay cover; they're very nondescript and look just slightly like they're really meant to be removed. Most of them will fall out if you give them a good solid whack into the computer.

Step 12c: Insert the CD-ROM cables through the open bay, then slide the CD-ROM drive in after. Some systems require you to attach runners or rails to the CD-ROM before you slide it in. These runners slip into small notches in the sides of the drive bay like a kitchen drawer. They're also a nuisance. That's because your PC doesn't come with extras and your kit probably didn't include any. You may have to call your PC manufacturer to get two more runners (you can also try a local computer store). You can tell if your system needs runners by looking at a component already installed (like your floppy drive). Are there small runners attached to its sides? If so, the CD-ROM drive will probably need them, too. Attach the runners now and slide the drive into place.

Step 12d: Secure the CD-ROM drive with very small screws. For systems without runners, the screws drive through the sides of the drive bay enclosure and into the CD-ROM drive. If your system uses runners, this step may not be necessary (some runners "click" into place), or you may secure the CD-ROM drive from the front. Where do you get the screws, though? Good question. Usually, I "borrow" them from other components that look like they're over-secured. Like my floppy drive, which had six screws holding it in. It really only needs three, and I can use the other three on the CD-ROM drive.

Step 12e: Connect power to the CD-ROM drive. At the back of your computer is its power supply. It has all sorts of wires coming out of it, all of which end in translucent plastic plugs that have four holes. Pick one and plug it into the power connector on the CD-ROM drive. If you don't have a free one, rush to Radio Shack or a local computer store and explain your situation. You want a Y cable for a PC power supply. Then just unplug one of the peripherals and plug the Y cable into it to split it into two.

If you have an external CD-ROM drive, you have two cards in your kit: the Sound Blaster and a smaller, 8-bit card. These two cards are connected by a ribbon cable that you can only plug in one way. Connect them together now. (The CD-ROM later plugs in to the back of the smaller 8-bit card.)

Step 13: Install the Sound Blaster.

Now you're ready to plug the Sound Blaster into an open slot. First, you've got to prepare your computer. It's still open, right? Okay, find an open 16-bit ISA slot (one that's next to either an 8-bit slot or extra 16-bit slot—you don't *need* an 8-bit slot—if you have the external CD-ROM that requires the extra card) and remove the metal plate that covers the opening in the back of the computer, as in Figure 2.5. (If you have an external CD-ROM drive kit, remove two of the metal plates on slots right next to each other.)

Figure 2.5 Removing the metal plate from the back of your computer

Now slide the card into place and screw its little metal flange to the back of the PC. Connect the speakers to the back of the card.

If you have an external CD-ROM kit, install the Sound Blaster in the lower of the two slots so that the smaller card can reside in the slot "on top" of the Sound Blaster (the short connecting cable is too short for you to plug them together the other way). Now you need to install the smaller card. To do so, slide it into the slot above the Sound Blaster. This may sound easy, but because the cable between the cards is so short, it's probably going to be somewhat frustrating. Break out your best curses before you attempt this. If you find it isn't working, get a friend and try installing the cards simultaneously. Seriously.

Step 14: Boot your system.

Your hardware is all installed. If the gods of PC installations are smiling on you, it's all installed properly. Just in case they aren't, don't reattach the cover just yet—it's a lot easier to pull out a card for a quick change if you don't have to drag the whole cover off.

Plug your computer back into the wall, and set it up so that you can see the monitor, type at the keyboard, and use the mouse. Now turn it on and let it boot.

If your system doesn't boot or you get an error message like "Hard disk failure. Press <F1> to continue," you have some kind of a resource conflict, probably either an IRQ or base memory address conflict. Go back to Step 2 to reascertain your free resources. If that doesn't work, try potluck settings. If this doesn't sound at all scientific, don't worry—it isn't.

Start by altering base memory addresses (the most common reason you'll get a hard disk failure message), then IRQs, then DMA channels. Be as scientific as you can, only altering one thing at a time. This advice may seem like a horrible cop-out, but, unfortunately, it's the best I can offer. There are

no perfect diagnostic tools that will tell you what system resources are free, so you never have a full guarantee that
your initial settings on your Sound Blaster will work.

Step 15: Run the Sound Blaster configuration software.

Now that your system has booted, you have to install some
software to make it work. Put the disk that has a name like
"Sound Blaster 16 Disk #1" into your disk drive (for our example, we'll say that's drive A). Type the following:

```
C:\>A:
A:\>INSTALL
```

You'll go into the Sound Blaster 16 setup.

The purpose of the setup is to add some software to your
computer and make some changes to it so that it can talk to
the Sound Blaster (see Figure 2.6). More specifically, the installation routine will add lines to your CONFIG.SYS and
AUTOEXEC.BAT files and install drivers (the software that
enables DOS and other software to talk to the Sound
Blaster) to your hard disk. During the installation, the software will ask you some simple questions about the card's
configuration. Refer to the Post-it note on your monitor (the
one on which you wrote your Sound Blaster's configuration
information) if you don't remember.

After you've finished running INSTALL, remove the Sound
Blaster diskette from your floppy drive and reboot your
computer. Watch for any error messages (if the installation
completed properly, which it probably did, you won't see
any). Now type the following:

```
A:\>C:
C:\>CD \SB16
C:\SB16\>TESTSB16
```

The TESTSB16 program will test your Sound Blaster to
make sure it's running perfectly. If you get an error message

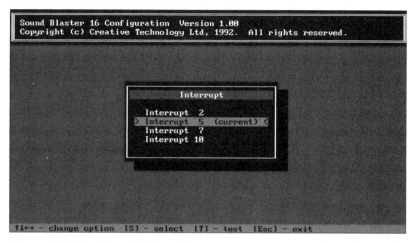

Figure 2.6 The Sound Blaster 16 setup program tests your settings before using them.

or TESTSB16 hangs, you probably have either a resource conflict (unlikely) or your system cannot do 16-bit DMA. Rerun SBCONFIG (there's a copy in the SB16 directory) and make sure that the installation program's settings agree with those on the card. If everything looks okay, turn off 16-bit DMA as in Figure 2.7.

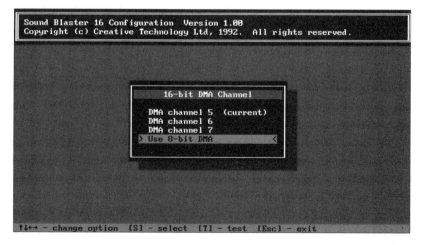

Figure 2.7 Some systems can't handle 16-bit DMA, so you'll use 8-bit instead.

That should eliminate any error messages. If you can't get sound from the speakers, check the obvious stuff:

✓ Are the speakers plugged into the card?
✓ Is the volume control on the back of the card turned up? (It's not labeled, so turn it all the way one direction, then all the way the other, then settle for a midpoint.)
✓ Is the volume on the speakers turned up?
✓ Are the speakers plugged in to power (or do they have batteries)?
✓ Are the DMA and IRQ set correctly?

The general thing about sound cards is that they usually either work or they don't. There's no middle ground where sometimes you get sound and sometimes you don't. So if all the obvious stuff is set correctly and you still aren't getting sound, you may just have a defective card. It's rare, but it happens. Call technical support (the phone number is in Appendix A).

Step 16: Install the CD-ROM drivers.

Once you've tested the Sound Blaster and everything's working, install the CD-ROM drivers from the CD-ROM driver diskette that came with the kit. Put that diskette into drive A (or whatever drive it goes into) and type the following:

```
C:\>A:
A:\>INSTALL
```

This routine will install all the drivers necessary to get DOS to talk to your CD-ROM drive. It will also ask you some questions about your Sound Blaster setup—specifically about the DMA. Refer to your Post-it for information.

Just to let you know, there are two sets of drivers that DOS needs in order to talk to a CD-ROM drive. The first is the hardware-dependent driver, so called because there's a different one for each vendor's CD-ROM drive on the market. CD-ROM drives aren't like diskette drives or hard drives. Aside from the really obvious (you can't write data onto them—they're read-only), there's no information in your PC's BIOS (Basic Input/Output System) for how to talk to a CD-ROM drive. (In case you don't know, the BIOS contains information for how to talk to just about every component that comes in a stripped-down PC—the diskette drive, the disk drive, the keyboard, the CPU, and so on.) So you (or, more precisely, your CD-ROM drive vendor) need to supply one.

Once the hardware-dependent driver is installed, DOS still needs something—the Microsoft CD Extensions (MSCDEX). MSCDEX (pronounced emm-ess-see-decks) plays some non-obvious role in the interaction of DOS with your CD-ROM drive. That role is to provide a common interface for applications to talk to. Rather than knowing how to talk to all the hardware-dependent drivers, your programs just have to know how to talk to MSCDEX, which will cheerfully talk to all the hardware-dependent drivers. With recent versions of DOS (6.0 and later) and Windows (3.1 and later), MSCDEX is included, but your multimedia kit vendor probably included a copy, too.

Anyway, this particular install routine will copy some more files into the `C:\SB16` directory and will modify your `CONFIG.SYS` and `AUTOEXEC.BAT` files to add support for your CD-ROM drive. After it's done, remove all floppy disks from the drives and reboot your computer. Your CD-ROM drive should come up as drive D or E (depending on what the next available drive is).

Step 17: Run Windows.

The Sound Blaster installation isn't quite done yet; you still need to run Windows (if you have it installed) to add all the Sound Blaster Windows utilities. To run Windows, just type

```
C:\>WIN
```

The Sound Blaster configuration will take care of itself. Congratulations. Your Sound Blaster should now be installed and working properly.

Reveal Kits

Reveal makes a few kits, but its killer kit is the Quantum, which includes about a billion CD titles and a pair of the best speakers on the market (40 or 80 watt, which is ten or twenty times what typical speakers can output). Since all the kits are built around the 16-bit Sound FX board, we'll limit this discussion to it.

(For Steps 1–9, please see the section entitled "The First Steps for Any Card," pages 27–38.)

Step 10: Take a guided tour of a Sound FX.

If all goes well, you're not going to have to change anything on your Sound FX, but if you do, it'll be useful to know where all the different thingamabobs are. So take a look at your Sound FX. It should look something like what's in Figure 2.8.

In case your board doesn't look like this, don't panic. Reveal changes the designs of its boards periodically (as do all hardware designers) so they can add new features or condense old ones into fewer chips (which makes the boards less expensive to manufacture).

Figure 2.8 A typical Sound FX

There are a few points you should take note of on the card. On the far right are all the external connectors. From top to bottom, they are line in, speaker output, microphone input, and the joystick/MIDI adapter plug. In case you forget, they're labeled. The one problem I have with the Sound FX is that there's no volume control on the card itself.

Moving onto the board proper, you'll see that just to the left of the external line-in connector that there are three white plugs, each of which has four pins. These are the audio connectors for the three CD-ROM drives that the Sound FX board supports. When you play audio CDs in your CD-ROM drive, the sound travels over a wire that connects to one of these three plugs. Why three? Because the Sound FX could come with any of three CD-ROM drives. The connectors are, from top to bottom, for the Sony, Panasonic (or Matsushita or Sanyo), and Mitsumi drives. Depending on the drive that came with your kit, you're going to be connecting a wire to one of these three connectors.

Keep moving left on the board and you'll run into two more sets of jumpers, labeled JP7 and JP5. JP7's job is to send a bit of electrical power (when it's closed) to the microphone port. For the most part, you won't need to do that because you'll be using either a battery-powered microphone or a dynamic microphone that doesn't need power.

JP5's job is to set the base memory address of the wave table portion of the Sound FX. By default, that address is at 0x534 (also written as 534H—same thing, just different ways of expressing a mathematical notation called hexadecimal that's used a lot when talking about PC memory).

Move a little more to the left (past a bunch of shiny metal parts) and you'll meet up with JP4, which you'll use to change the base memory address of the rest of the Sound FX. By default, pins 3 and 4 will be connected, giving the board a base memory address of 0x330.

Now move to the far left of the board, and find one more set of jumpers, JP3. These jumpers help you select which CD-ROM drive you're going to be using with your board. By default, it's the Panasonic/Matsushita/Sanyo (pins 1 and 2 are joined, as are pins 3 and 4). This set of jumpers works with the three connectors above it. These connectors are where you plug in your CD-ROM drive's ribbon cable. From top to bottom, they are for the Panasonic/Matsushita/Sanyo,

Mitsumi, and Sony drives. The Panasonic and Mitsumi drive connectors are the same size (forty pins); the Sony drive uses a thirty-four-pin connector. In case you're wondering how to tell what kind of drive you have, you'll find the manufacturer's name on all the drives (except that a Panasonic drive will likely be labeled Matsushita-Kotobuki or Sanyo).

Sound FX CD-ROM Drive Note

The Sound FX can support any of three CD-ROM drives: a Sony, a Mitsumi, or a Panasonic (or Matsushita, the parent company, or Sanyo). Why? A few reasons. First, Reveal's kits are in high demand. Reveal knows it can satisfy the demand for sound cards, but they need several suppliers to satisfy the demand for CD-ROM drives. So they build logic onto their sound cards to support several different CD-ROM drives, then order CD-ROM drives from several manufacturers. Since performance on the CD-ROM drives doesn't vary dramatically, both you and Reveal benefit: Reveal makes a sale, and you get your kit quickly.

What's odd is that the Reveal manual made it clear in my manual that I was only to use the settings for the Panasonic drive. That's right: the circuitry is in place for other drives, but they didn't seem to be shipping one.

Step 11: Configure the Sound FX.

Remember that Post-it you were supposed to write your free IRQs and your used DMAs and base memory addresses on way back in Step 2? Look at it, then compare it with the Sound FX's default setup in Table 2.13.

Table 2.13 Sound FX Defaults

Thing	Setting
Base IRQ	2
Wave table IRQ	7
8-bit DMA	1
16-bit DMA	Disabled
Base memory	0x330
Wave table base memory	0x534

So if you happen to have these base memory addresses, IRQs, and DMAs free, you can just plug and go.

If you're wondering why the sound card takes so many resources, it's because it handles so many functions. First, it gets its own IRQ. In addition, its wave table synthesizer gets an IRQ. Next, it needs two DMA channels, one for talking 8 bits at a time, one for 16. The Sound FX by default turns 16-bit DMA off because not all systems can handle it. It also gets two base memory addresses, one for the regular sounds, and one for all the wave table sounds.

If you don't have these resources free, you may have to move a few jumpers. Move them now. When you're done, write down the final configuration of your card on a Post-it note and attach it to your monitor. Much of the Sound FX configuration can be done entirely through software during the installation, so don't worry about trying to resolve IRQ conflicts here—you'll do that later.

Tables 2.14 through 2.16 show what each of the important jumpers on your Sound FX do when you move them.

Table 2.14 Sound FX Base I/O Addresses

JP4, Pin 1	JP4, Pin 2	JP4, Pin 3	JP4, Pin 4	Resulting Base I/O Address
Off	Off	Off	Off	0x350
On	On	Off	Off	0x340
Off	Off	On	On	0x330 (Default)
On	On	On	On	0x320

Table 2.15 Wave Table Interface Base I/O Addresses

JP5, Pin 1	JP5, Pin 2	JP5, Pin 3	JP5, Pin 4	Resulting Base I/O Address
Off	Off	Off	Off	0xF44
On	On	Off	Off	0x534 (Default)
Off	Off	On	On	0x608
On	On	On	On	0xE84

Table 2.16 CD-ROM Selection

JP3, Pin 1	JP3, Pin 2	JP3, Pin 3	JP3, Pin 4	CD-ROM Drive
Off	Off	Off	Off	Disabled
On	On	Off	Off	Sony
Off	Off	On	On	Mitsumi
On	On	On	On	Matsushita/Panasonic (Default)

A Configuration Example

Let's take an example. Let's say that your kit shipped with a Panasonic drive and that none of the board's settings will work in your computer. Your Post-it note tells you that you only have the resources listed in Table 2.17 free.

Table 2.17 Just as an Example . . .

Resource	Your Free Resources
IRQ	10
Base memory	0x320
DMA	2

What are you going to do? The answer is, not much. The only thing you have to change on the board itself is the base memory address. To get the board to 0x320, just attach the jumpers over all the pins in JP4. Your board is now almost ready.

Step 12: Prepare the CD-ROM drive.

You're almost ready to plug your sound card into an open slot. There are two scenarios you could be following: internal CD-ROM drive or external CD-ROM drive. Their installations are slightly different.

If you have an internal CD-ROM drive, you should take this opportunity to attach the wires that connect the sound card to the internal CD-ROM drive. It's a lot easier to attach them before inserting the CD-ROM drive into a drive bay because you can see what you're doing and maneuver your fingers more easily.

There are two wires you'll need to attach. The first is about a foot long, two inches wide, and flat. It's called a ribbon cable. The second is also about a foot long, but it looks round—more like a regular wire. The ribbon cable carries data between the CD-ROM drive and the sound card; the other cable carries the sound from the CD-ROM drive to the sound card when you play regular audio CDs in your CD-ROM drive. All the connectors on the back of the CD-ROM drive have distinctive shapes, and the cables you have will only fit into one slot.

Attach the ribbon cable. Some ribbon cables, but not most, have on their connectors a small flange that ensures that you can't insert the cable into the slot incorrectly (unless you use a *lot* of force). It's kind of like sliding tab A into slot B. And the direction does matter. So look closely at the CD-ROM drive, specifically just above the connector where the ribbon cable goes. You should see, somewhere, a label that says "Bus." Just below that, you'll see some numbers. Look for the number 1. That 1 identifies pin 1 of the connector. Now look at the ribbon cable itself; see that one edge of it is a different color from the rest (probably red). That side of the cable should plug into the connector near the number 1. Remember: red, one. When you're connecting the cable to the sound card, you're going to attach the red side to pin 1 again.

Now attach the other wire. It's the wire that carries audio sound from the CD-ROM drive to the sound card when you play audio CDs. You'll probably find its connector at the right of the CD-ROM drive labeled "Audio." Both ends are different shapes, so if the end you're using doesn't fit right, try the other end. In addition, it has little tabs on it, so that it can go in only one way (right-side up); if you find you're exerting a lot of force, flip the wire over and try it the other way.

Now your wires are attached. Time to insert the drive into an open bay. Actually installing your CD-ROM drive is going to be a bit different from computer type to computer type. The basic procedure is pretty similar, but the specifics vary greatly. Here's the basic lineup.

Step 12a: Open the case (I know you already have yours open, but I'm being thorough).

Step 12b: Pop out a 5¼-inch, half-height external drive bay cover. The front of your computer probably has at least one drive bay cover; they're very nondescript and look just slightly like they're really meant to be removed. Most of them will fall out if you give them a good solid whack into the computer.

Step 12c: Insert the CD-ROM cables through the open bay, then slide the CD-ROM drive in after. Some systems require you to attach runners to the CD-ROM before you slide it in. These runners slip into small notches in the sides of the drive bay like a kitchen drawer. They're also a nuisance. That's because your PC doesn't come with extras and your kit probably didn't include any. You may have to call your PC's manufacturer or a local computer store to get two more runners. You can tell if your system needs runners by looking at a component already installed (like your floppy drive). Are there small runners attached to its sides? If so, the CD-ROM drive will probably need them, too. Attach the runners now and slide the drive into place.

Step 12d: Secure the CD-ROM drive with very small screws. For systems without runners, the screws drive through the sides of the drive bay enclosure and into the CD-ROM drive. If your system uses runners, this step may not be necessary (some runners "click" into place), or you may secure the CD-ROM drive from the front. Where do you get the screws, though? Good question. Usually, I "borrow" them from other components that look like they're over-secured. Like my floppy drive, which had six screws holding it in. It really only needs three, and I can use the other three on the CD-ROM drive.

Step 12e: Connect power to the CD-ROM drive. At the back of your computer is its power supply. It has all sorts of wires coming out of it, all of which end in translucent plastic plugs that have four holes. Pick one and plug it into the power connector on the CD-ROM drive. If you don't have a free one, rush to Radio Shack or a local computer store and explain your situation. You want a Y cable for a PC power

supply. Then just unplug one of the peripherals and plug the
Y cable into it to split it into two.

Step 13: Install the Sound FX.

Now you're ready to plug the Sound FX into an open slot.
First you've got to prepare your computer. It's still open,
right? Okay, find an open 16-bit ISA slot and remove the
metal plate that covers the opening in the back of the computer, as in Figure 2.9. (If you have an external CD-ROM
drive kit, remove two of the metal plates on slots right next
to each other.)

Figure 2.9 Removing the metal plate from the back of your computer

Now slide the card into place and screw its little metal flange to the back of the PC. Connect the speakers to the back of the card.

Step 14: Boot your system.

Your hardware is all installed. If the gods of PC installations are smiling on you, it's all installed properly. Just in case they aren't, don't reattach the cover just yet. It's a lot easier to pull out a card for a quick change if you don't have to drag the whole cover off.

Plug your computer back into the wall, and set it up so that you can see the monitor, type at the keyboard, and use the mouse. Now turn it on and let it boot.

If your system doesn't boot or you get an error message like "Hard disk failure. Press <F1> to continue," you have some kind of a resource conflict, probably either an IRQ or base memory address conflict. Go back to Step 2 to reascertain your free resources. If that doesn't work, try potluck settings. If this doesn't sound at all scientific, don't worry—it isn't.

Start by altering base memory addresses (the most common reason you'll get a hard disk failure message), then IRQs, then DMA channels. Be as scientific as you can, only altering one thing at a time. This advice may seem like a horrible cop-out, but, unfortunately, it's the best I can offer. There are no perfect diagnostic tools that will tell you what system resources are free, so you never have a full guarantee that your initial settings on your Sound FX will work.

Step 15: Run the Sound FX configuration software.

Now that your system has booted, you have to install some software to make it work. Put the disk that has a name like "Sound FX Disk #1" into your disk drive (for our example, we'll say that's drive A). Now run Windows (the command is `WIN`). Sound FX setup only runs from Windows. Now pull down Program Manager's File menu and select Run. In the resulting dialog box, type `A:\SETUP`. You'll go into the Sound FX setup.

The purpose of the setup is to add some software to your computer and make some changes to it so that it can talk to the Sound FX card. More specifically, the installation routine will add lines to your CONFIG.SYS and AUTOEXEC.BAT files and install drivers (the software that enables DOS and other software to talk to the Sound FX card) to your hard disk. During the installation, the software will ask you some simple questions about the card's configuration. Refer to the Post-it note on your monitor (the one you wrote your Sound FX's configuration information on) if you don't remember.

Some notes during your installation of the software. First, SETUP will ask you if you want to run an express installation or a custom installation. You can probably take the express, but if you want to see what's being set where, try the custom (if you mess up, you can always rerun the installation and choose express). Next it'll ask where to put its software, with the default being C:\SOUNDFX. Unless you have a really compelling reason, leave it there. It'll also ask you if you want to use the Sound FX as your CD-ROM drive controller. The answer is Yes. When it asks you what type of CD-ROM drive you're using, tell it Panasonic. Then, when it asks you what drive letter to assign to the CD-ROM drive, accept whatever it offers unless you have a really strong reason not to. Finally, it'll ask where a file called MSCDEX.EXE is. It's probably in C:\DOS.

After you've finished running the setup routine, remove the Sound FX diskette from your floppy drive, exit from Windows, and reboot your computer and go back into Windows. Watch for any error messages (if the installation completed properly, which it probably did, you won't see any).

If you can't get sound from the speakers, check the obvious stuff:

✓ Are the speakers plugged into the card?
✓ Is the volume on the speakers turned up?

✓ Are the speakers plugged in to power (or do they have batteries)?

✓ Are the DMA and IRQ set correctly?

The general thing about sound cards is that they usually either work or they don't. There's no middle ground where sometimes you get sound and sometimes you don't. So if all the obvious stuff is set correctly and you still aren't getting sound, you may just have a defective card. It's rare, but it happens. Call technical support (the phone number is in Appendix A).

Congratulations. Your Sound FX should now be installed and working properly.

Media Vision Kits

Media Vision makes several kits all based on its Pro Audio Spectrum card. The installation for this card is incredibly simple and virtually automated: plug it in and run their software. (For Steps 1–9, please see the section entitled "The First Steps for Any Card," pages 27–38.)

Step 10: Take a guided tour of the Pro Audio Spectrum.

Take a gander at Figure 2.10. There are a few points you should take note of on the card. On the far right are all the external connectors. From top to bottom, they are line in, microphone input, speaker output, and the joystick/MIDI adapter plug. In case you forget, they're labeled. The one problem I have with the Pro Audio Spectrum is that there's no volume control on the card itself. Since the Labtec speakers that come with the kit have a volume control, this isn't a big deal unless you're using headphones.

Moving onto the board proper, you'll see just to the left of and above the external line-in connector that there are three white plugs, each of which has four pins. These are the audio connectors for the three CD-ROM drives that the Pro

Figure 2.10 A typical Pro Audio Spectrum

In case your board doesn't look like this, don't panic. Media Vision changes the designs of its boards periodically (as do all hardware designers) so that they can add new features or condense old ones into fewer chips (which makes the boards less expensive to manufacture).

Audio Spectrum board supports. When you play audio CDs in your CD-ROM drive, the sound travels over a wire that connects to one of these three plugs. Why three? Because the Pro Audio Spectrum could come with any of three CD-ROM drives. The connectors are, from right to left, for the Sony, Panasonic/Matsushita/Sanyo, and Mitsumi drives. Depending on the drive that came with your kit, you're going to be connecting a wire to one of these three connectors. (Most kits come with a Panasonic drive that's labeled as though it comes from Sanyo.)

Keep moving left on the board and you'll run into a bunch of pins sticking out. These are for the wave table synthesis upgrade that you can purchase separately to get better wave sound.

Directly below this is a jumper labeled J8. J8 controls what's called DMA 1 sharing. Most computers can have a couple of devices sharing DMA 1, so the Pro Audio Spectrum comes with sharing disabled (the jumper covers pins 2 and 3). If, for some incredibly reason, you know you want to share DMA 1 with another device, move the jumper to pins 1 and 2.

Below and to the right of J8 are J18 and J19. J18 enables you to connect a Roland MPU-401 sound device to the Pro

Audio Spectrum. It's on by default, and I see no reason to change it. J19 controls whether the Pro Audio Spectrum's joystick port is enabled. Since a system can have only one joystick, if your computer comes with a joystick built in, you'll have to move the jumper on J19 to cover both pins.

Now move to the far left of the board, and find all the plugs for CD-ROM drives. The Pro Audio Spectrum can support drives from Sony, Panasonic/Matsushita/Sanyo, and Mitsumi. The Sony drive will be labeled Sony. The Panasonic drive will be labeled Matsushita or Sanyo, and the Mitsumi drive will be labeled Mitsumi. The Panasonic and Mitsumi drive connectors are the same size (forty pins); the Sony drive uses a thirty-four-pin connector.

Pro Audio Spectrum CD-ROM Drive Note

The Pro Audio Spectrum can support any of three CD-ROM drives: a Sony, a Mitsumi, or a Panasonic (often called Matsushita or Sanyo). Why? A few reasons. First, Media Vision's kits are in high demand. Media Vision knows it can satisfy the demand for sound cards, but they need several suppliers to satisfy the demand for CD-ROM drives. So they build logic onto their sound cards to support several different CD-ROM drives, then order CD-ROM drives from several manufacturers. Since performance on the CD-ROM drives doesn't vary dramatically, both you and Media Vision benefit: Media Vision makes a sale, and you get your kit quickly.

Step 11: Configure the Pro Audio Spectrum.

If you have to change any of the jumpers, do it now. Don't worry about configuring IRQs, DMAs, or base memory addresses—the installation software will take care of that automatically.

Step 12: Prepare the CD-ROM drive.

You're almost ready to plug your sound card into an open slot. First you have to install your internal CD-ROM drive. Take this opportunity to attach the wires that connect the sound card to the internal CD-ROM drive. It's a lot easier to attach them before inserting the CD-ROM drive into a drive bay because you can see what you're doing and maneuver your fingers more easily.

There are two wires you'll need to attach. The first is about a foot long, two inches wide, and flat. It's called a ribbon cable. The second is also about a foot long, but it looks round—more like a regular wire. The ribbon cable carries data between the CD-ROM drive and the sound card; the other cable carries the sound from the CD-ROM drive to the sound card when you play regular audio CDs in your CD-ROM drive. All the connectors on the back of the CD-ROM drive have distinctive shapes, and the cables you have will fit into only one slot.

Attach the ribbon cable. Some ribbon cables, but not most, have on their connectors a small flange that ensures that you can't insert the cable into the slot incorrectly (unless you use a *lot* of force). It's kind of like sliding tab A into slot B. And the direction does matter. So look closely at the CD-ROM drive, specifically just above the connector where the ribbon cable goes. You should see, somewhere, a label that says "Interface Connection." Just below that, you'll see some numbers. Look for the number 1. That 1 identifies pin 1 of the connector. Now look at the ribbon cable itself; see that one edge of it is a different color from the rest (probably red). That side of the cable should plug into the connector near the number 1. Remember: red, one. When you're connecting the cable to the sound card, you're going to attach the red side to pin 1 again.

Now attach the other wire. It's the wire that carries audio sound from the CD-ROM drive to the sound card when you play audio CDs. You'll probably find its connector at the right of the CD-ROM drive labeled "Audio." Both ends are different shapes, so if the end you're using doesn't fit right, try the other end. In addition, it has little tabs on it, so it can go in only one way (right-side up). If you find you're exerting a lot of force, flip the wire over and try it the other way.

Now your wires are attached. Time to insert the drive into an open bay. Actually installing your CD-ROM drive is going to be a bit different from computer type to computer type. The basic procedure is pretty similar, but the specifics vary greatly. Here's the basic lineup.

Step 12a: Open the case (I know you already have yours open, but I'm being thorough).

Step 12b: Pop out a 5¼-inch, half-height external drive bay cover. The front of your computer probably has at least one drive bay cover; they're very nondescript and look just slightly like they're really meant to be removed. Most of them will fall out if you give them a good solid whack into the computer.

Step 12c: Insert the CD-ROM cables through the open bay, then slide the CD-ROM drive in after. Some systems require you to attach runners to the CD-ROM before you slide it in. These runners slip into small notches in the sides of the drive bay like a kitchen drawer. They're also a nuisance. That's because your PC doesn't come with extras and your kit probably didn't include any. You may have to call your PC manufacturer or a local computer store to get two more runners. You can tell if your system needs runners by looking at a component already installed (like your floppy drive). Are there small runners attached to its sides? If so, the CD-ROM drive will probably need them, too. Attach the runners now and slide the drive into place.

Step 12d: Secure the CD-ROM drive with very small screws. For systems without runners, the screws drive through the sides of the drive bay enclosure and into the CD-ROM drive. If your system uses runners, this step may not be necessary (some runners "click" into place), or you may secure the CD-ROM drive from the front. Where do you get the screws, though? Good question. Usually, I "borrow" them from other components that look like they're over-secured. Like my floppy drive, which had six screws holding it in. It really only needs three, and I can use the other three on the CD-ROM drive.

Step 12e: Connect power to the CD-ROM drive. At the back of your computer is its power supply. It has all sorts of wires coming out of it, all of which end in translucent plastic plugs that have four holes. Pick one and plug it into the power connector on the CD-ROM drive. If you don't have a free one, use the Y cable that comes with the Media Vision kit to split an existing cable into two outputs.

Step 13: Install the Pro Audio Spectrum.

Now you're ready to plug the Pro Audio Spectrum into an open slot. First, you've got to prepare your computer. It's still open, right? Okay, find an open 16-bit ISA slot and remove the metal plate that covers the opening in the back of the computer, as in Figure 2.11.

Figure 2.11 Removing the metal plate from the back of your computer

Now slide the card into place and screw its little metal flange to the back of the PC. Connect the speakers to the back of the card. It's important to have the speakers connected so you can hear the sound test.

Step 14: Boot your system.

Your hardware is all installed. If the gods of PC installations are smiling on you, it's all installed properly. Just in case they aren't, don't reattach the cover just yet. It's a lot easier to pull out a card for a quick change if you don't have to drag the whole cover off.

Plug your computer back into the wall, and set it up so that you can see the monitor, type at the keyboard, and use the mouse. Now turn it on and let it boot.

If you get an error message, turn your system off and make sure all the cards are all the way in their slots and everything's connected together tightly.

Step 15: Run the Pro Audio Spectrum configuration software.

Now that your system has booted, you have to install some software to make it work. Put the disk that has a name like "Media Vision Multimedia Kit Installation Disk Disk 1 of 2" into your disk drive (for our example, we'll say that's drive A). Now run Windows (the command is WIN). Pro Audio Spectrum setup only runs from Windows. Now pull down Program Manager's File menu and select Run. In the resulting dialog box, type A:\SETUP. (Assuming that the floppy is in your A drive.) You'll go into the Pro Audio Spectrum setup.

The purpose of the setup is to add some software to your computer and make some changes to it so that it can talk to the Pro Audio Spectrum card (see Figure 2.12). More specifically, the installation routine will add lines to your CONFIG.SYS and AUTOEXEC.BAT files and install drivers (the software that enables DOS and other software to talk to the Pro Audio Spectrum card) to your hard disk. The Pro Audio Spectrum installation is completely automated, so you shouldn't have to do anything—just select Standard Installation and watch it do its thing. It'll reboot the system automatically, discover where the card is, and test it automatically.

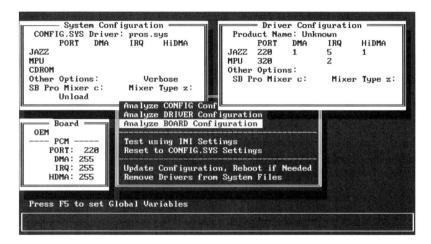

Figure 2.12 Run \MEDVSN\DIAG\DIAG if you have problems during setup.

If you can't get sound from the speakers, check the obvious stuff:

✓ Are the speakers plugged into the card?

✓ Is the volume on the speakers turned up?

✓ Are the speakers plugged in to power (or do they have batteries)?

✓ Are the DMA and IRQ set correctly?

The general thing about sound cards is that they usually either work or they don't. There's no middle ground in which sometimes you get sound and sometimes you don't. So if all the obvious stuff is set correctly and you still aren't getting sound, you may just have a defective card. It's rare, but it happens. Call technical support (the phone number is in Appendix A).

Congratulations, your Pro Audio Spectrum should now be installed and working properly.

Installing a Generic Kit

I'm the Great Carnac (remember him from the Carson show?). Even without knowing what kind of multimedia kit you have, I can tell you how to install it. That's because there's really no magic to installing the card and CD-ROM drive. If you have even a little bit of mechanical aptitude (and everybody—even my dad—does) and a lot of patience, you should have no problem. (For Steps 1–9, see the section entitled "The First Steps for Any Card," pages 27–38.)

Step 10: Take a guided tour of your sound card.

If all goes well, you're not going to have to change anything on your sound card, but if you do, it'll be useful to know where all the different thingamabobs are. So take a look at your card. It should look something like what's in Figure 2.13.

There are a few points you should take note of on the card. On the far right are all the external connectors. You'll definitely have at least one—a "line out." That's the fancy technical term for the place you plug your speakers or headphones in. It'll also probably have a "line in," which is where you plug in audio components that can supply a signal directly to the sound card, like an audio CD player or even a tape deck. There will probably be at least one more ⅛-inch jack (as they're called) on the back, this one for microphone input. Microphones require different electrical treatment from other stereo components, so they need a separate jack. Don't plug a microphone into your line-in plug. It won't work and may damage the board. Finally, you'll probably have a combined MIDI and joystick port, which is shaped vaguely like the letter "D." That's where you'll plug in a joystick or your musical instrument digital interface (MIDI) components, such as a keyboard.

Figure 2.13 A typical sound card

Moving onto the board proper, you'll see a mishmash of chips, resistors, and diodes. Ignore them. From here in you're looking for three different types of elements: jumpers, CD-ROM drive data plugs, and CD-ROM drive audio plugs. Jumpers consist of two metal prongs that stick up out of your board. They may or may not be covered by a small piece of metal embedded in black (usually) plastic. Jumpers are very simple electrical switches: When the piece of metal is over both metal prongs, the circuit is closed and electricity flows through it; when the metal isn't over the two prongs, the circuit is open and electricity doesn't flow. You'll use jumpers to set various aspects of your board's behavior.

It's possible that your sound card doesn't have any jumpers. You'll configure it through software. How does this work? How can software talk to a piece of hardware if it doesn't know its DMA, base memory, and IRQ? Some of it is just blind luck. Your sound card manufacturer took a guess about what DMA and IRQ would be unused. These are the two critical bits of information that must be unique for software to talk to a card. If, however, something in your system already uses the ones that your card comes with by default, your card may be unconfigurable—the setup software won't be able to find it.

Software configuration is both a blessing and a curse. It's really convenient to be able to plug in a sound card without worrying about getting its IRQ, DMA, and base memory address all set correctly first. That means you won't be pulling the board out of your computer to reset jumpers should something go wrong. But not all that glitters is gold. You're at the mercy of the software, and it's often the case that vendors that make good hardware don't make good software. Figuring out jumper settings can be a pain but at least it's straightforward. Much of the installation software I've seen feels as though it were translated directly from the original Greek by someone with only a rudimentary understanding of how mere mortals think. As the saying goes, "You pays your money and you takes your chances."

The CD-ROM drive data plug (or plugs—some boards have more than one) looks like a collection of jumpers all put together. There should be about thirty-four or forty pins poking out of the board. They may or may not be surrounded by a plastic frame. Usually they're located at the left end of the board, positioned either horizontally or vertically. This is where you plug in the long, flat ribbon cable that came with your kit. If there's a plastic corral around all the pins, it probably has a break in it at one point. That break accommodates a tab that's on the ribbon cable and ensures that you can't insert the cable upside down. Even if there's no corral, you should find that there are numbers on the board itself, usually a number 1 or 2 at one end and a number 33, 34, 39, or 40 at the other. Because pin 1 of the board must connect to pin 1 on the CD-ROM drive, it's important to make sure that everything lines up properly. That's why one side of your ribbon cable will be red, either a nice solid red, or a dotted-line red. That redness represents the side that's supposed to line up with pin 1.

Somewhere else on your board, usually near the top and usually either in the center or over to the right side you'll find the "CD audio in" connector. To it connects the round wire (probably gray) that came with your kit. What's all this for? When you play audio CDs in your CD-ROM drive, the sound travels over a round wire separate from the flat ribbon cable. Because an audio signal is so different from a data signal, it requires a separate wire. Does this mean you won't be able to hear any music if you don't connect the round wire? No. Some music, like that in a video game, for example, has been digitized and comes over the flat ribbon cable. But audio CDs (the kind you buy in a record store) can't pass information over the ribbon cable, so they have this separate wire.

Some kits will have more than one CD-ROM drive data plug and more than one CD audio in connector. Why? Because the many sound cards could come with more than one manufacturer's CD-ROM drives. Most popular are Panasonic (also called by its parent company's name, Matsushita), Mitsumi, and Sony. In case you're wondering how to tell what kind of drive you have, you'll find the manufacturer's name on all the drives (except that a Panasonic drive will likely be labeled Matsushita).

In such cases, you'll find a set of jumpers on the board to enable you to select which CD-ROM drive you're going to be using with your board. These jumpers are often located where you plug in your CD-ROM drive's ribbon cable. On most sound cards, the default is the Panasonic. Which connector goes with which drive? If they aren't labeled, here's a guide to help you figure it out: the Panasonic and Mitsumi drive connectors are the same size (forty pins); the Sony drive uses a smaller thirty-four pin connector. Telling the Panasonic from the Mitsumi plug can be difficult.

CD-ROM Drive Note

Many sound cards can support any of several CD-ROM drives: usually one from Sony, Mitsumi, or Panasonic (or Matsushita, the parent company). Why? A few reasons. First, multimedia kits are in high demand. Vendors know they can satisfy the demand for sound cards, but they need several suppliers to satisfy the demand for CD-ROM drives. So they build logic onto their sound cards to support several different CD-ROM drives, then order CD-ROM drives from several manufacturers. Since performance from double-speed CD-ROM drive to double-speed CD-ROM drive doesn't vary dramatically, both you and the manufacturer benefit: they make a sale, and you get your kit quickly.

Step 11: Configure the card.

Remember that Post-it you were supposed to write your free IRQs and your used DMAs and base memory addresses on way back in Step 2? Look at it. Now open the manual that came with your card. Check the table of contents for mention of the hardware settings of your card (they might be in an appendix). Fill in Table 2.18 with the information you garner from your card.

Table 2.18 Fill in Your Sound Card's Defaults

Thing	Setting
Base IRQ	
Second IRQ	
8-bit DMA	
16-bit DMA	
Base memory	
Wave table base memory	

Now compare your Post-it to the information in this table. If they line up right, you can plug and go. If not, you're going to have to check your manual for how to change your sound card's settings. You may change these settings entirely with jumpers, entirely through software, or use some combination of the two.

If you're wondering why the sound card takes so many resources, it's because it handles so many functions. First, it gets its own IRQ. In addition, its wave table synthesizer may get an IRQ. Next, it needs two DMA channels, one for talking 8 bits at a time, one for 16. Not all computers can handle 16-bit DMA. The card also gets two base memory addresses, one for the regular sounds, and one for all the wave table sounds.

If you don't have these resources free, you may have to move a few jumpers. Move them now. When you're done, write down the final configuration of your card on a Post-it note and attach it to your monitor.

Step 12: Prepare the CD-ROM drive.

You're almost ready to plug your sound card into an open slot. There are two scenarios you could be following: internal CD-ROM drive and external CD-ROM drive. Their installations are slightly different.

If you have an internal CD-ROM drive, you should take this opportunity to attach the wires that connect the sound card to the internal CD-ROM drive. It's a lot easier to attach them before inserting the CD-ROM drive into a drive bay because you can see what you're doing and maneuver your fingers more easily.

There are two wires you'll need to attach. The first is about a foot long, two inches wide, and flat. It's called a ribbon cable. The second is also about a foot long, but it looks round—more like a regular wire. The ribbon cable carries data between the CD-ROM drive and the sound card; the other cable carries the sound from the CD-ROM drive to the sound card when you play regular audio CDs in your CD-ROM drive. All the connectors on the back of the CD-ROM drive have distinctive shapes, and the cables you have will only fit into one slot.

Attach the ribbon cable. Some ribbon cables, but not most, have on their connectors a small flange that ensures that you can't insert the cable into the slot incorrectly (unless you use a *lot* of force). It's kind of like sliding tab A into slot B. And the direction does matter. So look closely at the CD-ROM drive, specifically just above the connector where the ribbon cable goes. It will probably be labeled "Main I/F" or "Bus." Just below that, you'll see some numbers. Look for the number 1. That 1 identifies pin 1 of the connector.

If you have a Sony drive, the pins may not be labeled, but pin 1 is on the right as you face the rear of the drive.

Now look at the ribbon cable itself; see that one edge of it is a different color from the rest (probably red). That side of the cable should plug into the connector near the number 1. Remember: red, one. When you're connecting the cable to the sound card, you're going to attach the red side to pin 1 again.

Now attach the other wire. It's the wire that carries audio sound from the CD-ROM drive to the sound card when you play audio CDs. You'll probably find its connector at the right of the CD-ROM drive labeled "Audio" or "Audio Out." Both ends of the wire are often different shapes, so if the end you're using doesn't fit right, try the other end. In addition, it has little tabs on it so it can go in only one way (right-side up). If you find you're exerting a lot of force, flip the wire over and try it the other way.

Now your wires are attached. Time to insert the drive into an open bay. Actually installing your CD-ROM drive is going to be a bit different from computer type to computer type. The basic procedure is pretty similar, but the specifics vary greatly. Here's the basic lineup.

Step 12a: Open the case (I know you already have yours open, but I'm being thorough).

Step 12b: Pop out a 5¼-inch, half-height external drive bay cover. The front of your computer probably has at least one drive bay cover; they're very nondescript and look just slightly like they're really meant to be removed. Most of them will fall out if you give them a good solid whack into the computer.

Step 12c: Insert the CD-ROM cables through the open bay, then slide the CD-ROM drive in after. Some systems require you to attach runners to the CD-ROM before you slide it in. These runners slip into small notches in the sides of the drive bay like a kitchen drawer. They're also a nuisance. That's because your PC doesn't come with extras and your kit probably didn't include any. You may have to call your PC manufacturer or a local computer store to get two more runners. You can tell if your system needs runners by looking at a component already installed (like your floppy drive). Are there small runners attached to its sides? If so, the CD-ROM drive will probably need them, too. Attach the runners now and slide the drive into place.

Step 12d: Secure the CD-ROM drive with very small screws. For systems without runners, the screws drive through the sides of the drive bay enclosure and into the CD-ROM drive. If your system uses runners, this step may not be necessary (some runners "click" into place), or you may secure the CD-ROM drive from the front. Where do you get the screws, though? Good question. Usually, I "borrow" them from other components that look like they're over-secured. Like my floppy drive, which had six screws holding it in. It really only needs three, and I can use the other three on the CD-ROM drive.

Step 12e: Connect power to the CD-ROM drive. At the back of your computer is its power supply. It has all sorts of wires coming out of it, all of which end in translucent plastic plugs that have four holes. Pick one and plug it into the power connector on the CD-ROM drive. If you don't have a free one, rush to Radio Shack or a local computer store and explain your situation. You want a Y cable for a PC power supply. Then just unplug one of the peripherals and plug the Y cable into it to split it into two.

Step 13: Install your sound card.

Now you're ready to plug the sound card into an open slot. First, you've got to prepare your computer. It's still open, right? Okay, find an open 16-bit ISA slot and remove the metal plate that covers the opening in the back of the computer, as in Figure 2.14.

Now slide the card into place and screw its little metal flange to the back of the PC. Connect the speakers to the back of the card.

Figure 2.14 Removing the metal plate from the back of your computer

Step 14: Boot your system.

Your hardware is all installed. If the gods of PC installations are smiling on you, it's all installed properly. Just in case they aren't, don't reattach the cover just yet. It's a lot easier to pull out a card for a quick change if you don't have to drag the whole cover off.

Plug your computer back into the wall, and set it up so that you can see the monitor, type at the keyboard, and use the mouse. Now turn it on and let it boot.

If your system doesn't boot or you get an error message like "Hard disk failure. Press <F1> to continue," you have some kind of a resource conflict, probably either an IRQ or base memory address conflict. Go back to Step 2 to reascertain your free resources. If that doesn't work, try potluck settings. If this doesn't sound at all scientific, don't worry—it isn't.

Start by altering base memory addresses (the most common reason you'll get a hard disk failure message), then IRQs, then DMA channels. Be as scientific as you can, only altering one thing at a time. This advice may seem like a horrible cop-out, but, unfortunately, it's the best I can offer. There are no perfect diagnostic tools that will tell you what system resources are free, so you never have a full guarantee that your initial settings on your sound card will work.

Step 15: Run your sound card configuration software.

This is the last step in the process and, thanks to the complete lack of standardization in the sound card software world, the step where I have to be the most vague. It's pretty clear that, now that your system has booted, you have to install some software to make it work.

Locate the installation floppies that came with your sound card. They'll probably have names like "Installation Disk 1," "Installation Disk 2," and so on, but they may not. Put the first disk into your disk drive (for our example, we'll say that's drive A).

Now check for drive A filenames ending in .EXE, like this:

```
C:\>DIR A:*.EXE
```

This will probably yield one or two files. Look for a file with a name like INSTALL.EXE or SETUP.EXE. and run it, something like this:

```
C:\>A:
A:\>INSTALL
```

If you get an error message like "This program requires Microsoft Windows," start Windows on your computer, select File, Run from the Program Manager's main menu, and type in the name of the file again. If not, you should be running your sound card's installation software. It will probably ask you for the configuration of your card (its base memory, IRQ, and DMA), so be ready to refer to your Post-it when it does.

The purpose of the setup is to add some software to your computer and make some changes to it so that it can talk to the sound card. More specifically, the installation routine will add lines to your CONFIG.SYS and AUTOEXEC.BAT files and install drivers (the software that enables DOS and other software to talk to the sound card) to your hard disk.

Some notes during your installation of the software. First, it will probably ask you where to put its software. Unless you have a really compelling reason, leave it wherever its default is. It may also ask you if you want to use your sound card as your CD-ROM drive controller. The answer is Yes. When it asks you what type of CD-ROM drive you're using, tell it. Then, if it asks you what drive letter to assign to the CD-ROM drive, accept whatever it offers unless you have a really strong reason not to. Finally, it may ask where a file called MSCDEX.EXE is. It's probably in C:\DOS.

After you've finished installing the software, remove the installation diskette from your floppy drive (exit from Windows if necessary) and reboot your computer. Watch for any error messages (if the installation completed properly, which it probably did, you won't see any). There should be a test program that the software installed. Run it now to make sure everything's working.

If you can't get sound from the speakers, check the obvious stuff:

✓ Are the speakers plugged into the card?
✓ Is the volume control on the back of the card turned up? (It's not labeled, so turn it all the way one direction, then all the way the other, then settle for a midpoint.)

✓ Is the volume on the speakers turned up?

✓ Are the speakers plugged in to power (or do they have batteries)?

✓ Are the DMA and IRQ set correctly?

The general thing about sound cards is that they usually either work or they don't. There's no middle ground in which you get sound sometimes, but not other times. So if all the obvious stuff is set correctly and you still aren't getting sound, you may just have a defective card. It's rare, but it happens. Call technical support (the phone number is in Appendix A).

Now, if the installation procedure didn't already accomplish this, you may have to install your CD-ROM drivers. There will probably be a separate diskette for this (at least, that's the way Creative Labs does it). Repeat the basic installation procedure with this diskette, reboot your computer, and test the CD-ROM drive by putting a CD into it and seeing if you can read it.

You should be up and running now.

3
Separate Installation

I beheld the wretch—the miserable monster whom I had created.

—MARY WOLLSTONECRAFT SHELLEY,
Frankenstein, 1818

. . . And from these parts, I knew I had created a monster. Installing a multimedia upgrade kit isn't so bad—at least you know that all the parts should work together. Adding a sound card to a system that already has a CD-ROM or vice versa can mean serious trauma. Why? Because the parts weren't guaranteed to work together from the start.

So in this chapter I'm going to try to help you install a sound card separate from a CD-ROM drive and vice versa. We'll deal with installing sound cards from Creative Labs, Reveal, and Media Vision, as well as general instructions for installing most any other sound card. Then we'll spend a bit of time installing a CD-ROM drive into your system.

What Makes It So Difficult?

Installing parts separately doesn't have to be difficult. If you already have a sound card, for example, you can call your manufacturer to find out what CD-ROM drives will connect to it and to get drivers from them. You can probably even purchase a CD-ROM drive from them that will be guaranteed to work.

However, installing a sound card when you already have a CD-ROM drive can be a bit of a hassle. This is because of what the computer industry calls standards.

The primary standard for attaching a CD-ROM drive to your computer is called the small computer systems interface, or SCSI (pronounced *scuzzy*). SCSI is a widely used standard for attaching to a computer all sorts of peripherals—scanners, disk drives, CD-ROM drives, and tape drives to name a few. To attach a CD-ROM drive to your computer, someone probably plugged what's called a SCSI host adapter into one of your system's bus slots, then plugged the CD-ROM drive into that.

So what? Nothing, maybe. If you install your sound card and just connect the CD-ROM drive to it with an audio cable, everything should work fine (provided you can find the cable). If, however, you unwisely try to plug the CD-ROM drive into the sound card's CD-ROM controller circuitry, you'll probably wind up spending a few days debugging things.

That's my roundabout way of saying that if you purchase a CD-ROM drive and sound card separately, and particularly if you don't purchase a CD-ROM drive that your sound card maker says will work with your sound card, don't try to have your sound card control your CD-ROM drive. Sometimes it does work, but when it doesn't, it's a major hassle.

An Overview

Following is the basic procedure for installing a sound card and a CD-ROM drive in any PC.

Installing a Sound Card

1. Check for free resources. This is where you make sure you have bus slots, IRQs, DMAs, and base memory addresses.

2. Configure your card. Make your card conform to your free IRQs, DMAs, and base memory by moving jumpers (if the card has them).

3. Install the card.

4. Connect the card to your CD-ROM drive.

5. Boot your computer.

6. Configure the card software.

7. Enjoy the fruit of your labor.

Installing a CD-ROM Drive

1. Check for free resources for your CD-ROM controller. Whether you use a SCSI host adapter, enhanced IDE controller, or some proprietary interface card (the last of which I strongly recommend against), you're going to need to know that you have free bus slots, IRQs, DMAs, base memory addresses, and, for an internal CD-ROM drive, a free drive bay and free power cable.

2. Configure your interface card. Make the card conform to your free IRQs, DMAs, and base memory by moving jumpers (if the card has them).

3. Install the interface card.

4. Install the CD-ROM drive.

5. Connect the CD-ROM drive's audio port to your sound card's audio input.

6. Boot the computer.

7. Configure your CD-ROM drivers.

8. Enjoy the fruit of your labor.

Of course, it never works out this easily, but you can see that it's a pretty simple process.

The First Steps for Any Sound Card

No matter what kind of card you have, you need to run through the following nine steps.

The key to an effortless installation lies in Steps 1 and 2. Remember to plan ahead.

Step 1: Determine that your PC meets your sound card's requirements.

Before you open your box or unscrew your case, check to make sure you have the following:

✓ ISA bus

✓ 386 or better CPU

✓ VGA monitor and video card

✓ 5 MB free hard disk space

✓ DOS 3 or later

✓ Windows 3.1 or later

This step is really kind of perfunctory because most PCs today meet every kit's requirements. Just in case, you'd better check.

Most sound cards will install into any IBM compatible with an ISA bus (also called an AT bus) and a 386 or better (486 or Pentium) processor. You'd better have at least a VGA monitor and video adapter (although some kits still support the old EGA standard) and about 5 MB of free disk space on your hard disk (you *do* have a hard disk, don't you?) for the drivers and other software the sound card will need to install. Oh, and you'll probably want at least DOS version 3 or later (version 6.22 is current). Finally, if you expect to do any work in Microsoft Windows you should have Windows 3.1 or later—I've never seen a sound card that supports previous versions.

Step 2: Determine free IRQs, DMAs, and base memory addresses.

Check for the following:

✓ Free IRQs

✓ Free DMAs

✓ Free base memory addresses

This step is kind of tricky. There's no really easy way to 100 percent guarantee that you'll get it right if you do it from software. Microsoft includes with MS-DOS 5 and later a utility called Microsoft System Diagnostics (MSD). As you can see in Figure 3.1, it's not very helpful.

MSD will probably give you a vague indication of what kind of IRQs, DMAs, and so on that you have. Make that *very* vague. The odds are pretty good that you're going to have to wait until your system is open before you can really make sure that you have this information right. If you look closely at Figure 3.1, you'll notice that it says my IRQ 5 is free. It isn't—there's a sound card there. Regardless, IRQs labeled (Reserved) are generally free.

```
 File  Utilities  Help
                              IRQ Status
   IRQ  Address    Description      Detected          Handled By

    0   09A8:04B7  Timer Click      Yes               SNAP.EXE
    1   C95E:1923  Keyboard         Yes               Block Device
    2   0430:0057  Second 8259A     Yes               Default Handlers
    3   0430:006F  COM2: COM4:      COM2:             Default Handlers
    4   D543:0096  COM1: COM3:      COM1: COM3: PS/2 StyMOUSE.EXE
    5   0430:009F  LPT2:            No                Default Handlers
    6   0430:00B7  Floppy Disk      Yes               Default Handlers
    7   0070:06F4  LPT1:            Yes               System Area
    8   0430:0052  Real-Time Clock  Yes               Default Handlers
    9   F000:EC2D  Redirected IRQ2  Yes               BIOS
   10   0430:00CF  (Reserved)                         Default Handlers
   11   0430:00E7  (Reserved)                         Default Handlers
   12   0430:00FF  (Reserved)                         Default Handlers
   13   F000:EC36  Math Coprocessor Yes               BIOS
   14   0430:0117  Fixed Disk       Yes               Default Handlers
   15   0430:012F  (Reserved)                         Default Handlers

                              OK

 IRQ Status: Displays current usage of hardware interrupts.
```

Figure 3.1 MSD isn't really great about letting you know what your free IRQs, DMAs, and base memory addresses are, but at least it's free.

Nonetheless, write down the free resource information MSD provides on a Post-it note. You'll need it in just a minute.

If you're really at a loss for the configuration information of the cards in your computer, there are several programs that can help. At work I use one called PC Tools for Windows from Central Point Software (see Figure 3.2). There's also one called SysInfo, and another called CheckIt Pro Analyst.

Truth to tell, though, PCs weren't designed with configuration-determining software in mind. There's no 100 percent sure piece of software available that will figure out every card you might have plugged into your computer. Sorry.

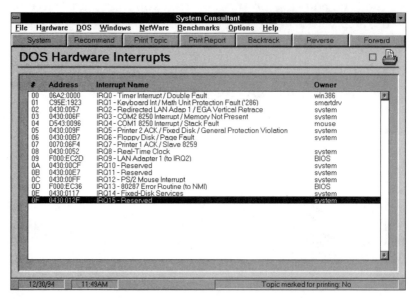

Figure 3.2 Even Central Point's System Consultant isn't 100 percent accurate.

The new Plug and Play standard (from Intel, Microsoft and Al, as in et al.) should help fix that, but that's future stuff, and you have to figure out your configuration today. Well, if MSD didn't give you a full report (how do you know? I'll tell you: it didn't) then wait a minute and I'll tell you what to do.

Step 3: Back up crucial software.

This may sound silly. It may sound ridiculous. It may sound like a pain in the buttocks. But. And I underline that: <u>But</u>. Heck, I'll underline it, italicize it, boldface it, and put it into a different font: ***But*** you had better do it. Start by backing up four critical files: AUTOEXEC.BAT, CONFIG.SYS,

WIN.INI, and SYSTEM.INI. (You should be doing this any-
time you change your files anyway, but do it now.) To do
this, put a formatted floppy into your floppy drive (I'll assume its drive A) and run these commands:

```
C:\>COPY \CONFIG.SYS A:
C:\>COPY \AUTOEXEC.BAT A:
C:\>COPY \WINDOWS\WIN.INI A:
C:\>COPY \WINDOWS\SYSTEM.INI A:
```

Now if you run into any problems when booting your computer, you can restore these four files, and things should be
fine.

Now you have to back up the software that came with your
sound card. This is for when (not if, when) your distribution
diskettes go south. It will happen: it always does. Try using
these commands (I'm assuming you have a hard disk):

```
C:\>MD DISTRIB
C:\>MD DISTRIB\DISK1
C:\>MD DISTRIB\DISK2
```

Repeat this command once for every distribution diskette so
that you have unique directories for each. Now place the
first of your distribution diskettes in your floppy drive. I'm
assuming you're using drive A. Now run these commands:

```
C:\>XCOPY /S A:*.* C:\DISTRIB\DISK1
```

Now put the second diskette into the drive and run the command again, but this time change the target directory to
C:\DISTRIB\DISK2. Keep doing it until all the diskettes
are backed up onto your hard drive.

Now you can create a second copy of your distribution floppies really easily: just XCOPY the files from the hard drive
onto a bunch of new floppies. You'll need to format one new
floppy for each of the distribution floppies that came with
your software:

```
C:\>FORMAT A:
```

When it asks you if you want to format another, say Yes until
you've formatted all the floppies you need. Now create nice
new labels for your floppies that tell you what's on them, and
XCOPY the data off the hard disk onto the floppies:

```
C:\>XCOPY /S C:\DISTRIB\DISK1\*.* A:\
```

And keep at it until you're out of directories. You should now
have a fully backed-up set of floppies. You can delete your
DISTRIB directories now. If you have MS-DOS 6 or later,
you can use this command:

```
C:\>DELTREE C:\DISTRIB
```

But if you have a previous DOS version, you're going to have
to go into each directory, delete all the files, then delete the
directory, like this:

```
C:\>DEL \DISTRIB\DISK1
C:\>RMDIR \DISTRIB\DISK1
```

And so on. Now you have a nice working (one hopes) copy of
your multimedia kit's distribution diskettes.

Step 4: Open your PC.

Let's make like Sherlock Holmes and crack your case. PC
enclosures come in two basic types: desktop and tower. The
desktop version sits comfortably on . . . well, on your desktop, usually with your monitor on top of it. The tower type
of case is usually too tall for your desktop—it dwarfs everything on your desk when you try to put it there.

In either case (pun intended), you're going to be dealing
with some kind of fastener to remove the enclosure that covers the guts of your computer. With most cases, these fasteners are screws of some kind, thumbscrews and Phillips
screws being the most common. In some cases, you may
have an advanced case design that uses some kind of screwless latch to pop open.

I'd like to say, "Read your owner's manual to see how to open your case." But, if you're like me, you no longer have your owner's manual. If you ever had one at all. Never fear: here are hints for opening both types of cases.

Screwless Case: These are usually the easier of the two to open. You'll know you have one if, somewhere on your enclosure, there's a small button that turns neither the computer nor "Turbo" on or off. Usually the latch is located either in the upper-middle of the front (as on IBM ValuePoint) or somewhere on the back. Push the button and hold it in.

Screwy Case: Look at the back of your computer. There are probably a bunch of screws there. Look at the edges of the back. You'll probably see five or six screws that pretty clearly secure the sides of the computer to the back. Just remove these.

Now wiggle the enclosure front-to-back. That's right, stand in front of your computer, lay your hands flat on the side of the computer, and give the enclosure a good hard jerk toward you, then away from you. The case (or a panel on the case) should move in one of the two directions. Pull or push it as far in that direction as it will go, then lift it up until it's clear of the rest of the computer. You're in.

Step 5: Recheck your DMAs, IRQs, and base memory while the case is open.

Check again for the following:

✓ Free IRQs
✓ Free DMAs
✓ Free base memory addresses

Now that you're inside your computer, you'll have a really great time verifying that MSD gave you totally inaccurate information about your system's configuration. How? By looking at each of the cards in your computer and checking to see what their settings are.

This is no small task for even the most knowledgeable PC people. Most cards don't have obvious settings; instead, they have jumpers with names like J0, J1, H5, and N21. They have DIP switches numbered 0–7 that have nothing to do with anything. And they *don't print what the jumpers and switches mean on the board*. Of all the boards I've plugged into computers, only Adaptec has the courtesy to assume that you're going to throw away their manual and to print what each of the jumper settings means. Some boards don't even have jumpers or DIP switches at all—they're configured through software.

Tables 3.1 and 3.2 list the common IRQ and DMA settings that are already in your PC. Since most card vendors don't let you use a setting that they already know is going to be in use, these tables will give you a leg up.

Table 3.1 Common IRQ Assignments

IRQ	What Uses It
0	System timer
1	Keyboard
2	Connection from PIC #1 to PIC #2
3	COM2; your PC's second communications port (look for a small-ish D-shaped connector on the back of your PC). You may have a mouse connected to it.
4	COM1; why somebody put COM2 before COM1 eludes me.
5	LPT2; your PC's second printer port
6	Floppy disk drive
7	LPT1; reversed again
8	Real-time clock
9	Connection from PIC #2 to PIC #1
10	Usually unused
11	Usually unused
12	Usually unused, unless you have a bus mouse (or PS/2-style mouse)
13	Usually unused
14	Hard disk
15	Usually unused

Table 3.2 Common Base Memory Address Assignments

Port	Usually Used For
0200	Sound cards
0278	LPT2
02E8	COM4 (if you have one, which you probably don't)
02F8	COM2
0330	SCSI host adapter
0378	LPT1
03B0	Video cards (which use through 03CF)
03E8	COM3 (which you probably don't have)
03F0	Floppy drives
03F8	COM1

Regardless, you've got to take a look just to make sure. So first you're going to have to pull your boards out of the slots they're in. In every computer I've seen, this is done by loosening a Phillips-head screw located toward the back of the computer. Each board gets its own screw. So look at each board and trace it to the back of your computer. When you run out of board, there will be a metal plate—the plate that's exposed through the back of the computer. It has a lip inside the computer, and, on top of this lip, you should see a screw. Remove it. But before you wrestle the board out of its slot, *remove any wires from its back*. Any wires that protrude out the back of your computer will hang up the board as you try to remove it.

Now pull the board out. This isn't as easy as it seems because the boards fit very tightly into their slots. Try grasping opposite ends of the board between your thumbs and index fingers, then lifting first the right side, then the left side. You're wiggling the board free. Take a look at Figure 3.3.

Figure 3.3 Remove boards by unscrewing, unplugging, and wiggling them.

Both DIP switches and jumpers are very small. As you work with them, (and you will work with them) you might want a small screwdriver or a pair of needle-nosed pliers.

Once the board's free of the computer, check it for jumpers or DIP switches. You're wondering, maybe, what's a jumper? Or a DIP switch? They're two ways of accomplishing basically the same thing: closing a circuit. With jumpers, you have a small piece of metal with plastic around it that either closes the gap between two electrical poles or doesn't. A DIP switch (stands for dual in-line packaging) is basically a little light switch; flick it to 0 and it's off (or "open"), flip it to 1 and it's on (or "closed").

If you're lucky, the board you're looking at has its jumpers and/or DIP switches labeled with their function. For example, jumper J1 might be labeled IRQ 5. That means if you close the jumper (put it over the two little wires poking out of the board), you'll set the board to IRQ 5. Look at your boards and see if you can determine more information about their configuration than MSD gave you. If you have the manuals for these components, you'll find out what the jumpers and DIP switches mean by looking in there (usually in an appendix).

Once you're done, replace all of them. It doesn't matter which slots you slide which boards into usually: any 16-bit ISA board can go into any 16-bit ISA slot, any 8-bit ISA card can go into any ISA slot at all, any PCI board can go into any PCI slot.

There may be a catch with some VESA-Local bus slots (called VL-bus slots for short). VL-bus slots are numbered (1, 2, and so on). Some VL-bus boards (like my Adaptec AHA-2842) need to go into a particular slot—the slot that matches the number that the board is configured for. Just make sure you install your VL-bus cards back into the slots they came from, and you'll have no problem.

How to tell a 16-bit slot from an 8-bit slot: The 16-bit slot has two parts—two separate slots—and is longer than an 8-bit slot.

Step 6: Verify that you have enough open bus slots.

Now that all your existing boards are back home, check to make sure you have enough bus slots for the card(s) you're about to install. Most sound cards require one 16-bit ISA slot.

Let's take an example. At work, I have a Compaq DeskPro 466i, which is a machine with only three 16-bit ISA slots. One of these slots goes to a SCSI host adapter for my external CD-ROM drive. A second is for my network card. The third goes to an internal fax/modem. (The DeskPro 466i has a video "card" built onto its motherboard, so I don't need a video card. It also has built-in sound capabilities, but they don't work under DOS, so . . .) Say I want to add a Sound Blaster multimedia upgrade kit. It may seem like I don't have a slot. But I do—after I remove my CD-ROM's SCSI host adapter. That's because the Sound Blaster can control a CD-ROM drive without a SCSI host adapter. So I remove the SCSI host adapter and add my Sound Blaster and hook my new CD-ROM drive up to it. And I now have an extra CD-ROM drive and controller that I can use in another computer.

The moral of this story is that it's pretty hard to run out of expansion slots.

Step 7: Install the sound card.

Now for the easy part: just install the sound board. But seriously, if you've done all the previous steps, actually plugging the board into your PC is going to be a breeze. The next four sections in this chapter are: "Creative Labs Sound Cards," "Reveal Sound Cards," "Media Vision Sound Cards," and "Installing a Generic Sound Card." Skip to the section that matches your sound card.

Creative Labs Sound Cards

Creative Labs makes a few varieties of its extremely popular Sound Blaster sound card. There's the Sound Blaster Pro (an 8-bit card), the Sound Blaster 16 (16-bit), the Sound Blaster 16 with Advanced Signal Processor or Wave Processor (a Sound Blaster 16 with either better MIDI or better wave table synthesis), and the Sound Blaster AWE 32 (another significantly enhanced 16-bit card). For three reasons, I'm going to show how to deal with only the plain old Sound Blaster 16:

1. It's by far the most popular.
2. If you know how to install it, you know basically how to install the others.
3. We have several other sound cards to cover here.

(For Steps 1–7, see the section entitled "The First Steps for Any Sound Card," pages 87–98.)

Step 8: Take a guided tour of a Sound Blaster.

If all goes well, you're not going to have to change anything on your Sound Blaster, but if you do, it'll be useful to know where all the different thingamabobs are. So take a look at your Sound Blaster. It should look something like what's in Figure 3.4.

Figure 3.4 A typical Sound Blaster

In case your board doesn't look like this, don't panic. Creative Labs changes the designs of its boards periodically (as do all hardware designers) so that they can add new features or condense old ones into fewer chips (which makes the boards less expensive to manufacture).

There are a few points you should take note of on the card. On the far right are all the external connectors. From top to bottom, they are line in, microphone input, the volume control, speaker output, and the joystick/MIDI adapter plug. Notice that they aren't labeled; this is one of the Sound Blaster's great shortcomings.

Moving on to the board proper, you'll see just to the left of all those connectors toward the top of the board what's called "Pin 1." I have no idea what pin 1 does. Keep going left and down a little bit and you'll see jumpers OPSL and OPSR, which turn on and off the Sound Blaster's internal amplifier (the thing that makes music loud). Default is on. Leave it there.

Now move up so that you're nearly at the top of the card, and move a bit left. You'll see a bunch of brass pins poking out of the board. These make up the connector for Sound Blaster add-ons. Don't worry about them unless you're planning to install something like a wave table upgrade.

Move directly up and you'll see two connectors. The one on the right is labeled "CD_IN," and the one to the left is

"PC_SPK." This is board-designer-speak for "the place where you plug your CD-ROM drive's audio output cable" and "the place where you plug your motherboard's PC speaker," respectively. You won't use PC_SPK.

Move left and to the center of the board. You're staring at a bunch of jumpers labeled IFSD, APSD, JYEN, I0S0, and I0S1. Such creative names. IFSD and APSD aren't documented, so you'll want to leave 'em alone. JYEN controls whether the Sound Blaster's joystick controller will work (by default it will). If your PC has a joystick port built in (most don't), remove the jumper from JYEN.

I0S0 and I0S1 together control the base I/O address of the Sound Blaster. Now we're getting somewhere—you could very well wind up changing the settings of these jumpers. By default, the Sound Blaster's base I/O address is 0x220 (which you'll sometimes see printed as 240H; same thing, different notation).

Keep moving left and a little down and you'll run into another bank of jumpers. These are MSEL, DAS0, DAS1, DBS0, DBS1, IS0, and IS1. MSEL controls the base I/O address of the MIDI portion of the Sound Blaster. By default, that's 0x330 (330H). Why are there two base I/O addresses on your Sound Blaster? Because the board itself is made up of a bunch of different components, all of which have different resource requirements. There's the wave table part (the one whose base I/O address is 0x220) and the MIDI part, for example. Different subsystems on the same board.

DAS0 and DAS1 together control the DMA channel of the 8-bit part of the Sound Blaster (channel 1 by default). DBS0 and DBS1 control the DMA of the 16-bit part of the Sound Blaster (channel 5 by default). Why are there two channels? Because not all systems support 16-bit DMA (which is superior). IS0 and IS1 together control the IRQ of the Sound Blaster (default is 5).

Keep moving left. If your board has more jumpers at the bottom, labeled JP18 and JP19, not to mention another bank labeled JP20 through JP24, you probably also have a bank at the top-left corner labeled PAN, SON, MIT, and DISABLE. This means that your board will support any one of three CD-ROM drives: a Panasonic (often called by the name of its parent company, Matsushita, or its sister company, Sanyo), a Sony, or a Mitsumi.

Step 9: Configure the Sound Blaster.

Remember that Post-it on which you were supposed to write your free IRQs and your used DMAs and base memory addresses on way back in Step 2? Look at it, then compare it with the Sound Blaster's default setup in Table 3.3.

Table 3.3 Sound Blaster Defaults

Thing	Setting
IRQ	5
8-bit DMA	1
16-bit DMA	5
Base memory	0x220
MIDI base memory	0x330

So if you happen to have these base memory addresses, IRQs, and DMAs free, you can just move one jumper, then plug and go.

The jumper you have to move is the one in the upper-left side of the card. Right now it's probably set to PAN. Move it to DISABLE. You're not going to be using the Sound Blaster to control your CD-ROM drive—presumably you already have it connected to some kind of controller in your system.

This is a very important configuration step.

If you're wondering why the sound card takes so many resources, it's because it handles so many functions. First, it gets its own IRQ. Simple. Next, a sound card needs two DMA channels, one for talking 8 bits at a time, one for 16. It also gets two base memory addresses, one for the regular sounds, and one for all the MIDI sounds. And the Mitsumi CD-ROM drive control logic on the sound card needs its own IRQ, DMA, and base memory address.

If you don't have these resources free, you're going to have to move a few jumpers. Move them now. When you're done, write down the final configuration of your card on a Post-it note and attach it to your monitor.

Tables 3.4 through 3.11 show what each of the important jumpers on your Sound Blaster does when you move them.

Table 3.4 Sound Blaster Base I/O Addresses

IOS0	IOS1	Resulting Audio Base I/O Address
On	On	0x220 (Default)
Off	On	0x240
On	Off	0x260
Off	Off	0x280

Table 3.5 MIDI Interface Base I/O Addresses

MSEL	Resulting MIDI Base I/O Address
On	0x330 (Default)
Off	0x300

Table 3.6 Sound Blaster IRQs

IS0	IS1	Resulting Audio IRQ
On	On	2
Off	On	5 (Default)
Off	On	7
Off	Off	10

Table 3.7 8-bit DMA Channels

DAS0	DAS1	Resulting 8-bit Audio DMA Channel
On	On	0
Off	On	1 (Default—don't change this)
On	Off	3

Table 3.8 16-bit DMA Channels

DBS0	DBS1	Resulting 16-bit Audio DMA Channel
On	On	5 (Default)
Off	On	6
On	Off	7

Table 3.9 Mitsumi CD-ROM Base I/O Addresses

JP19	JP18	Resulting Mitsumi CD-ROM Interface Base I/O Address
On	On	0x310
On	Off	0x320
Off	On	0x340 (Default)
Off	Off	0x350

Table 3.10 Mitsumi CD-ROM IRQs

JP20	JP21	JP22	Resulting Mitsumi CD-ROM Interface IRQ
On	Off	Off	11 (Default)
Off	On	Off	10
Off	Off	On	3

Table 3.11 Mitsumi CD-ROM DMA Channels

JP24	JP23	Resulting Mitsumi CD-ROM DMA Channel
Off	On	7 (Default)
On	Off	6

A Configuration Example

Let's take an example. Your Post-it note tells you that you have only the resources listed in Table 3.12 free.

Table 3.12 Just as an Example . . .

Resource	Your Free Resources
IRQ	10
Base memory	0x280
DMA	1 and 6

What are you going to do?

First, let's move that jumper in the upper-left corner of the board from PAN to DISABLE.

Now let's reconfigure your IRQ. By default, the Sound Blaster comes at IRQ 5. Find jumpers IS0 and IS1 (kind of at the lower left of the board). You want both jumpers off the pins, so pull off the jumper on IS1 (the one on IS0 should already be off). Reattach them so they hang off one pin.

Now let's set your base memory. By default, the Sound Blaster's at 0x220. Again, you want both jumpers to be off the pins to get 0x280, so remove the jumpers from IOS1 and IOS0. Reattach them so they hang off one pin.

Now the DMA channels. By default, they're at 1 and 5, so you only have to change the 16-bit channel. That's a good thing because most software that supports the Sound Blaster *only* supports 8-bit DMA through channel 1. If something else is at channel 1 (which is pretty unlikely), change *it,* not the Sound Blaster. To change your 16-bit DMA channel to 6, find jumpers DBS0 and DBS1. By default, both are jumpered; remove the connector between the two pins of DBS0 and hang it so it attaches to only one pin.

Step 10: Install the Sound Blaster.

Now you're ready to plug the Sound Blaster into an open slot. First, you've got to prepare your computer. It's still open, right? Okay, find an open 16-bit ISA slot (one that's next to an 8-bit slot or extra 16-bit slot if you have the external CD-ROM that requires the extra card) and remove the metal plate that covers the opening in the back of the computer, as in Figure 3.5. (If you have an external CD-ROM drive that works with the Sound Blaster, remove two of the metal plates on slots right next to each other.)

Figure 3.5 Removing the metal plate from the back of your computer

Now slide the card into place and screw its little metal flange to the back of the PC. Connect the speakers to the back of the card.

Step 11: Connect the Sound Blaster to your CD-ROM drive.

You'll need a special cable for this—a CD audio cable, which has two plastic blocks at either end. One end plugs into a port on your CD-ROM drive—the port labeled something like "Audio Out" or just "Audio." The other end plugs into a port on your Sound Blaster.

Look at the upper-center of your Sound Blaster and you'll see two connectors. The one on the right is labeled "CD_IN" and the one to the left is "PC_SPK." This is board-designer-speak for "the place you plug your CD-ROM drive's audio output cable" and "the place you plug your motherboard's PC speaker," respectively. Plug the other end of your CD audio cable into the port labeled CD_IN.

Step 12: Boot your system.

Your hardware is all installed. If the gods of PC installations are smiling on you, it's all installed properly. Just in case they aren't, don't reattach the cover just yet—it's a lot easier to pull out a card for a quick change if you don't have to drag the whole cover off.

Plug your computer back into the wall, and set it up so that you can see the monitor, type at the keyboard, and use the mouse. Now turn it on and let it boot.

If your system doesn't boot or you get an error message like "Hard disk failure. Press <F1> to continue," you have some kind of a resource conflict, probably either an IRQ or base memory address conflict. Go back to Step 2 to reascertain your free resources. If that doesn't work, try potluck settings. If this doesn't sound at all scientific, don't worry—it isn't.

Start by altering base memory addresses (the most common reason you'll get a hard disk failure message), then IRQs, then DMA channels. Be as scientific as you can, only altering one thing at a time. This advice may seem like a horrible cop-out, but, unfortunately, it's the best I can offer. There are no perfect diagnostic tools that will tell you what system resources are free, so you never have a full guarantee that your initial settings on your Sound Blaster will work.

Step 13: Run the Sound Blaster configuration software.

Now that your system has booted, you have to install some software to make it work. Put the disk that has a name like

"Sound Blaster 16 Disk #1" into your disk drive (for our example, we'll say that's drive A). Type the following:

```
C:\>CD A:
A:\>INSTALL
```

You'll go into the Sound Blaster 16 setup.

The purpose of the setup routine is to add some software to your computer and make some changes to it so that it can talk to the Sound Blaster (see Figure 3.6). More specifically, the installation routine will add lines to your CONFIG.SYS and AUTOEXEC.BAT files and install drivers (the software that enables DOS and other software to talk to the Sound Blaster) to your hard disk. During the installation, the software will ask you some simple questions about the card's configuration. Refer to the Post-it note on your monitor (the one on which you wrote your Sound Blaster's configuration information) if you don't remember.

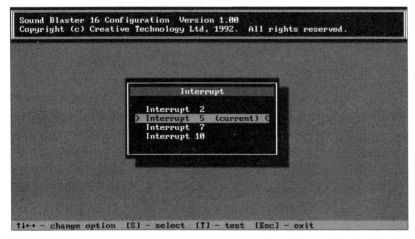

Figure 3.6 The Sound Blaster 16 setup program can test your settings before locking them in.

After you've finished running INSTALL, remove the Sound Blaster diskette from your floppy drive and reboot your computer. Watch for any error messages (if the installation completed properly, which it probably did, you won't see any). Now type the following:

```
A:\>C:
C:\>CD \SB16
C:\SB16\>TESTSB16
```

The TESTSB16 program will test your Sound Blaster to make sure it's running perfectly. If you get an error message or TESTSB16 hangs, you probably have either a resource conflict (unlikely) or your system cannot do 16-bit DMA. Rerun SBCONFIG (there's a copy in the SB16 directory) and make sure that the installation program's settings agree with those on the card. If everything looks okay, turn off 16-bit DMA as in Figure 3.7.

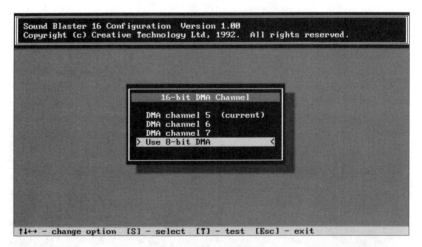

Figure 3.7 Some systems can't handle 16-bit DMA, so you'll use 8-bit instead.

That should eliminate any error messages. If you can't get sound from the speakers, check the obvious stuff:

✓ Are the speakers plugged into the card?

✓ Is the volume control on the back of the card turned up? (It's not labeled, so turn it all the way one direction, then all the way the other, then settle for a midpoint.)

✓ Is the volume on the speakers turned up?

✓ Are the speakers plugged in to power (or do they have batteries)?

The general thing about sound cards is that they usually either work or they don't. There's no middle ground on which sometimes you get sound and sometimes you don't. So if all the obvious stuff is set correctly and you still aren't getting sound, you may just have a defective card. It's rare, but it happens. Call technical support (the phone number is in Appendix A).

Step 14: Run Windows.

The Sound Blaster installation isn't quite done yet—you still need to run Windows (if you have it installed) to add all the Sound Blaster Windows utilities. To run Windows, just type:

```
C:\>WIN
```

The Sound Blaster configuration will take care of itself. Congratulations, your Sound Blaster should now be installed and working properly.

Reveal Sound Cards

Here's what to do if you purchased a 16-bit Reveal Sound FX Wave 32 board. (For Steps 1–7, see the section entitled "The First Steps for Any Sound Card," pages 87–98.)

Step 8: Take a guided tour of a Sound FX.

If all goes well, you're not going to have to change anything on your Sound FX; but if you do, it'll be useful to know where all the different thingamabobs are. So take a look at your Sound FX. It should look something like what's in Figure 3.8.

In case your board
doesn't look like this,
don't panic. Reveal
changes the designs of
its boards periodically
(as do all hardware de-
signers) so they can add
new features or con-
dense old ones into fewer
chips (which makes the
boards less expensive to
manufacture).

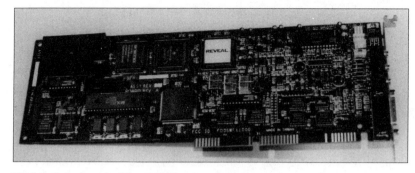

Figure 3.8 A typical Sound FX

There are a few points you should take note of on the card.
On the far right are all the external connectors. From top to
bottom, they are line in, speaker output, microphone input,
and the joystick/MIDI adapter plug. In case you forget,
they're labeled. The one problem I have with the Sound FX
is that there's no volume control on the card itself.

Moving onto the board proper, you'll see just to the left of the
external line-in connector that there are three white plugs,
each of which has four pins. These are the audio connectors
for the three CD-ROM drives that the Sound FX board supports. When you play audio CDs in your CD-ROM drive, the
sound travels over a wire that connects to one of these three
plugs. The connectors are, from top to bottom, for the Sony,
Panasonic, and Mitsumi drives. Depending on the drive you
have, you're going to be connecting a wire to one of these
three connectors.

Keep moving left on the board and you'll run into two more
sets of jumpers, labeled JP7 and JP5. JP7's job is to send a
bit of electrical power (when it's closed) to the microphone
port. For the most part, you won't need to do that because
you'll be using either a battery-powered microphone or a dynamic microphone that doesn't need power.

JP5's job is to set the base memory address of the wave table
portion of the Sound FX. By default, that address is at 0x534

(also written as 534H—same thing, just different ways of expressing a mathematical notation called hexadecimal that's used a lot when talking about PC memory).

Move a little more to the left (past a bunch of shiny metal parts) and you'll meet up with JP4, which you'll use to change the base memory address of the rest of the Sound FX. By default, pins 3 and 4 will be connected, giving the board a base memory address of 0x330.

Now move to the far left of the board and find one more set of jumpers—JP3. These jumpers help you select which CD-ROM drive you're going to be using with your board. By default, it's the Panasonic (pins 1 and 2 are joined, as are pins 3 and 4). This set of jumpers works with the three connectors above it. These connectors are where you plug in your CD-ROM drive's ribbon cable. From top to bottom, they are for the Panasonic, Mitsumi, and Sony drives. The Panasonic and Mitsumi drive connectors are the same size (forty pins); the Sony drive uses a thirty-four-pin connector. In case you're wondering how to tell what kind of drive you have, you'll find the manufacturer's name on all the drives (except that a Panasonic drive will likely be labeled Matsushita or Sanyo).

Step 9: Configure the Sound FX.

Remember that Post-it on which you were supposed to write your free IRQs and your used DMAs and base memory addresses way back in Step 2? Look at it, then compare it with the Sound FX's default setup in Table 3.13.

Table 3.13 Sound FX Defaults

Thing	Setting
Base IRQ	2
Wave table IRQ	7
8-bit DMA	1
16-bit DMA	Disabled
Base memory	0x330
Wave table base memory	0x534

So if you happen to have these base memory addresses, IRQs, and DMAs free, you can just make one change and then plug and go.

Don't miss this step. Here's the change you have to make. Look for the jumpers at JP3 and remove *all* of them. That will disable the Sound FX as a CD-ROM controller. You already have a CD-ROM controller, don't you?

If you're wondering why the sound card takes so many resources, it's because it handles so many functions. First, it gets its own IRQ. In addition, its wave table synthesizer gets an IRQ. Next, it needs two DMA channels, one for talking 8 bits at a time, one for 16. The Sound FX by default turns 16-bit DMA off because not all systems can handle it. It also gets two base memory addresses, one for the regular sounds, and one for all the wave table sounds.

If you don't have these resources free, you may have to move a few jumpers. Move them now. When you're done, write down the final configuration of your card on a Post-it note and attach it to your monitor. Much of the Sound FX configuration can be done entirely through software during the installation, so don't worry about trying to resolve IRQ or DMA conflicts here—you'll do that later.

Tables 3.14 through 3.16 show what each of the important jumpers on your Sound FX does when you move them.

Table 3.14 Sound FX Base I/O Addresses

JP4, Pin 1	JP4, Pin 2	JP4, Pin 3	JP4, Pin 4	Resulting Base I/O Address
Off	Off	Off	Off	0x350
On	On	Off	Off	0x340
Off	Off	On	On	0x330 (Default)
On	On	On	On	0x320

Table 3.15 Wave Table Interface Base I/O Addresses

JP5, Pin 1	JP5, Pin 2	JP5, Pin 3	JP5, Pin 4	Resulting Base I/O Address
Off	Off	Off	Off	0xF44
On	On	Off	Off	0x534 (Default)
Off	Off	On	On	0x608
On	On	On	On	0xE84

Table 3.16 CD-ROM Selection

JP3, Pin 1	JP3, Pin 2	JP3, Pin 3	JP3, Pin 4	CD-ROM Drive
Off	Off	Off	Off	Disabled
On	On	Off	Off	Sony
Off	Off	On	On	Mitsumi
On	On	On	On	Matsushita/Panasonic (Default)

A Configuration Example

Let's take an example. Say that your computer has a Panasonic drive compatible with your Sound FX, and that none of the board's settings will work in your computer. Your Post-it note tells you that you only have the resources listed in Table 3.17 free.

Table 3.17 Just as an Example . . .

Resource	Your Free Resources
IRQ	10
Base memory	0x320
DMA	2

What are you going to do? The answer is, not much. The only things you have to change on the board itself are the base memory address and the CD-ROM support. To get the board to 0x320, just attach the jumpers over all the pins in JP4. Now remove the jumpers on JP3. Your board is now ready.

Step 10: Install the Sound FX.

Now you're ready to plug the Sound FX into an open slot.
First, you've got to prepare your computer. It's still open,
right? Okay, find an open 16-bit ISA slot and remove the
metal plate that covers the opening in the back of the computer, as in Figure 3.9.

Figure 3.9 Removing the metal plate from the back of your computer

Now slide the card into place and screw its little metal flange to the back of the PC. Connect the speakers to the back of the card.

Step 11: Boot your system.

Your hardware is all installed. If the gods of PC installations are smiling on you, it's all installed properly. Just in case they aren't, don't reattach the cover just yet. It's a lot easier to pull out a card for a quick change if you don't have to drag the whole cover off.

Plug your computer back into the wall, and set it up so that you can see the monitor, type at the keyboard, and use the mouse. Now turn it on and let it boot.

If your system doesn't boot or you get an error message like "Hard disk failure. Press <F1> to continue," you have some kind of a resource conflict, probably either an IRQ or base memory address conflict. Go back to Step 2 to reascertain your free resources. If that doesn't work, try potluck settings. If this doesn't sound at all scientific, don't worry—it isn't.

Start by altering base memory addresses (the most common reason you'll get a hard disk failure message), then IRQs, then DMA channels. Be as scientific as you can, only altering one thing at a time. This advice may seem like a horrible cop-out, but, unfortunately, it's the best I can offer. There are no perfect diagnostic tools that will tell you what system resources are free, so you never have a full guarantee that your initial settings on your Sound FX will work.

Step 12: Run the Sound FX configuration software.

Now that your system has booted, you have to install some software to make it work. Put the disk that has a name like "Sound FX Disk #1" into your disk drive (for our example, we'll say that's drive A). Now run Windows (the command is WIN). Sound FX setup only runs from Windows. From the Program Manager, select File, Run, then type A:\SETUP. You'll go into the Sound FX setup.

The purpose of the setup is to add some software to your computer and make some changes to it so that it can talk to the Sound FX card. More specifically, the installation routine will add lines to your CONFIG.SYS and AUTOEXEC.BAT files and install drivers (the software that enables DOS and other software to talk to the Sound FX card) to your hard disk.

Some notes during your installation of the software. First, SETUP will ask you if you want a Custom or Express installation. Choose Custom. Next, it'll ask where to put its software, with the default being C:\SOUNDFX. Unless you have a really compelling reason, leave it there. It'll also ask you if you want to use the Sound FX as your CD-ROM drive controller. The answer is No.

Finally, and most important, when it asks what kind of CD-ROM drive you're using, set it to Disable. Although you have a CD-ROM drive, the Sound FX won't be controlling it, so it doesn't need to know about it.

After you've finished running SETUP, remove the Sound FX diskette from your floppy drive, exit from Windows, and reboot your computer and go back into Windows. Watch for any error messages (if the installation completed properly, which it probably did, you won't see any).

If you can't get sound from the speakers, check the obvious stuff:

✓ Are the speakers plugged into the card?
✓ Is the volume on the speakers turned up?
✓ Are the speakers plugged in to power (or do they have batteries)?

The general thing about sound cards is that they usually either work or they don't. There's no middle ground, where sometimes you get sound and sometimes you don't. So if all the obvious stuff is set correctly and you still aren't getting sound, you may just have a defective card. It's rare, but it happens. Call technical support (the phone number is in Appendix A).

Congratulations, your Sound FX should now be installed and working properly.

Media Vision Sound Cards

Media Vision makes several kits all centered around its Pro Audio Spectrum card. The installation for this card is incredibly simple and virtually automated: plug it in and run their software. The only possible catch I found was that the installation program runs only under Windows. If you have an older system without Windows, you'll need to install a copy. You should have it anyway, if you ask me. (For Steps 1–7, see the section entitled "The First Steps for Any Sound Card," pages 87–98.)

Step 8: Take a guided tour of your Pro Audio Spectrum.

Check out Figure 3.10. There are a few points you should take note of on the card. On the far right are all the external connectors. From top to bottom, they are line in, microphone input, speaker output, and the joystick/MIDI adapter plug. In case you forget, they're labeled. The one problem I have with the Pro Audio Spectrum is that there's no volume control on the card itself. Since the Labtec speakers that come with the kit have a volume control, this isn't a big deal unless you're using headphones.

In case your board
doesn't look like this,
don't panic. Media Vision
changes the designs of
its boards periodically
(as do all hardware
designers) so that
they can add new
features or condense old
ones into fewer chips
(which makes the boards
less expensive to
manufacture).

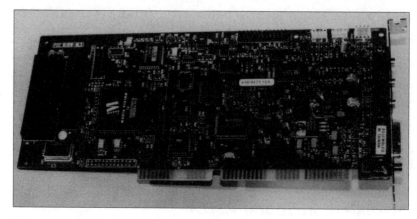

Figure 3.10 A typical Pro Audio Spectrum

Moving onto the board proper, you'll see just to the left of
and above the external line-in connector that there are three
white plugs, each of which has four pins. These are the
audio connectors for the three CD-ROM drives that the Pro
Audio Spectrum board supports. When you play audio CDs
in your CD-ROM drive, the sound travels over a wire that
connects to one of these three plugs. Why three? Because the
Pro Audio Spectrum can come in a kit that could come with
any of three CD-ROM drives. The connectors are, from right
to left, for the Sony, Panasonic, and Mitsumi drives.
Depending on the drive that came with your kit, you're going
to be connecting a wire to one of these three connectors.
(Most kits come with a Panasonic drive that's labeled as
though it comes from Sanyo—they're sister companies.)

Keep moving left on the board and you'll run into a bunch of
pins sticking out. These are for the wave table synthesis upgrade that you can purchase separately to get better wave
sound.

Directly below this is a jumper labeled J8, which controls
what's called DMA 1 sharing. Most computers can have a
couple of devices sharing DMA 1, so the Pro Audio Spectrum
comes with sharing disabled (the jumper covers pins 2 and
3). If, for some incredibly odd reason, you want to share DMA
1 with another device, move the jumper to pins 1 and 2.

Below and to the right of J8 are J18 and J19. J18 enables you to connect a Roland MPU-401 sound device to the Pro Audio Spectrum. It's on by default, and I see no reason to change it. J19 controls whether the Pro Audio Spectrum's joystick port is enabled. Since a system can have only one joystick, if your computer comes with a joystick built in, you'll have to move the jumper on J19 to cover both pins.

Now move to the far left of the board, and find all the plugs for CD-ROM drives. The Pro Audio Spectrum can support drives from Sony, Panasonic, and Mitsumi. The Sony drive will be labeled Sony. The Panasonic drive will be labeled Matsushita or Sanyo, and the Mitsumi drive will be labeled Mitsumi. The Panasonic and Mitsumi drive connectors are the same size (forty pins); the Sony drive uses a thirty-four-pin connector.

Step 9: Configure the Pro Audio Spectrum.

If you have to change any of the jumpers, do it now. Don't worry about configuring IRQs, DMAs, or base memory addresses—the installation software will take care of that automatically.

Step 10: Install your sound card.

Now you're ready to plug the Pro Audio Spectrum into an open slot. First, you've got to prepare your computer. It's still open, right? Okay, find an open 16-bit ISA slot and remove the metal plate that covers the opening in the back of the computer, as in Figure 3.11.

Now slide the card into place and screw its little metal flange to the back of the PC. Connect the speakers to the back of the card. It's important to have the speakers connected so that you can hear the sound test.

Figure 3.11 Removing the metal plate from the back of your computer

Step 11: Boot your system.

Your hardware is all installed. If the gods of PC installations are smiling on you, it's all installed properly. Just in case they aren't, don't reattach the cover just yet. It's a lot easier to pull out a card for a quick change if you don't have to drag the whole cover off.

Plug your computer back into the wall, and set it up so that you can see the monitor, type at the keyboard, and use the mouse. Now turn it on and let it boot.

If you get an error message, turn your system off and make sure all the cards are all the way in their slots and everything's connected together tightly.

Step 12: Run the Pro Audio Spectrum configuration software.

Now that your system has booted, you have to install some software to make it work. Put the disk that has a name like "Media Vision Multimedia Kit Installation Disk 1 of 2" into your disk drive (for our example, we'll say that's drive A). Now run Windows (the command is WIN). Pro Audio Spectrum setup only runs from Windows. From the Program Manager select File, Run, then type A:\SETUP. (Assuming that the floppy is in your A drive.) You'll go into the Pro Audio Spectrum setup.

The purpose of the setup is to add some software to your computer and make some changes to it so that it can talk to the Pro Audio Spectrum. More specifically, the installation routine will add lines to your CONFIG.SYS and AUTOEXEC.BAT files and install drivers (the software that enables DOS and other software to talk to the Pro Audio Spectrum card) to your hard disk. The Pro Audio Spectrum installation is completely automated, so you shouldn't have to do anything— just select Standard Installation and watch it do its thing. It'll reboot the system automatically, discover where the card is, and test it automatically, something like what's in Figure 3.12.

If you can't get sound from the speakers, check the obvious stuff:

✓ Are the speakers plugged into the card?

✓ Is the volume on the speakers turned up?

✓ Are the speakers plugged in to power (or do they have batteries)?

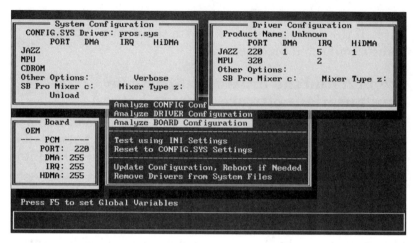

Figure 3.12 Problem? Run \MEDVSN\DIAG\DIAG.

The general thing about sound cards is that they usually either work or they don't. There's no middle ground, where you get sound sometimes, but not other times. So if all the obvious stuff is set correctly and you still aren't getting sound, you may just have a defective card. It's rare, but it happens. Call technical support (the phone number is in Appendix A).

Congratulations, your Pro Audio Spectrum should now be installed and working properly.

Installing a Generic Sound Card

Okay, maybe "generic" isn't the best term. But it's the best word that would fit in a subheading. So anyway, you purchased a sound card that isn't from Creative Labs, Reveal, or Media Vision and you want to install it. (For Steps 1–7, see the section entitled "The First Steps for Any Sound Card," pages 87–98.)

Step 8: Take a guided tour of your sound card.

If all goes well, you're not going to have to change anything on your sound card; but if you do, it'll be useful to know where all the different thingamabobs are. So take a look at your card. It'll probably look something like what's in Figure 3.13.

Figure 3.13 A typical sound card

In case your board doesn't look like this, don't panic. This is just supposed to be representative of sound cards in general, not an exact duplicate of yours.

There are a few points you should take note of on the card. On the far right are all the external connectors. You'll definitely have at least one—a "line out." That's the fancy technical term for the place where you plug in your speakers or headphones. It'll also probably have a "line in," which is where you plug in audio components that can supply a signal directly to the sound card, like an audio CD player or even a tape deck. There will probably be at least one more ⅛-inch jack (as they're called) on the back, this one for microphone input. Microphones require different electrical treatment from other stereo components, so they need a separate jack. Don't plug a microphone into your line-in plug. It won't work and may damage the board. Finally, you'll probably have a combined MIDI and joystick port, which is shaped vaguely like the letter "D." That's where you'll plug in a joystick or your musical instrument digital interface (MIDI) components, such as a keyboard.

Moving onto the board proper, you'll see a mishmash of chips, resistors, and diodes. Ignore them. From here in you're looking for two different types of elements: jumpers and CD-ROM drive audio plugs. Jumpers consist of two metal prongs that stick up out of your board. They may or may not be covered by a small piece of metal embedded in black (usually) plastic. Jumpers are very simple electrical switches: When the piece of metal is over both metal prongs, the circuit is closed and electricity flows through it; when the metal isn't over the two prongs, the circuit is open and electricity doesn't flow. You'll use jumpers to set various aspects of your board's behavior.

It's possible that your sound card doesn't have any jumpers. You'll configure it through software. How does this work? How can software talk to a piece of hardware if it doesn't know its DMA, base memory, and IRQ? Some of it is just blind luck. Your sound card manufacturer took a guess about what DMA and IRQ would be unused. These are the two critical bits of information that must be unique for software to talk to a card. If, however, something in your system already uses the ones that your card comes with by default, your card may be unconfigurable—the setup software won't be able to find it.

Software configuration is both a blessing and a curse. It's really convenient to be able to plug in a sound card without worrying about getting its IRQ, DMA, and base memory address all set correctly first. That means you won't be pulling the board out of your computer to reset jumpers should something go wrong. But not all that glitters is gold. You're at the mercy of the software and it's often the case that vendors that make good hardware don't make good software. Figuring out jumper settings can be a pain but at least it's straightforward. Much of the installation software I've seen feels as though it were translated directly from the original Greek by someone with only a rudimentary understanding of how mere mortals think. As the saying goes, "You pays your money and you takes your chances."

Somewhere else on your board, usually near the top and usually either in the center or over to the right side, you'll find the "CD audio in" connector. To it connects the round wire (probably gray) that came with your kit. What's all this for? When you play audio CDs in your CD-ROM drive, the sound travels over a round wire separate from the flat ribbon cable. Because an audio signal is so different from a data signal, it requires a separate wire. Does this mean you won't be able to hear any music if you don't connect the round wire? No. Some music, like that in a video game for example, has been digitized and comes over a flat ribbon cable and arrives to your sound card through the magic that is a PC. But audio CDs (the kind you buy in a record store) can't pass information over the ribbon cable, so they have this separate wire.

Some cards will have more than one CD audio-in connector. Why? Because the many sound cards could come with more than one manufacturer's CD-ROM drives. Most popular are Panasonic (also called by its parent company's name, Matsushita), Mitsumi, and Sony. In case you're wondering how to tell what kind of drive you have, you'll find the manufacturer's name on all the drives (except that a Panasonic drive will likely be labeled Matsushita).

Step 9: Configure the card.

Remember that Post-it on which you were supposed to write your free IRQs and your used DMAs and base memory addresses way back in Step 2? Look at it. Now open the manual that came with your card. Check the table of contents for mention of the hardware settings of your card (they might be in an appendix). Fill in Table 3.18 with the information you garner from your card.

Table 3.18 Fill in Your Sound Card's Defaults

Item	Setting
Base IRQ	
Second IRQ	
8-bit DMA	
16-bit DMA	
Base memory	
Wave table base memory	

Now compare your Post-it to the information in this table. If they line up right, you're almost ready to plug and go. If not, you're going to have to check your manual for how to change your sound card's settings. You may change these settings entirely with jumpers, entirely through software, or use some combination of the two.

One change you should make right now is to find the jumper that controls whether your sound card thinks that it's a CD-ROM drive controller. Find it and disable it—you're not going to be using the sound card to control your CD-ROM drive.

If you're wondering why the sound card takes so many resources, it's because it handles so many functions. First, it gets its own IRQ. In addition, its wave table synthesizer may get an IRQ. Next, it needs two DMA channels, one for talking 8 bits at a time, one for 16. Not all computers can handle 16-bit DMA. The card also gets two base memory addresses, one for the regular sounds, and one for all the wave table sounds.

If you don't have these resources free, you may have to move a few jumpers. Move them now. When you're done, write down the final configuration of your card on a Post-it note and attach it to your monitor.

Step 10: Install your sound card.

Now you're ready to plug the sound card into an open slot. First, you've got to prepare your computer. It's still open, right? Okay, find an open 16-bit ISA slot and remove the metal plate that covers the opening in the back of the computer, as in Figure 3.14.

Now slide the card into place and screw its little metal flange to the back of the PC. Connect the speakers to the back of the card.

Figure 3.14 Removing the metal plate from the back of your computer

Step 11: Attach your sound card's CD audio-in port to your CD-ROM drive.

Using a small, round cable with funny-looking plastic connectors at either end, attach the audio-out port (or just audio) on the CD-ROM drive to one of the CD audio-in connectors on the sound card. This will enable your CD-ROM drive to pass audio signals directly to your sound card when appropriate.

Step 12: Boot your system.

Your hardware is all installed. If the gods of PC installations are smiling on you, it's all installed properly. Just in case they aren't, don't reattach the cover just yet. It's a lot easier to pull out a card for a quick change if you don't have to drag the whole cover off.

Plug your computer back into the wall, and set it up so that you can see the monitor, type at the keyboard, and use the mouse. Now turn it on and let it boot.

If your system doesn't boot or you get an error message like "Hard disk failure. Press <F1> to continue," you have some kind of a resource conflict, probably either an IRQ or base memory address conflict. Go back to Step 2 to reascertain your free resources. If that doesn't work, try potluck settings. If this doesn't sound at all scientific, don't worry—it isn't.

Start by altering base memory addresses (the most common reason you'll get a hard disk failure message), then IRQs, then DMA channels. Be as scientific as you can, only altering one thing at a time. This advice may seem like a horrible cop-out, but, unfortunately, it's the best I can offer. There are no perfect diagnostic tools that will tell you what system resources are free, so you never have a full guarantee that your initial settings on your sound card will work.

Step 13: Run your sound card configuration software.

This is the last step in the process and, thanks to the complete lack of standardization in the sound card software world, the step where I have to be the most vague. It's pretty clear that, now that your system has booted, you have to install some software to make it work.

Locate the installation floppies that came with your sound card. They'll probably have names like "Installation Disk 1," "Installation Disk 2," and so on, but they may not. Put the

first disk into your disk drive (for our example, we'll say
that's drive A).

Now take a directory of what's on drive A and look for files
whose name ends .EXE, like this:

```
C:\>DIR A:*.EXE
```

This will probably yield one or two files. Look for a file with
a name like INSTALL.EXE or SETUP.EXE and run it, something like this:

```
C:\>A:
A:\>INSTALL
```

If you get an error message like "This program requires
Microsoft Windows," start Windows on your computer, and
from the Program Manager select File, Run, and type in the
name of the file again. If not, you should be running your
sound card's installation software. It will probably ask you
for the configuration of your card (its base memory, IRQ,
and DMA), so be ready to refer to your Post-it when it does.

The purpose of the setup routine is to add some software to
your computer and make some changes to it so that it can
talk to the sound card. More specifically, the installation routine will add lines to your CONFIG.SYS and AUTOEXEC.BAT
files and install drivers (the software that enables DOS and
other software to talk to the sound card) to your hard disk.

Some notes during your installation of the software. First, it
will probably ask you where to put its software. Unless you
have a really compelling reason, leave it wherever its default is. It may also ask you if you want to use your sound
card as your CD-ROM drive controller. The answer is No.

After you've finished installing the software, remove the installation diskette from your floppy drive (exit from
Windows if necessary) and reboot your computer. Watch for
any error messages (if the installation completed properly,

which it probably did, you won't see any). There should be a test program that the software installed. Run it now to make sure everything's working.

If you can't get sound from the speakers, check the obvious stuff:

✓ Are the speakers plugged into the card?
✓ Is the volume control on the back of the card turned up? (It's not labeled, so turn it all the way one direction, then all the way the other, then settle for a midpoint.)
✓ Is the volume on the speakers turned up?
✓ Are the speakers plugged in to power (or do they have batteries)?

The general thing about sound cards is that they usually either work or they don't. There's no middle ground, where you get sound sometimes, but not other times. So if all the obvious stuff is set correctly and you still aren't getting sound, you may just have a defective card. It's rare, but it happens. Call technical support (the phone number is in Appendix A).

You should be up and running now.

Adding a CD-ROM Drive to Your System

I'm going to assume here that you have a working sound card in your computer and you want to know how to make it interact with your new CD-ROM drive. It's really simple. Except that installation part.

Your CD-ROM drive will connect (most likely) either to a port on your sound card or to its own controller. In the case of the former, you should call right now and make sure that your sound card will support whatever CD-ROM drive you purchased and ask where you can get the latest drivers for it (see Appendix A). In the case of the latter, you're going to have a little hardware setup to do.

Let's take each case separately, attaching it to a sound card first.

Attaching a CD-ROM Drive to Your Sound Card

There are nine basic steps to attaching a CD-ROM drive to an existing sound card, and they're pretty simple.

Step 1: Make sure your sound card will support it.

Before you even think of purchasing a CD-ROM drive for your sound card, you should call the maker of the sound card to make sure the two are compatible. The phone numbers for technical support for some major vendors are in Appendix A.

If you haven't yet bought your CD-ROM drive, give 'em a call and ask what CD-ROM drives their sound card supports—make sure you get make and model numbers. If the sound card vendor also sells these CD-ROM drives, don't think twice about price: purchase it from them directly. You'll save yourself an incredible headache later.

If the sound card vendor doesn't sell the CD-ROM drives and you know somebody who does, ask that vendor to supply you with drivers that will work through your sound card.

The reason for all this confusion is that a CD-ROM drive isn't always a CD-ROM drive. Although two units may look exactly the same, they may not support the same interface, so when you go to plug the drive into its controller, whatever that controller is, it may not work. This is what's called the problem of the stupid proprietary interface, and I run into it all the time. But that's another story.

Once you, the vendor, and your cat are satisfied that your CD-ROM drive will work with your sound card, proceed to Step 2.

Step 2: Back up your CD-ROM driver diskettes.

This may sound silly. It may sound ridiculous. It may sound like a pain in the buttocks. But. And I underline that: <u>But</u>. Heck, I'll underline it, italicize it, boldface it, and put it into a different font: ***But*** you had better do it. Start by backing up four critical files: AUTOEXEC.BAT, CONFIG.SYS, WIN.INI, and SYSTEM.INI. (You should be doing this any time you change your files anyway, but do it now.) To do this, put a formatted floppy into your floppy drive (I'll assume its drive A) and run these commands:

```
C:\>COPY \CONFIG.SYS A:
C:\>COPY \AUTOEXEC.BAT A:
C:\>COPY \WINDOWS\WIN.INI A:
C:\>COPY \WINDOWS\SYSTEM.INI A:
```

Now, if you run into any problems when booting your computer, you can restore these four files and things should be fine.

Next, back up your distribution diskettes (the ones that came with the CD-ROM drive). This is for when (not if, when) your distribution diskettes go south. It will happen: it always does.

Take the diskette(s) that came with your CD-ROM drive and try using these commands (I'm assuming you have a hard disk):

```
C:\>MD DISTRIB
C:\>MD DISTRIB\DISK1
C:\>MD DISTRIB\DISK2
```

Repeat this command once for every distribution diskette, so you have unique directories for each. Now place the first of your distribution diskettes in your floppy drive. I'm assuming you're using drive A. Now run these commands:

```
C:\>XCOPY /S A:*.* C:\DISTRIB\DISK1
```

Now put the second diskette into the drive and run the command again, but this time change the target directory to C:\DISTRIB\DISK2. Keep doing it until all the diskettes are backed up onto your hard drive.

Now, you can create a second copy of your distribution floppies really easily: just XCOPY the files from the hard drive onto a bunch of new floppies. You'll need to format one new floppy for each of the distribution floppies that came with your software:

```
C:\>FORMAT A:
```

When it asks you if you want to format another, say Yes until you've formatted all the floppies you need. Now create nice new labels for your floppies that tell you what's on them, and XCOPY the data off the hard disk onto the floppies:

```
C:\>XCOPY /S C:\DISTRIB\DISK1\*.* A:\
```

And keep at it until you're out of directories. You should now have a fully backed-up set of floppies. You can delete your DISTRIB directories now. If you have MS-DOS 6 or later, you can use this command:

```
C:\>DELTREE C:\DISTRIB
```

But if you have a previous DOS version, you're going to have to go into each directory, delete all the files, then delete the directory, like this:

```
C:\>DEL \DISTRIB\DISK1
C:\>RMDIR \DISTRIB\DISK1
```

And so on. Now you have a nice, working (one hopes) copy of your multimedia kit's distribution diskettes.

Step 3: Open your PC.

Let's make like Hercule Poirot and crack your case. PC enclosures come in two basic types: desktop and tower. The

desktop version sits comfortably on . . . well, on your desktop, usually with your monitor on top of it. The tower type
of case is usually too tall for your desktop—it dwarfs everything on your desk when you try to put it there.

In either case (pun intended), you're going to be dealing
with some kind of fastener to remove the enclosure that covers the guts of your computer. With most cases, these fasteners are screws of some kind, thumbscrews and Phillips
screws being the most common. In a very few cases, you
have an advanced case design that uses some kind of screwless latch to pop open.

I'd like to say, "Read your owner's manual to see how to
open your case." But, if you're like me, you no longer have
your owner's manual. If you ever had one at all. Never fear:
here are hints for opening both types of cases.

Screwless Case: These are usually the easier of the two to
open. You'll know you have one if somewhere on your enclosure there's a small button that turns neither the computer
nor "Turbo" on or off. Usually, the latch is located either in
the upper-middle of the front (as on IBM ValuePoint) or
somewhere on the back. Push the button and hold it in.

Screwy Case: Look at the back of your computer. There is
probably a bunch of screws there. Look at the edges of the
back. You'll probably see five or six screws that pretty
clearly secure the sides of the computer to the back. Just remove these.

Now wiggle the enclosure front-to-back. That's right, stand
in front of your computer, lay your hands flat on the side of
the computer, and give the enclosure a good hard jerk toward you, then away from you. The case (or a panel on the
case) should move in one of the two directions. Pull or push
it as far in that direction as it will go, then lift it up until it's
clear of the rest of the computer. You're in.

Step 4: Install the CD-ROM drive itself.

You already have a sound card in an open slot. There are two scenarios you could be following: internal CD-ROM drive and external CD-ROM drive. Their installations are slightly different.

If you have an internal CD-ROM drive, you should take this opportunity to attach the wires that connect the sound card to the internal CD-ROM drive. It's a lot easier to attach them before inserting the CD-ROM drive into a drive bay because you can see what you're doing and maneuver your fingers more easily.

There are two wires you'll need to attach. The first is about a foot long, two inches wide, and flat. It's called a ribbon cable. The second is also about a foot long, but it looks round—more like a regular wire. The ribbon cable carries data between the CD-ROM drive and the sound card; the other cable carries the sound from the CD-ROM drive to the sound card when you play regular audio CDs in your CD-ROM drive. All the connectors on the back of the CD-ROM drive have distinctive shapes, and the cables you have will only fit into one slot.

Attach the ribbon cable. Some ribbon cables, but not most, have on their connectors a small flange that ensures that you can't insert the cable into the slot incorrectly (unless you use a *lot* of force). It's kind of like sliding tab A into slot B. And the direction does matter. So look closely at the CD-ROM drive, specifically just above the connector where the ribbon cable goes. You should see, somewhere, a label that says "Bus." Just below that, you'll see some numbers. Look for the number 1. That 1 identifies pin 1 of the connector. Now look at the ribbon cable itself; see that one edge of it is a different color from the rest (probably red). That side of the cable should plug into the connector near the number 1. Remember: red, one. When you're connecting the cable to the sound card, you're going to attach the red side to pin 1 again.

Now attach the other wire. It's the wire that carries audio sound from the CD-ROM drive to the sound card when you play audio CDs. You'll probably find its connector at the right of the CD-ROM drive labeled "Audio." Both ends are different shapes, so if the end you're using doesn't fit right, try the other end. In addition, it has little tabs on it so it can go in only one way (right-side up), so if you find you're exerting a lot of force, flip the wire over and try it the other way.

Now your wires are attached. Time to insert the drive into an open bay. Actually installing your CD-ROM drive is going to be a bit different from computer type to computer type. The basic procedure is pretty similar, but the specifics vary greatly. Here's the basic lineup:

Step 4a: Open the case (I know, you already have yours open, but I'm being thorough).

Step 4b: Pop out a 5¼ -inch, half-height external drive bay cover. The front of your computer probably has at least one drive bay cover; they're very nondescript and look just slightly like they're really meant to be removed. Most of them will fall out if you give them a good solid whack into the computer.

Step 4c: Insert the CD-ROM cables through the open bay, then slide the CD-ROM drive in after. Some systems require you to attach runners to the CD-ROM before you slide it in. These runners slip into small notches in the sides of the drive bay like a kitchen drawer. They're also a nuisance. That's because your PC doesn't come with extras and your kit probably didn't include any. You may have to call your manufacturer to get two more runners. You can tell if your system needs runners by looking at a component already installed (like your floppy drive). Are there small runners attached to its sides? If so, the CD-ROM drive will probably need them, too. Attach the runners now and slide the drive into place.

Step 4d: Secure the CD-ROM drive with very small screws. For systems without runners, the screws drive through the sides of the drive bay enclosure and into the CD-ROM drive. If your system uses runners, this step may not be necessary (some runners "click" into place), or you may secure the CD-ROM drive from the front. Where do you get the screws, though? Good question. Usually, I "borrow" them from other components that look like they're oversecured. Like my floppy drive, which had six screws holding it in. It really only needs three, and I can use the other three on the CD-ROM drive.

Step 4e: Connect power to the CD-ROM drive. At the back of your computer is its power supply. It has all sorts of wires coming out of it, all of which end in translucent plastic plugs that have four holes. Pick one and plug it into the power connector on the CD-ROM drive. If you don't have a free one, rush to Radio Shack or a local computer store and explain your situation. You want a Y cable for a PC power supply. Then just unplug one of the peripherals and plug the Y cable into it to split it into two.

Step 5: Flip whatever switch on your sound card there is to make it support your CD-ROM drive.

If you purchase a sound card without a CD-ROM drive, that doesn't mean it *can't* support a CD-ROM drive, just that support is turned off. Turning support off is usually a simple matter of moving a jumper from one set of pins to another. Conversely, turning support on is just as simple as moving it back—you may not even have to pull out the sound card!

Let's take the Sound Blaster 16, for example. Look at the upper-left side. Do you see jumpers labeled PAN, SON, MIT, and DISABLE? If so, you should see that a jumper covers DISABLE. That means your Sound Blaster isn't currently set up to act as your CD-ROM controller. But it also means that your board *will* support any one of three CD-ROM drives: a

Panasonic (often called by the name of its parent company, Matsushita), a Sony, or a Mitsumi.

Depending on the vendor of the CD-ROM drive you purchased, move this jumper to either PAN (Panasonic or Matsushita), SON (Sony), or MIT (Mitsumi). You may have to remove the card from the system to get at these jumpers. If so, all you have to do is disconnect all the cables from it, unscrew the screw that holds it in (located at the back of your case), and yank. Getting it back in simply reverses the process. But don't reinstall it yet—you're going to have to get at some other parts of the board for Step 6.

Step 6: Connect the two.

Now your sound card is ready, your CD-ROM is installed and has its cables dangling. Connect 'em. There are two wires (plus the power cable) coming off the back of the CD-ROM drive: a wide, flat one (called a ribbon cable) that goes into a wide, flat connector on the CD-ROM drive, and a skinny, round one that goes into a port on the sound card that probably has a name like CD_AUDIO or AUDIO_IN.

If your sound card will support several CD-ROM drive types (like the Sound Blaster we were talking about earlier), you'll probably have a variety of places you could attach the wide, flat cable and even the round one. Fortunately, at least in the case of the ribbon cable, those places are labeled. Look closely at your sound board. You should see a place where a bunch of brass pins poke up—thirty-four or forty of them.

You may have to remove the card from the system to get at these pins. If so, all you have to do is disconnect all the cables from it, unscrew the screw that holds it in (located at the back of your case), and yank. Getting it back in simply reverses the process.

Now that you're looking at the pins, see if there are labels nearby that correspond to the labels on the CD-ROM selection jumpers, like PAN, SON, and MIT. The Panasonic and

Mitsumi connectors each have forty pins; the Sony connector has thirty-four. Depending on the type of CD-ROM drive you have, plug it into the appropriate connector.

Similarly, you may have multiple audio-input connectors—one for each CD-ROM drive type. These connectors will probably be located near the right side of the sound card. Attach the round cable to the appropriate connector.

Now reinstall your sound card.

Step 7: Boot your system.

Make sure everything comes up. It should—you haven't made any really major changes.

Step 8: Install the CD-ROM driver.

This can be as simple as inserting your driver diskette into your floppy drive and typing INSTALL, or as complicated as having to modify your AUTOEXEC.BAT and CONFIG.SYS files. So put the floppy into your floppy drive (I'll assume it's drive A for my example) and type DIR /W A: to see what's on the drive. If there's an INSTALL.EXE or SETUP.EXE or anything that looks like its job is to install your drivers, run it by typing A: then the name of the file.

If not, and you just see a file with a name like SBCD.SYS, you're going to have to modify your CONFIG.SYS and AUTOEXEC.BAT by hand. This isn't actually very hard.

First, make a place on your hard drive for the files from the floppy—try calling it CDROM—then copy the files from the floppy into that directory:

```
C:\>MD \CDROM
C:\>COPY /S A:*.* C:\CDROM
```

The files should now be on your hard drive.

Using a text editor such as DOS 5's EDIT, modify your
CONFIG.SYS by adding a pair of lines like this at the bottom:

```
DEVICE=C:\CDROM\SBCD.SYS /D:MSCD001 /P:240
LASTDRIVE=E
```

This line adds the CD-ROM driver to your system. The
/D:MSCD001 says that this is the first CD-ROM drive in
your system, the /P:240 tells the driver what base memory address to look at to access the drive. You'll have to figure out what switches work with your driver (with any luck,
you have a manual, otherwise call technical support with
the number in Appendix A). Save and exit.

Now use your text editor again to add a line like this to the
end of your AUTOEXEC.BAT:

```
C:\CDROM\MSCDEX.EXE /D:MSCD001 /V /M:15
```

This line adds the MSCDEX driver to your system at the
next available drive letter. This is a pretty standard syntax
for this driver. If MSCDEX.EXE isn't located in your CDROM
directory, look for it in \DOS or \WINDOWS. Save and exit.

Step 9: Reboot.

Press Ctrl+Alt+Del to reboot your computer. It should come
up with a working CD-ROM drive at letter D or E.

Running a CD-ROM Drive off Its Own Controller

Depending on the type of CD-ROM drive you have, you
could be facing anything from a simple installation to a
"Don't plan to start this at 4 P.M. on a Friday" installation. I
hate to say it, but even with first-class technical resources,
installing a CD-ROM drive and its controller can be a pain.

Make sure you get a con-
troller that will work with
your CD-ROM drive.
There are three basic setups you could have: an Enhanced
IDE CD-ROM drive, a SCSI CD-ROM drive, and a proprietary CD-ROM drive. Each of these will have its own type
of controller and will require slightly different drivers.

Enhanced IDE controllers are (as of this writing) still rare—
the preference is for plain old IDE. But they're becoming incredibly popular, and if you buy a system today, you should
look for built-in Enhanced IDE. My IBM ValuePoint
100DX4/Dp, for example, has one built in (although I can't
find CD-ROM drivers that work with it for the life of me).
The key, at least in the initial stages until all the compatibility bugs are worked out, will be getting a money-back
guarantee on the CD-ROM drive you purchase. That way, if
it doesn't work, you can return it.

SCSI is a familiar CD-ROM drive interface. It has several
caveats that the other two solutions don't. For example,
each device attached to your SCSI host adapter has to have
its own ID number. That makes it a little more confusing.
However, it's more powerful than Enhanced IDE because
you can have longer cables (up to 18 feet) and attach more
devices to one host adapter (up to seven, and those seven
devices can be other host adapters, so you can theoretically
have forty-nine devices off a single SCSI host adapter, but
let's not get too wild).

Proprietary CD-ROM interfaces are, thankfully, dying.
Although they're virtually hassle-free, they are . . . well,
proprietary. I've had it drilled into me so hard that proprietary is bad that I almost can't remember why. But the big
thing about proprietary interfaces is that if one component
goes bad, you can have a heck of a time finding someone to
replace or repair it.

With all three solutions, you may wind up purchasing not
only a CD-ROM drive, but a controller board, too. That's
definitely true for proprietary interfaces, and usually true
for SCSI interfaces (since some systems build SCSI onto the
motherboard, you may not need another board) and
Enhanced IDE interfaces (older systems will need a card;
newer ones will probably have an Enhanced IDE interface
built in). As with any board installation, you're going to
have to do a little two-step to get things to work right.

The basic procedure is as follows:

1. Determine free resources.
2. Set up the board.
3. Install the board.
4. Install the CD-ROM drive.
5. Connect them.
6. Boot the computer and install the drivers.
7. Reboot.

We'll go into a little more depth soon, but remember that you really only have seven basic steps.

The First Steps for Any Controller Card

No matter what kind of CD-ROM drive you have, you need to run through the following nine steps.

Step 1: Determine that your PC meets your drive kit's requirements.

Before you open your brand new CD-ROM drive's box or un-screw your case, check to make sure you have the following:

✓ ISA bus
✓ 2 MB free hard disk space
✓ DOS 3 or later

This step is really kind of perfunctory because most PCs today meet every CD-ROM drive/controller combination's requirements, but just in case, you'd better check.

Most CD-ROM drive/controller combinations will install into any IBM-compatible with an ISA bus (also called an AT bus). You'd better have at least 2 MB of free disk space on your hard disk (you *do* have a hard disk, don't you?) for the drivers and other software you'll need to install. Oh, and you'll probably want at least DOS version 3 or later (version 6.22 is current).

Step 2: Determine free IRQs and DMAs.

If you're installing a board into your system, check for the following:

✓ Free IRQs

✓ Free DMAs

This step is kind of tricky. There's no really easy way to 100 percent guarantee that you'll get it right if you do it from software. Microsoft includes with MS-DOS 5 and later a utility called Microsoft System Diagnostics (MSD). As you can see in Figure 3.15, it's not very helpful.

```
 File  Utilities  Help
                             IRQ Status
   IRQ  Address     Description       Detected           Handled By

    0  09A8:04B7  Timer Click       Yes                SNAP.EXE
    1  C95E:1923  Keyboard          Yes                Block Device
    2  0430:0057  Second 8259A      Yes                Default Handlers
    3  0430:006F  COM2: COM4:       COM2:              Default Handlers
    4  D543:0096  COM1: COM3:       COM1: COM3: PS/2 StyMOUSE.EXE
    5  0430:009F  LPT2:             No                 Default Handlers
    6  0430:00B7  Floppy Disk       Yes                Default Handlers
    7  0070:06F4  LPT1:             Yes                System Area
    8  0430:0052  Real-Time Clock   Yes                Default Handlers
    9  F000:EC2D  Redirected IRQ2   Yes                BIOS
   10  0430:00CF  (Reserved)                           Default Handlers
   11  0430:00E7  (Reserved)                           Default Handlers
   12  0430:00FF  (Reserved)                           Default Handlers
   13  F000:EC36  Math Coprocessor  Yes                BIOS
   14  0430:0117  Fixed Disk        Yes                Default Handlers
   15  0430:012F  (Reserved)                           Default Handlers

                            ═══ OK ═══

 IRQ Status: Displays current usage of hardware interrupts.
```

Figure 3.15 MSD isn't really great about letting you know what your free IRQs and DMAs are, but at least it's free.

MSD will probably give you a vague indication of what kind of IRQs, DMAs, and so on you have. Make that *very* vague. For example, my IRQ 5 is occupied by a sound card, but it doesn't show up in Figure 3.15. Generally, areas marked (Reserved) should be free, but the odds are pretty good that you're going to have to wait until your system is open before you can really make sure that you have this information right.

Nonetheless, write down the free resource information MSD provides on a Post-it note. You'll need it in just a minute.

If you're really at a loss for the configuration information of the cards in your computer, there are several programs that can help. At work I use one called PC Tools for Windows from Central Point Software (shown in Figure 3.16). There's also one called SysInfo, and another called CheckIt Pro Analyst. Truth to tell, though, PCs weren't designed with configuration-determining software in mind. There's no 100 percent sure piece of software available that will figure out every card you might have plugged into your computer. Sorry.

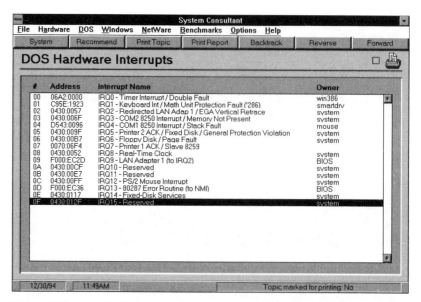

Figure 3.16 PC Tools System Consultant looks better but isn't more accurate.

The new Plug and Play standard (from Intel, Microsoft and Al, as in et al.) should help fix that, but that's future stuff, and you have to figure out your configuration today. Well, if MSD didn't give you a full report (how do you know? I'll tell you: it didn't) then wait a minute and I'll tell you what to do.

Step 3: Back up your crucial software.

This may sound silly. It may sound ridiculous. It may sound like a pain in the buttocks. But. And I underline that: <u>But</u>. Heck, I'll underline it, italicize it, boldface it, and put it into a different font: ***But*** you had better do it. Start by backing up four critical files: AUTOEXEC.BAT, CONFIG.SYS, WIN.INI, and SYSTEM.INI. (You should be doing this any-time you change your files anyway, but do it now.) To do this, put a formatted floppy into your floppy drive (I'll as-sume its drive A) and run these commands:

```
C:\>COPY \CONFIG.SYS A:
C:\>COPY \AUTOEXEC.BAT A:
C:\>COPY \WINDOWS\WIN.INI A:
C:\>COPY \WINDOWS\SYSTEM.INI A:
```

Now if you run into any problems when booting your com-puter, you can restore these four files and things should be fine.

Now you have to back up the software that came with your CD-ROM drive. This is for when (not if, when) your distrib-ution diskettes go south. It will happen: it always does. Try using these commands (I'm assuming you have a hard disk):

```
C:\>MD DISTRIB
C:\>MD DISTRIB\DISK1
C:\>MD DISTRIB\DISK2
```

Repeat this command once for every distribution diskette, so you have unique directories for each. Now place the first of your distribution diskettes in your floppy drive. I'm as-suming you're using drive A. Now run these commands:

```
C:\>XCOPY /S A:*.* C:\DISTRIB\DISK1
```

Now put the second diskette into the drive and run the com-mand again, but this time change the target directory to C:\DISTRIB\DISK2. Keep doing it until all the diskettes are backed up onto your hard drive.

Now you can create a second copy of your distribution floppies really easily: just XCOPY the files from the hard drive onto a bunch of new floppies. You'll need to format one new floppy for each of the distribution floppies that came with your software:

```
C:\>FORMAT A:
```

When it asks you if you want to format another, say Yes until you've formatted all the floppies you need. Now create nice, new labels for your floppies that tell you what's on them, and XCOPY the data off the hard disk onto the floppies:

```
C:\>XCOPY /S C:\DISTRIB\DISK1\*.* A:\
```

And keep at it until you're out of directories. You should now have a fully backed-up set of floppies. You can delete your DISTRIB directories now. If you have MS-DOS 6 or later, you can use this command:

```
C:\>DELTREE C:\DISTRIB
```

But if you have a previous DOS version, you're going to have to go into each directory, delete all the files, then delete the directory, like this:

```
C:\>DEL \DISTRIB\DISK1
C:\>RMDIR \DISTRIB\DISK1
```

And so on. Now you have a nice, working (one hopes) copy of your distribution diskettes.

Step 4: Open your PC.

Let's make like Nero Wolfe and crack your case. PC enclosures come in two basic types: desktop and tower. The desktop version sits comfortably on . . . well, on your desktop, usually with your monitor on top of it. The tower type of case is usually too tall for your desktop—it dwarfs everything on your desk when you try to put it there.

In either case (pun intended), you're going to be dealing with some kind of fastener to remove the enclosure that covers the guts of your computer. With most cases, these fasteners are screws of some kind, thumbscrews and Phillips screws being the most common. In a very few cases, you have an advanced case design that uses some kind of screwless latch to pop open.

I'd like to say, "Read your owner's manual to see how to open your case." But if you're like me, you no longer have your owner's manual. If you ever had one at all. Never fear: Here are hints for opening both types of cases.

Screwless Case: These are usually the easier of the two to open. You'll know you have one if somewhere on your enclosure there's a small button that turns neither the computer nor "Turbo" on or off. Usually, the latch is located either in the upper-middle of the front (as on IBM ValuePoint) or somewhere on the back. Push the button and hold it in.

Screwy Case: Look at the back of your computer. There are probably a bunch of screws there. Look at the edges of the back. You'll probably see five or six screws that pretty clearly secure the sides of the computer to the back. Just remove these.

Now wiggle the enclosure front-to-back. That's right, stand in front of your computer, lay your hands flat on the side of the computer, and give the enclosure a good hard jerk toward you, then away from you. The case (or a panel on the case) should move in one of the two directions. Pull or push it as far in that direction as it will go, then lift it up until it's clear of the rest of the computer. You're in.

Step 5: Recheck your DMAs and IRQs while the case is open.

If you're installing a card, check again for the following:

✓ Free IRQs
✓ Free DMAs

Now that you're inside your computer, you'll have a really great time verifying that MSD gave you totally inaccurate information about your system's configuration. How? By looking at each of the cards in your computer and checking to see what their settings are.

This is no small task for even the most knowledgeable PC people. Most cards don't have obvious settings—they have jumpers with names like J0, J1, H5, and N21. They have DIP switches numbered 0–7 that have nothing to do with anything. And they *don't print what the jumpers and switches mean on the board.* Of all the boards I've plugged into computers, only Adaptec has the courtesy to assume that you're going to throw away their manual and to print what each of the jumper settings means. Some boards don't even have jumpers or DIP switches at all—they're configured through software.

Regardless, you've got to take a look just to make sure. So first you're going to have to pull your boards out of the slots they're in. In every computer I've seen, this is done by loosening a Phillips-head screw located toward the back of the computer. Each board gets its own screw. So look at each board, and trace it to the back of your computer. When you run out of board, there will be a metal plate—the plate that's exposed through the back of the computer. It has a lip inside the computer, and, on top of this lip, you should see a screw. Remove it. But before you wrestle the board out of its slot, *remove any wires from its back.* Any wires that protrude out the back of your computer will hang up the board as you try to remove it.

Now pull the board out as in Figure 3.17. This isn't as easy as it seems because the boards fit very tightly into their slots. Try grasping opposite ends of the board between your thumbs and index fingers, then lifting first the right side, then the left side. You're wiggling the board free.

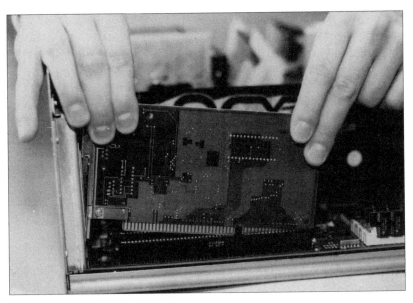

Figure 3.17 Shake, wiggle, and roll.

Once the board's free of the computer, check it for jumpers or DIP switches. What's a jumper? Or a DIP switch? They're two ways of accomplishing basically the same thing: closing a circuit. With jumpers, you have a small piece of metal with plastic around it that either closes the gap between two electrical poles or doesn't. A DIP switch (stands for dual in-line packaging) is basically a little light switch; flick it to 0 and it's off (or "open"), flip it to 1 and it's on (or "closed").

If you're lucky, the board you're looking at has its jumpers and/or DIP switches labeled with their function. For example, jumper J1 might be labeled IRQ 5. That means if you close the jumper (put it over the two little wires poking out of the board) you'll set the board to IRQ 5. Look at your boards and see if you can determine more information about their configuration than MSD gave you. If you have the manuals for these components, you'll find out what the jumpers and DIP switches mean by looking in there (usually in an appendix).

Both DIP switches and jumpers are very small. As you work with them, (and you will work with them), you might want a small screwdriver or pair of needle-nosed pliers.

How to tell a 16-bit slot from an 8-bit slot: The 16-bit slot has two parts—two separate slots—and is longer than an 8-bit slot.

Once you're done, replace all of them. It doesn't matter which slots you slide which boards into usually: any 16-bit ISA board can go into any 16-bit ISA slot, any 8-bit ISA card can go into any ISA slot at all, and any PCI board can go into any PCI slot.

There may be a catch with some VESA-Local bus slots (called VL-bus slots for short). VL-bus slots are numbered (1, 2, and so on). Some VL-bus boards (like my Adaptec AHA-2842) need to go into a particular slot—the slot that matches the number that the board is configured for. Just make sure you install your VL-bus cards back into the slots they came from and you'll have no problem.

Step 6: Verify that you have enough open bus slots.

Again, if you're installing a card, check to make sure you have enough bus slots for the card you're about to install. Most SCSI cards require one 16-bit ISA slot, but many proprietary cards and low-end SCSI cards require only an 8-bit ISA slot.

Step 7: Verify that you have an open drive bay (internal CD-ROM only).

This is kind of like the previous step. If you have an internal CD-ROM (you'll know because it'll look kind of unfinished in back), you need a half-height 5¼-inch external drive bay. Half-height bays are about 1½ inches tall, by the way. If you don't have a free bay, see if something that occupies one of your bays can be moved to an internal bay. Ideal candidates are hard disk drives, which really don't need to be exposed at all.

Moving something to an internal bay can be a royal PITA (an acronym for pain in the behind). If you're lucky, you'll just have to remove a few really small screws. If you aren't, you're going to have to deal with positioning special rails.

This is a case where having a decent mechanical aptitude is the only thing that will help. Look at the other drives and whatnot and see how they're attached, then make your CD-ROM drive ready to look like that. If your computer needs rails, for example, attach rails to the CD-ROM drive. A good kit (such as Reveal's) will include a bunch of different kinds of rails.

Step 8: Verify that you have a power cord (internal CD-ROM only).

If you have an internal CD-ROM drive, take a look at your PC's power supply (the large shiny box near the back). Make sure that there's at least one free plug coming out of it. This plug should be about one inch across and has four holes in it. If you don't have a free plug, you can go to Radio Shack or a local computer store and buy a power cable splitter. Just go in and ask the person behind the counter for a Y cable that will split the cable from a PC power supply into two usable plugs.

Step 9: Install everything.

Now for the easy part—just install all these pieces. But seriously, if you've done all the previous steps, actually plugging the board into your PC is going to be a breeze.

Step 10: Take a guided tour of your controller card.

If all goes well, you're not going to have to change anything on your controller card, but if you do, it'll be useful to know where all the different thingamabobs are. So crack your controller's manual and familiarize yourself with the various doodads on it.

Step 11: Configure the controller card.

Look at the manual for your controller card and write its default settings into Table 3.19. Now remember that Post-it you were supposed to write your free IRQs and your used DMAs and base memory addresses on way back in Step 2?

Look at it, then compare it with what you just put into
Table 3.19.

Table 3.19 Your Controller's Defaults

Item	Setting
IRQ	
DMA	
Base memory	

So if you happen to have these base memory addresses,
IRQs, and DMAs free, you can just plug and go.

If you don't have these resources free, you're probably going
to have to move a few jumpers. Use your manual to determine how to configure them and move them now. When
you're done, write down the final configuration of your card
on a Post-it note and attach it to your monitor.

Step 12: Prepare the CD-ROM drive.

You're almost ready to plug your controller card into an
open slot. But first, you've got to prepare your CD-ROM
drive. There are two scenarios you could be following: internal CD-ROM drive and external CD-ROM drive. Their installations are slightly different.

If you have an internal CD-ROM drive, you should take this
opportunity to attach the wires that connect the sound card
to the internal CD-ROM drive. It's a lot easier to attach
them before inserting the CD-ROM drive into a drive bay
because you can see what you're doing and maneuver your
fingers more easily.

There are two wires you'll need to attach. The first is about
a foot long, two inches wide, and flat. It's called a ribbon
cable, and it goes to your CD-ROM drive's controller. The
second is also about a foot long, but it looks round—more
like a regular wire. The round cable carries the sound from
the CD-ROM drive to your sound card. All the connectors on

the back of the CD-ROM drive have distinctive shapes, and the cables you have will generally only fit into one slot.

Attach the ribbon cable. Some, but not most, ribbon cables have on their connectors a small flange that ensures that you can't insert the cable into the slot incorrectly (unless you use a *lot* of force). It's kind of like sliding tab A into slot B. And the direction does matter. So look closely at the CD-ROM drive, specifically just above the connector where the ribbon cable goes. You should see, somewhere, a label that says "Bus." Just below that, you'll see some numbers. Look for the number 1. That 1 identifies pin 1 of the connector. Now look at the ribbon cable itself; see that one edge of it is a different color from the rest (probably red). That side of the cable should plug into the connector near the number 1. Remember: red, one. When you're connecting the cable to the sound card, you're going to attach the red side to pin 1 again.

Now attach the other wire. You'll probably find its connector at the right of the CD-ROM drive labeled "Audio." Both ends are different shapes, so if the end you're using doesn't fit right, try the other end. In addition, it has little tabs on it so that it can go in only one way (right-side up). If you find you're exerting a lot of force, flip the wire over and try it the other way.

Now your wires are attached. Time to insert the drive into an open bay. Actually installing your CD-ROM drive is going to be a bit different from computer type to computer type. The basic procedure is pretty similar, but the specifics vary greatly. Here's the basic lineup:

Step 12a: Open the case (I know you already have yours open, but I'm being thorough).

Step 12b: Pop out a 5¼-inch, half-height external drive bay cover. The front of your computer probably has at least one drive bay cover; they're very nondescript and look just slightly like they're really meant to be removed. Most of them will fall out if you give them a good solid whack into the computer.

Step 12c: Insert the CD-ROM cables through the open bay, then slide the CD-ROM drive in after. Some systems require you to attach runners to the CD-ROM before you slide it in. These runners slip into small notches in the sides of the drive bay like a kitchen drawer. They're also a nuisance. That's because your PC doesn't come with extras and your kit probably didn't include any. You may have to call your manufacturer to get two more runners. You can tell if your system needs runners by looking at a component already installed (like your floppy drive). Are there small runners attached to its sides? If so, the CD-ROM drive will probably need them, too. Attach the runners now and slide the drive into place.

Step 12d: Secure the CD-ROM drive with very small screws. For systems without runners, the screws drive through the sides of the drive bay enclosure and into the CD-ROM drive. If your system uses runners, this step may not be necessary (some runners "click" into place), or you may secure the CD-ROM drive from the front. Where do you get the screws, though? Good question. Usually, I "borrow" them from other components that look like they're over-secured. Like my floppy drive, which had six screws holding it in. It really only needs three, and I can use the other three on the CD-ROM drive.

Step 12e: Connect power to the CD-ROM drive. At the back of your computer is its power supply. It has all sorts of wires coming out of it, all of which end in translucent plastic plugs that have four holes. Pick one and plug it into the power connector on the CD-ROM drive. If you don't have a free one, rush to Radio Shack or a local computer store and explain your situation. You want a Y cable for a PC power supply. Then just unplug one of the peripherals and plug the Y cable into it to split it into two.

If you have an external CD-ROM drive, you don't have to do anything yet.

Step 13: Install the CD-ROM controller.

Now you're ready to plug the CD-ROM controller into an open slot. First you've got to prepare your computer. It's still open, right? Okay, find an open 16-bit ISA slot (or an 8-bit slot if that's all your controller needs) and remove the metal plate that covers the opening in the back of the computer, as in Figure 3.18.

Eight-bit cards will work in 16-bit slots.

Figure 3.18 Removing the metal plate from the back of your computer

Now slide the card into place and screw its little metal flange to the back of the PC. Connect the speakers to the back of the card.

If you have an external CD-ROM kit, install the controller card then connect the CD-ROM drive to its external port with what probably looks like a thick, round cable.

Step 14: Boot your system.

Your hardware is all installed. If the gods of PC installations are smiling on you, it's all installed properly. Just in case they aren't, don't reattach the cover just yet—it's a lot easier to pull out a card for a quick change if you don't have to drag the whole cover off.

Plug your computer back into the wall, and set it up so that you can see the monitor, type at the keyboard, and use the mouse. Now turn it on and let it boot.

If your system doesn't boot or you get an error message like "Hard disk failure. Press <F1> to continue," you have some kind of a resource conflict, probably either an IRQ or base memory address conflict. Go back to Step 2 to reascertain your free resources. If that doesn't work, try potluck settings. If this doesn't sound at all scientific, don't worry—it isn't.

Start by altering base memory addresses (the most common reason you'll get a hard disk failure message), then IRQs, then DMA channels. Be as scientific as you can, only altering one thing at a time. This advice may seem like a horrible cop-out, but, unfortunately, it's the best I can offer. There are no perfect diagnostic tools that will tell you what system resources are free, so you never have a full guarantee that your initial settings will work.

Step 15: Run the CD-ROM driver installation software.

Now that your system has booted, you have to install some software to make the CD-ROM drive work. You should have a diskette with drivers that came with the CD-ROM drive—the one you backed up earlier in this process. Put it into your disk drive (for our example, we'll say that's drive A). Type the following:

```
C:\>DIR/W A:
```

Look for files with names like INSTALL.EXE or SETUP.EXE. These are the common names for installation programs that copy the software that'll make your CD-ROM drive accessible (called "drivers") onto your computer.

If you see a file like this (say its name is INSTALL.EXE), run it, like this:

```
C:\>A:
A:\>INSTALL
```

The installation procedure should prompt you for whatever information it needs and make all the modifications to your system that it needs to make.

If your diskette doesn't have a file like this, you're going to have to improvise a little. Say that you see a file with a name like IBMIDECD.SYS. You're going to have to modify your CONFIG.SYS and AUTOEXEC.BAT by hand to include this driver and the Microsoft CD-ROM extensions (called MSCDEX for short). This isn't actually very hard.

First, make a place on your hard drive for the files from the floppy—try calling it CDROM—then copy the files from the floppy into that directory:

```
C:\>MD \CDROM
C:\>COPY /S A:*.* C:\CDROM
```

The files should now be on your hard drive.

Using a text editor such as DOS 5's EDIT, modify your
CONFIG.SYS by adding at the bottom two lines like this:

```
DEVICE=C:\CDROM\IBMIDECD.SYS /D:MSCD001 /P:240
LASTDRIVE=E
```

This line adds the CD-ROM driver to your system. The
/D:MSCD001 says that this is the first CD-ROM drive in
your system, the /P:240 tells the driver what base memory address to look at to access the drive. You'll have to figure out what switches work with your driver (with any luck,
you have a manual; otherwise call technical support using
the number in Appendix A). Save and exit.

Now use your text editor again to add a line like this to the
end of your AUTOEXEC.BAT:

```
C:\CDROM\MSCDEX.EXE /D:MSCD001 /V /M:15
```

This line adds the MSCDEX driver to your system at the
next available drive letter. This is a pretty standard syntax
for this driver. If MSCDEX.EXE isn't located in your CDROM
directory, look for it in \DOS or \WINDOWS. Save and exit.

Step 16: Reboot.

Press Ctrl+Alt+Del to reboot your computer. It should come
up with a working CD-ROM drive at letter D or E.

4
Using Your
Sound Card

I must get out of these wet clothes and into a dry Martini.
—ROBERT CHARLES BENCHLEY, 1939

Every multimedia kit comes with a little software in addition to its installation and configuration programs. These are the applications that enable you to play audio CDs, record and play wave files, and record and play MIDI files. Mostly, these little applications (called "applets") are useful but a bit lame. If you're lucky, your multimedia kit came with some extra software—games, "edutainment" CDs, reference works, and so on. Even so, you're going to want to purchase some more.

So it's time for me to do you two favors: explain how to get the most out of your applets, and give you some advice (cleverly disguised as my opinions) on what software you should purchase for your newly multimediaed PC.

Playing Audio CDs

Playing audio CDs is pretty simple. You don't even need a sound card. Here's how it works: You put a CD into your CD-ROM drive, and use some software that sends a signal to your CD-ROM drive's controller. That signal tells the CD-ROM drive to play the audio tracks on your CD. As your CD-ROM drive starts to play the music, it passes it through a digital-to-analog converter, which is a circuit that changes the binary zeroes and ones on the audio CD into a sound that we can understand. That sound comes out in two ways: through a port on the back of the sound card and through the ⅛-inch jack on the front of the CD-ROM drive.

If you have a sound card that's connected to the port on the back of your CD-ROM drive by a thin, round wire, your sound card can pick up these audio signals. That thin, round wire carries analog signals from the CD-ROM drive to the sound card. Even if you don't have an analog transfer wire, however, you can still hear what your CD-ROM drive is doing by plugging a pair of headphones into the jack on the front of the CD-ROM drive itself.

Best of all, depending on your software, you have all the functions of a very sophisticated CD player right in your PC. Of course, you can't access any data CDs while you're playing your Def Leppard, but those are the trade-offs of life.

Most sound cards come with two sets of software: one that runs under DOS, and one for Windows. Your manual will have full instructions for how to use these very simple applications.

Under DOS, the applications tend to be . . . well, less than fascinating, but kind of neat. For example, with the Media Vision Pro Audio Spectrum, there are seven programs to control your CD player under DOS: CDEJECT, CDPAUSE, CDRESUME, CDPLAY, CDSTOP, CDRESET, and CDSTATUS. They're located in the \MEDVSN\DIAG directory. You can probably guess what the first five do. CDRESET can get you out of trouble if your CD player is doing odd things. CDSTATUS just tells you what your CD player is doing.

Let's play a CD. If you just want to play the whole CD once, you can type CDPLAY and be done. But you can also skip around a little (although not as much as in Windows). CDPLAY takes three parameters: the number of the CD drive (which you can figure out by typing CDSTATUS), the number of the track you want to start with, and the number of the last track you want to play.

Let's say I want to play tracks 5 through 8 on my CD. I'd
use this command:

```
C:\>\MEDVSN\CDPLAY 3 5 8
```

My CD-ROM drive's number is 3, and I want to start with
track 5 and play through track 8. After I type this command, the CD player will start, and I'll get my DOS prompt
back.

That's the only one of these commands that takes any fancy
parameters. After that, you use CDPAUSE to pause play,
CDSTOP to stop it, CDEJECT to eject the CD, and so on.

Under Windows, things get more interesting. Taking those
commands we just ran for the Pro Audio Spectrum,
Windows puts a really nice interface on top (as in Figure
4.1). This utility is called Midisoft Sound Impression. All the
sound cards' utilities look a bit like this, so let's follow some
simple examples.

Put an audio CD into the drive. To run Midisoft Sound
Impression, double-click on its icon in the Media Vision
Multimedia Tools group (or wherever you had the installa-
tion place your multimedia tools).

You're only interested in the bottom part right now—the
part that looks a little like a CD player's face. Some of the
controls will look familiar if you know what CD players look
like. For example, along the bottom on the right are the
standard controls (from left to right) for Play, Pause, Stop,
Rewind, Fast Forward, Skip Back One Track, and Skip
Forward One Track. Directly above these controls are the
digital readouts for what track you're on and how far into it
you are. Unfortunately, you can't program these directly,
even if, for example, you know that you want to start at
minute 2:32 on track 4.

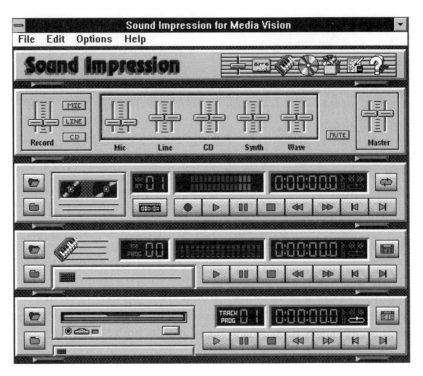

Figure 4.1 Media Vision's Midisoft Sound Impression tool

On the far left of this readout are the controls to initialize a CD and to close a CD. You won't find anything like these on your typical CD player. Through a clever mathematical operation, your CD player can tell one CD from another. Here's what they do: They use the number of tracks and the time on each track to arrive at a unique ID number for each disc.[1] So your Bach Toccata CD is uniquely identified. Your computer can store all sorts of information about your CDs by referencing this number. Unfortunately, the Media Vision tool doesn't, but some do. However, you must click on the upper button—the initialize button—before you can play an audio CD.

To the right of the digital readouts is the programming button. Click on it to program your CD player. You'll see something like what's in Figure 4.2.

---

1. Did you know that every audio CD can also have a unique number burned into it? Most CD manufacturers don't take advantage of this, so we need the "count the number of tracks and figure their lengths" workaround, but eventually, there should be a unique ID.

Figure 4.2 Programming your CD player

To program your CD player to play the tracks you want in the order you want, first click on the X off to the right. That will clear the program, giving you a clean slate to start from. Now, click on the track numbers in the bottom row that you want to appear above in the order you want them to appear. Say you wanted to play track 4 twice, then track 2, then track 1. Just click like that.

There's another setting you can make: repeat. If you want your program (or the whole CD) to play over and over, click on the oval-shaped loop with the two arrows in it. To return to the CD player to play your program, just click on the right arrow.

To eject the CD, just click on the closed folder over to the left of the main CD screen. On some CD players, you can also click on the button that's directly on the screen CD player's face. That didn't work on mine, though. Some CD players require you to manually eject the CD.

Recording and Playing Wave Files

Wave files (often called .WAV files) are actual recorded, digitized sounds. Generally, they're pretty short, because it takes up a lot of disk space to digitize a sound. How much space? Just take a look in Table 4.1 to get an idea of how much space 10 seconds of wave audio can occupy.

Table 4.1 We're All Famous for Ten Seconds—There Isn't Disk Space for More.

Sample Rate	8-bit Mono	8-bit Stereo	16-bit Mono	16-bit Stereo
11kHz	110K	220K	220K	440K
22kHz	220K	440K	440K	880K
44kHz	440K	880K	880K	1.76MB

Okay, what's this mono/stereo, 8-bit/16-bit thing? You're probably already familiar with the concept of monaural audio: one microphone records everything. The sense you get while listening to monaural (or mono) sound is that the sound is coalescing in the middle of your head (best heard with headphones). Stereo sound adds a second channel, so you can tell right from left and sometimes get a sense of the depth of whatever was recorded. When you listen to stereo sound, it will feel more spacious.

Eight-bit and 16-bit refer to sample sizes; 16-bit samples sound considerably better. If an 8-bit sample is like a chain link fence, a 16-bit sample is like a window screen. See Appendix C for more information on how this works.

If you have Windows, you already have some wave sounds, and you probably got more when you installed your sound card. Here's how to play them on a Media Vision Pro Audio Spectrum, which is pretty representative.

Run the Midisoft Sound Impression software (double-click on its icon in the Media Vision Multimedia Tools directory). Go to the section that looks like a cassette player (see Figure 4.3). This is the wave player.

You'll see again the familiar controls across the bottom from the middle to the right side. In order, they are Record, Play, Pause, Stop, Rewind, Fast Forward, Skip Back One Track, and Skip Forward One Track. Above the last of these controls is an oval with two arrows. That's for making whatever wave file you're playing repeat indefinitely. At the far left of

Figure 4.3 The wave table player

the panel are two other icons: on top, an open folder, on bottom, a closed folder. They open and save files, respectively.

So let's open a wave file and see what we can do. Click on the open folder and open the file \MEDVSN\DIAG\PCM0822S.WAV. This is a nice excerpt from a Bach Brandenberg Concerto. Click on the Play button. You're playing. And that's all there is to it.

To create a wave file on your Pro Audio Spectrum, you'll need to bring up the Midisoft Sound Impression tool. You want the wave tool (the one that looks like a tape deck) the master volume control, and the control for the device that you're going to be capturing from (if you're capturing from a MIDI file or from the CD player).

The first thing you need to do is set up the input so that you're capturing from the proper device. You do this from the master volume control. Let's say that you're going to be capturing from microphone: Click on the Mic button at the left of the master volume control, then set the volume for Mic about halfway up, click on the CD, then turn everything else down to zero. If you hear feedback (a whistling sound coming from your speakers), you can either move the microphone

Setting input and output volume controls is important: it controls the quality of what you'll record. Follow these instructions.

farther from the speakers or turn down the microphone input volume until it disappears.

Now click on the red Record button of the wave panel and start talking (or playing the basset horn or dropping pins or whatever it is you want to capture). When you're through, click on the Stop button.

Now adjust the master volume so that the Wave control is about halfway up and the Mic control is at zero, and play back what you just recorded.

One thing I noticed is that my Pro Audio Spectrum wasn't recording in stereo from the CD. Seems there's no way to get it to do that, either.

To record from the CD player (and probably violate a copyright in the process), click on the CD button on the master volume control panel, then adjust the CD volume so it's up halfway. Start recording, then play the CD tracks you want to record. When you're through, stop recording, stop playing, adjust the Wave volume so it's up halfway (you don't have to turn the CD input volume down if you aren't going to play a CD), and click on Play in the Wave portion of the mixer control panel.

Recording and Playing MIDI Files

Musical Instrument Digital Interface is what you get when you spell out MIDI. MIDI is a good way to synthesize musical instruments and other typical sounds without having to actually record them as you do with wave files. Unlike wave files, MIDI files can store a lot of music in very little space. That's because they contain the information about what note you want, the volume, and the instrument (to name a few) but not the actual sound. They rely on the sound card to make that synthesis.

There are two types of synthesis you can get on a sound card. The simpler is FM synthesis, which uses a kind of best guess system to figure out what a sound should sound like. You want a clarinet, and it has a little digital sine wave that looks a bit like a clarinet's. In all, it sounds pretty fake. Slightly better is wave table synthesis, where the sound card actually stores small samples of each instrument and transposes those samples to the pitch you want to hear. The larger your sample, the better the sound. Most samples are only 8-bits wide and don't cover a very wide frequency range, but they're still better than FM synthesized sounds.

To play MIDI music on a Media Vision Pro Audio Spectrum, you use the Midisoft Sound Impression tool. Double-click on it, but this time go to the segment with the keyboard on it and click on the open folder. You'll see something like what's in Figure 4.4.

Figure 4.4 Playing MIDI sounds

As with the other components, you have controls arrayed across the bottom from the center to the right side. They are Play, Pause, Stop, Rewind, Fast Forward, Skip Back One Track, and Skip Forward One Track, from left to right. Also, on the left side on top of each you have the open and save icons. Open a MIDI file now—you'll find one in \MEDVSN\MSOFTRS. Try ITALCO.MID to hear a little more Bach (the Italian Concerto). Now click on the Play button. Nice, huh? Click on the Stop button. Now click on the gray area beneath the track counter (the thing with the digital 01 in it). You'll see the name of the file you're playing and how long it is.

Some MIDI files have multiple tracks just like CDs. I don't have any, but if you do (or you make some) you can control which tracks you play and the order you play them in by clicking on the icon on the far right of the control panel.

Now click on the digital number. You'll see something like Figure 4.5.

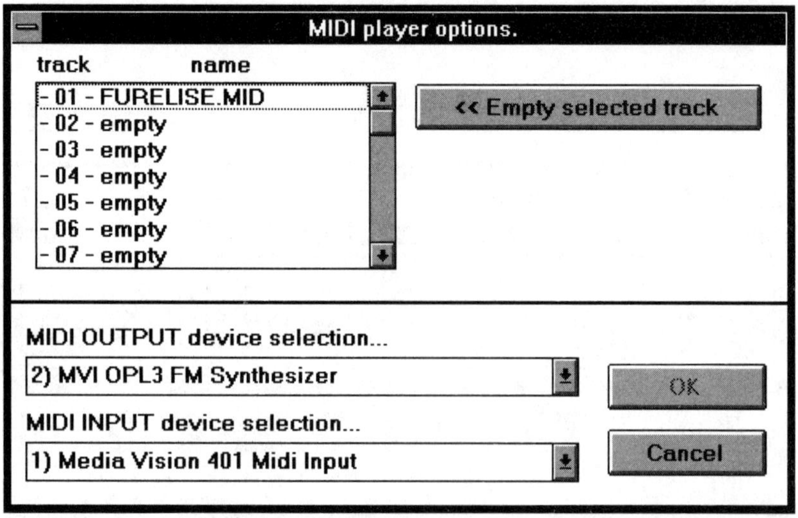

Figure 4.5 Adjusting MIDI sounds

This is the advanced feature setup control here. You'll probably never have to use it, but you can control which MIDI device your computer uses (if it has more than one) and empty out certain tracks from a multiple-track MIDI file.

Recording MIDI files is a bit more complicated. It requires three things: a MIDI input device, a sequencer, and an output device. Some kits supply you with all three, some with only one or two. The input device can be something like a keyboard you plug into the MIDI port on the back of your sound card, or you can use your computer's keyboard and mouse. The sequencer is what takes your input and arranges

it into separate voices, sets tempo, and prepares it so that
the output device (in this case, the synthesizer on your
sound card) can play it.

Media Vision supplies a sequencer called Recording Session
with the Pro Audio Spectrum. When you run it, you'll see a
screen that looks a lot like a musical score, as in Figure 4.6.

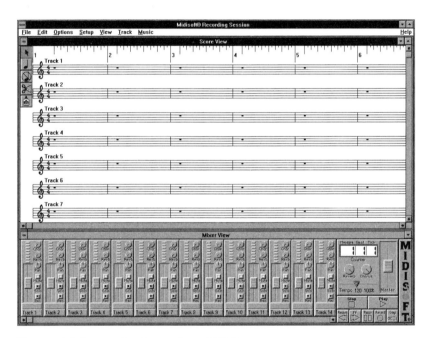

Figure 4.6 A typical software-based MIDI sequencer

As you can see, you start out with silence. This is how John
Cage composed his landmark *4'3"*. (If you don't know what
I'm talking about, it's okay. It's a music nerd joke.) You now
draw notes on the page, assign musical instruments to each
voice, and play back what you've composed. Not every sound
card comes with a sequencer. The Creative Labs Sound
Blaster 16 I have, for example, didn't come with one.

Some notes on playing back your creations. First of all, as I've already said, there are two types of synthesizer widely available in sound cards today: FM synthesis and wave table synthesis. Neither sounds quite as good as the real thing, but FM synthesis is far inferior. If you get at all serious about MIDI, you're going to want a wave table upgrade to your sound card if it doesn't already have one (most don't yet, but it's becoming the standard). Most of these upgrades plug into a special expansion connector on the sound card and cost from $100 to $300.

Do you want to connect a MIDI device to your sound card? It's pretty easy. First, power down both the device (let's say it's a keyboard) and the computer. If you leave either on, you can damage it when you plug one into the other. Now you need a cable to connect the keyboard to the sound card. Most sound cards don't come with this cable. Fortunately, the sound card end of the cable is very standard (there are a couple of keyboard connectors I've found). So all you have to do is go into the store where you bought your keyboard, explain what you're trying to do, and they'll sell you a cable (if one didn't already come with the keyboard). The price on these cables ranges from $10 up, depending on length and what it's made of. I found one for $200. Needless to say, I didn't buy it.

Software to Buy

Your hardware's up and running, so it's time to use it. If you bought a multimedia kit, it probably came with a few software titles. Here are the ones that I keep in my arsenal.

Games: The Real Reason You Bought All This Stuff

Doom II

Operating System: DOS
Processor: 386 or better
Retail Price: $40.00
Creator: id Software

The best shoot-'em-up to be had. You are a space marine, alone, against thousands of demons from Hell. Your job is (you'll never guess) to save the human race. Armed initially only with a pistol, you have to make your way through thirty levels of mazes (thirty-two if you find the two hidden levels) and kill everything. Why is it so great? The graphics are stunningly realistic (read bloody) and the sounds . . . well, if you're like me, you'll be afraid to play this alone in the dark. I've now played it about a dozen times to conclusion (I bet you *never* figure out how to win) and keep coming back for more. Oh, and if you have a network handy, you can play with (or against) your friends.

I did have some problems getting it to work with sound cards other than the Sound Blaster 16. Sometimes I'd get music but no sound effects (it's no fun unless you hear the monsters breathing—and shrieking), sometimes I'd get nothing at all. It's particularly bad when you're trying to use a "Sound Blaster compatible" sound card. Turns out that a lot of these cards aren't very compatible.

The Seventh Guest

Operating System:	DOS
Processor:	386 or better
Retail Price:	$99.00
Creator:	Virgin Interactive Entertainment/ Philips Media Games/Trilobyte, Inc.

If *Doom II* is the best shoot-'em-up, then *The Seventh Guest* is the best solve-the-puzzle. The stunningly rendered graphics make you really feel like you're in the Stoff mansion, solving devious puzzles. This is another "don't play it alone in the dark game." You'll get the distinct impression you're not alone. Because you aren't. There's a narrator with a nasty sense of humor who dishes out "hints" that are nearly as cryptic as the puzzles. It took two of us about a month of off-and-on playing to make our way through this whole thing. I was honestly sorry when we won.

There are all sorts of problems you can expect from this resource-hungry game. For instance, half of the sound cards I tried it with wouldn't make a peep. If you buy it, make sure you can return it—all 1,000MB of it (it comes on two CDs).

Sam 'n Max Hit the Road

Operating System: DOS
Processor: 386 or better
Retail Price: $56.00
Creator: LucasArts

"Caution, naked bunny with an attitude," reads the box. That's not all there is in this game. Your job is to guide Sam the detective and his sidekick Max through a bunch of puzzles as they search for their quarry. "Gee, so what," right? Okay, here's the twist: Sam is a brown dog in a raincoat who thinks he's Sam Spade. Max is the aforementioned naked bunny, and he does indeed have a nasty attitude. And their quarry: Bruno the Bigfoot, who escaped from a circus. The game is, in a word, funny. At times, I laughed until tears rolled down my cheeks. At other times, I wanted to throttle the damn game. The puzzles are often unsolvable without a trip to the hint book (which LucasArts thoughtfully includes with the game).

I had no problems with the game on any of the hardware I tried it with. Granted, my test wasn't completely scientific, but hey, it worked.

Myst

Operating System: Windows
Processor: 386 or better
Retail Price: $55.00
Creator: Brøderbund Software

This is one of those games that you either love or you hate. Most of my friends love it. I hated it. The plot is convoluted, but the graphics are stunning. There is no real animation. Instead the game consists of a bunch of still frames so gorgeously rendered that you'll think they're photographs.

Here's the basic plot: You've somehow traveled through the universe to wind up . . . somewhere. Your job is to figure out where you are, gather the pages of a book, and (of course) save somebody. If you're seriously into puzzle games (*hard* puzzle games, I think) you'll like *Myst*.

The only problems I had with *Myst* were speed. I wouldn't even attempt to run this on a 386. Best speed is probably on a 66MHz 486DX/2 with 8MB of RAM and a double-speed CD-ROM drive. At least.

The Journeyman Project

Operating System:	Windows
Processor:	386 or better
Retail Price:	$79.95
Creator:	Quadra Interactive/Presto Studios

The concept is neat: You're the time police (like in the Jean-Claude Van Damme movie *Time Cop)* and have to protect time. There are many puzzles to solve. The first one seemed to be getting out of your bedroom. I had the damnedest time figuring out how to navigate. Kept trying to walk through walls. The animation is good, but it's not smooth, as it is in an interactive game like *Doom II*. Instead, you click on a button, then you see (in a tiny corner of the screen) the hallway pass by on either side. Movement is S-L-O-W. So's the plot. I'm putting this game here because the premise is interesting. But it's not worth the $79.95 they're asking.

I found no hardware incompatibilities, but you'd be best off running this on a 60MHz Pentium or better.

SimCity 2000

Operating System:	DOS
Processor:	386 or better
Retail Price:	$54.95
Creator:	Maxis

This game is addictive. You're the mayor of a town and your job is to plan that town's development by zoning areas, building roads, trains, airports, electrical systems, and so on. The graphics aren't the greatest, but the intellectual challenge and the number of variations are. It's like a kind of video chess, only you're never quite sure of the rules. It plays on everything.

Sherlock Holmes, Consulting Detective

Operating System:	DOS
Processor:	386 or better
Retail Price:	$69.95
Creator:	Viacom New Media

Small video clips highlight this game, where your job is elementary, my dear Dr. Watson: Solve the puzzles. Was it Col. Mustard in the library with the rope? Fun for fans of puzzles and mysteries, but not a stunning multimedia play.

Commanche CD

Operating System:	DOS
Processor:	386 or better
Retail Price:	$74.95
Creator:	NovaLogic

Another shoot-'em-up, only this time you're a helicopter pilot. There's no plot to speak of, but some of the graphics work (taken, apparently, from some kind of computerized X-ray rendering technology) is pretty neat. The landscape whizzes along below you as you launch stingers, rockets, and hellfires at enemy helicopters and tanks. It's not worth $74.95, but if you can get it for about $30 someplace, give it a whirl.

The one catch to this game is that it doesn't work with `EMM386.EXE`, the expanded memory manager that DOS uses. Every time you want to play it, you're going to have to comment out this line in your `CONFIG.SYS` by starting it with REM. Oh, and there's no real sound, only some crackling noises and bad music.

Edutainment: Instructional Games for Kids

Just Grandma and Me

Operating System: DOS
Processor: 386 or better
Retail Price: $40.00
Creator: Brøderbund Software

Click, click, click. "Haw, har, har!" Click. "Heh." Click, click. "Guffaw!" Those are the sounds that were coming from down the hall as a group of my friends (ages twenty-five and up) played *Just Grandma and Me*. This game is just too darn funny. Of course, kids love it, too. How can you not love a game with lines like, "I found a nice seashell for Grandma, but it was full of crab." Accompanied, of course, by an animated picture of this kid—kind of a brown egg with arms and legs—being attacked by a crab.

It teaches reading and encourages kids to try things. You can click, for example, on various items and they'll do things. At one point, you click on a piece of paper and it becomes a paper airplane that flies through the rest of the story.

Runs on anything. Get it, whether you're a five-year-old or a fifty-year-old kid.

Arthur's Teacher Trouble

Operating System: DOS
Processor: 386 or better
Retail Price: $40.00
Creator: Brøderbund Software

The sequel to *Just Grandma and Me* uses the same tools with a different plot. In this case, Arthur must put up with Mr. Ratburn (read aloud as *RrrrrAT-burn*) and win a spelling tournament. If your kid loves *Just Grandma and Me* . . . well, pick up Arthur at the same time.

TuneLand

Operating System: Windows
Processor: 386 or better
Retail Price: $49.95
Creator: 7th Level

7th Level is making some of the most innovative stuff
around these days, and TuneLand is a great example. You
travel around *TuneLand* exploring while the characters sing
and act out the rhymes from our childhood. It won't teach
your child how to read as *Grandma* does, but it's worth a
look.

The Tale of Peter Rabbit

Operating System: DOS
Processor: 386 or better
Retail Price: $22.48
Creator: Knowledge Adventure

I have a 2-foot-tall stuffed Peter Rabbit in my bedroom. I've
had it since I was twenty-one. So you know I'd like this
reading of Beatrix Potter's tales. Again, the idea is for kids
to explore by clicking on objects to hear their names spoken.

Reference: Who Did What When?

Microsoft Bookshelf

Operating System: Windows
Processor: 386 or better
Retail Price: $99.00
Creator: Microsoft

You're going to see Microsoft's name a lot in this section.
They do good stuff, but *Bookshelf* is definitely (to me, any-
way) the best. It's the encyclopedia of encyclopediae, includ-
ing *The Concise Columbia Encyclopedia, The American
Heritage Dictionary, Roget's II Electronic Thesaurus,
Bartlett's Familiar Quotations, The Concise Columbia
Dictionary of Quotations,* the *Hammond Atlas,* and *The*

World Almanac and Book of Facts. Rarely is so much information gathered in one place. And it's easy to use and kind
of fun. *You need this program.*

VideoHound Multimedia

Operating System: Windows
Processor: 386 or better
Retail Price: $79.95
Creator: Visible Ink Software

Woody Leonhard turned me on to this particular application, which includes irreverent reviews of thousands of
movies. There are also stills from movies and photos of your
favorite actors.

Microsoft Cinemania

Operating System: Windows
Processor: 386 or better
Retail Price: $79.95
Creator: Microsoft

I didn't like the content as much as *VideoHound*, but the
presentation is typical Microsoft slick. If you're into movies,
you need *Cinemania* and *VideoHound*.

Microsoft Encarta

Operating System: Windows
Processor: 386 or better
Retail Price: $139.00
Creator: Microsoft

One of the best multimedia encyclopedias you can get, if
not *the* best. There are animations, sound clips, stills, and
lots of text all linked together (don't know how to pronounce
"Titian"? Click on it). Get this to go next to *Microsoft
Bookshelf*.

Mayo Clinic Family Health Book

Operating System: Windows
Processor: 386 or better
Retail Price: $69.95
Creator: IVI Publishing

Ouch. "Where does it hurt, honey?" Here. "Okay, let's look that up. Seems you have a subdural hematoma." A what? "A nasty bruise." Oh.

If you have any questions about health matters, the *Family Health Book* will have the answers. It's well-designed, but not as detailed as I'd like. But I've never met a medical book that could explain everything in one page, either, so I'm probably a chronic malcontent.

Microsoft Musical Instruments

Operating System: Windows
Processor: 386 or better
Retail Price: $79.00
Creator: Microsoft

I can name that instrument in one note. Thanks to *Musical Instruments*, anyway. I'm a firm believer that everyone should be subjec— uh, encouraged to take music lessons. If you can't, at least spend some time learning what each instrument sounds like and what its history is. After all, you never know when your life is going to depend on knowing the range of the sitar.

Wines of the World

Operating System: Windows
Processor: 386 or better
Retail Price: $59.95
Creator: Multicom Publishing

"I wanna go to Miaaaaami." The whine of New York. But seriously, I'm into wines. (Give me a straw and a bottle of Opus One and I'm happy.) If you are, too, *Wines of the World* will help you put a location to that Bordeaux and keep track of your vintages. It's fun learning this stuff.

5
Q&A

The only stupid question is the question unasked.

—Proverb

There are far too many questions in the world ever to be answered. But that's not going to keep me from trying. With a little help from some friends who really know computers cold and a little help from a program called Microsoft TechNet, I'm going to try to answer any questions you have about your multimedia PC.

Wish me luck.

How to Read This Chapter

I've broken this chapter into three major sections: "Creative Labs Sound Blaster Questions," "Media Vision Questions," and "Miscellaneous." The Creative Labs cards are by far the best selling on the market, so my friends and I have had the most experience with them, so we have the most questions. Media Vision has the second most cards installed, so ditto. After that, we lumped CD-ROM drive questions, questions about other sound cards, and so on into the "Miscellaneous" section. If you're a Sound Blaster or Pro Audio Spectrum owner and you can't find your problem in the section for your card, flip to the "Miscellaneous" section to see what's there.

Creative Labs Sound Blaster Questions

Audio CDs Don't Work

Problem: You just installed Microsoft Windows Sound System 2.0 over your Creative Labs Sound Blaster 16 and now your CD-ROM doesn't play music CDs.

Solution: By default, Windows Sound System turns CD audio off. You've got to turn it on, so first run the Audio Control application (you'll find it in the Windows Sound System group in Program Manager). Display the expanded view by double-clicking on the volume slider switch. Now just select the CD option to turn it on. To adjust the volume of CD music, move the slider for the CD option.

Choppy Sound

Problem: Sounds stutter or sound choppy when using Sound Blaster or Sound Blaster Pro.

Solution: You've probably misidentified the IRQ to whatever application you're running. You'll need to figure out what IRQ the Sound Blaster is at, then tell your application. The best way to determine what IRQ the Sound Blaster is using is to use the test utility the Creative Labs supplied with your card.

Look for your SBCONFIG program and run it. For the Sound Blaster it's in a directory called C:\SB. For the Sound Blaster Pro, look in C:\SBPRO. For the Sound Blaster 16, look in C:\SB16. In DOS, switch to this directory and run the installation routine, like this:

```
C:\>CD SB
C:\SB\>SBCONFIG
```

SBCONFIG will test your card's setup information. It will prompt you either to accept the defaults or press T so it can test to see where your sound card is. Always let it test. It may hang your system, particularly when it's testing for

16-bit DMA. If so, reboot and try again, but this time tell it
to use 8-bit DMA instead of 16-bit. Make a note of the IRQ,
DMA, and base memory address it finds and set up your application to use this IRQ.

For example, to set the correct settings for Microsoft Flight
Simulator 5.0, choose Preferences from the Options menu,
then choose Sound. Supply the information you noted after
running SBCONFIG, then exit and restart Flight Simulator.

System Hangs

Problem: Your program stops responding (it hangs) after
you've been using it for a while on a Sound Blaster 16.

Solution: You have an old version of the Sound Blaster 16
driver. Dial into the Creative Labs bulletin board service at
(405) 742-6660 (8 bits, 1 stop-bit, no parity) to download the
newest. Or call Creative Labs at (800) 998-1000 and have it
mailed to you—but be aware that they'll charge you shipping and handling to mail it.

"Sound Blaster in Use"

Problem: You have a Sound Blaster and are trying to use a
DOS application under Windows, but you get the error mes-
sage "Unable to Play Sound: Sound Blaster Is in Use by
Another Application."

Solution: Your SYSTEM.INI is missing a line that points to
the virtual sound device driver (called VSBPD.386) in its
[386Enh] section. All you have to do is edit SYSTEM.INI
and add the line device=vsbpd.386 to the [386Enh] section and make sure that file is in your \WINDOWS\SYSTEM
directory.

Let's add the line to SYSTEM.INI first. From Windows
Program Manager, select File, Run, and type SYSEDIT.
Press Enter. You'll see a kind of text editor. From the avail-
able windows, select the one titled SYSTEM.INI. Page

through this file until you find the [386Enh] section. Now add the line

```
device=vsbpd.386
```

anywhere in the [386Enh] section. Save and exit.

Now open File Manager (it's in the Windows Main group) and look in the directory \WINDOWS\SYSTEM. If you can find a file called VSBPD.386, you're fine. If not, you've got to copy it there. By default, Sound Blaster installations (no matter which card you have) put it in a subdirectory called WINDRV. So you'll be looking in a directory called something like \SB\WINDRV, or \SB16\WINDRV, or \SBP\WINDRV, depending on whether you have a Sound Blaster, a Sound Blaster 16, or a Sound Blaster Pro. Copy VSBPD.386 into \WINDOWS\SYSTEM.

Now restart Windows and try again.

Won't Play MIDI Files

Problem: Your Sound Blaster Pro doesn't play MIDI files correctly from Windows.

Solution: Your SYSTEM.INI is probably missing a few important lines. First, determine your Sound Blaster Pro's IRQ, base memory address, and its DMA channel. You can do this by running (from DOS) TEST-SBP from the \SBP directory. From the Windows Program Manager, select File, Run, type SYSEDIT and press the Enter key. If your base memory address (also called a port) is 220, its IRQ (also called an interrupt) is 7, and its DMA channel is 1 (those are the defaults), add the following lines to the bottom of the file:

```
[SoundBlaster]
port=220
int=7
dma=1
```

Save and exit, then restart Windows and try playing your MIDI files again.

Distorted MIDI Files

Problem: Under Windows, MIDI files don't play or are distorted (like you're missing the bass line) on your Sound Blaster Pro.

Solution: For some reason, your system may have the wrong MIDI synthesizer driver specified in your SYSTEM.INI. Creative Labs makes two versions of the Sound Blaster Pro, the CT1330 and the CT1600. They're built around different—and incompatible—MIDI chips. You're going to have to figure out what the correct one is and check it against your driver. So first, open your PC and look at your Sound Blaster Pro. Check for the number 1330 or 1600 somewhere on the card. Whichever one you have is the model number of your card.

Now plug the card back in and restart your computer. Go into Windows. From the Program Manager, select File, Run, type SYSEDIT, and press the Enter key. Select the SYSTEM.INI window and go to the section labeled [Drivers]. Find the line that starts MIDI=. If the thing after the = is SBPFM.DRV, you're set up for the CT1330 card; if it's SBP2FM.DRV, you're set up for the CT1600.

If the wrong driver's being used, you need to follow a few simple steps. First, you've got to get the right driver. Call Creative Labs technical support at (405) 742-6622 and explain your situation. They should respond by either mailing you a new driver or explaining how to get the correct one—check their bulletin board at (405) 742-6660.

With the new driver in hand (on a floppy disk, presumably), you're ready to begin. From Windows, run the Control Panel (it's in the Main group), double-click on the Drivers icon, and select the driver called Creative Sound Blaster Pro MIDI Synthesizer. Now choose Remove, then restart Windows.

Restart the Control Panel and go back into the Drivers sub-section. Choose Add, and choose Unlisted or Updated Driver. It'll prompt you for a path to a new driver, so supply it (if it's a floppy, it may be A:\). Double-click on Creative Sound Blaster Pro MIDI Synthesizer from the list of drivers. It'll ask you for your Sound Blaster Pro's hardware settings, so supply them. Then restart Windows. Your MIDI should now work.

Windows GPFs

Problem: Your system experiences general protection faults (GPFs) from Windows when you try to play music on your Sound Blaster 16.

Solution: Your computer probably doesn't handle 16-bit DMA. What's probably actually happening is that you're trying to play a compressed audio clip from a program like Microsoft *Dinosaurs*. You're going to have to tell your Sound Blaster *not to use 16-bit DMA*. Lucky you. Here's what you've got to do in a nutshell: run SBCONFIG from DOS and disable 16-bit DMA, then from Windows Control Panel, tell your Sound Blaster driver not to use 16-bit DMA. Here's the step-by-step.

From DOS, go to the SB16 directory and run SBCONFIG:

```
C:\>CD SB16
C:\SB16>SBCONFIG
```

Now let it go through all its various steps (just select Autoscan for everything but 16-bit DMA), but when it asks you if you want to test for 16-bit DMA, tell it to use 8-bit DMA instead.

Alternately, if you feel macho, you can skip running SBCONFIG and edit your AUTOEXEC.BAT file by hand (located in C:\) and modify the line that says SET BLASTER so that the parameter after H matches the parameter after D, like this

Before

```
SET BLASTER=A240 I5 D1 H5 P330 T6
```

After

```
SET BLASTER=A240 I5 D1 H1 P330 T6
```

Now go into Windows and run the Control Panel, and double-click on the Drivers icon. Select Sound Blaster 16 Wave/MIDI driver, and click on Setup. Under the HDMA setting, set it to DMA. Choose OK, then choose Restart Windows Now. Everything should be fine.

If you click on Setup and you find that you can't modify HDMA, you have a later version of the Sound Blaster 16 driver set and are going to have to do a little manual digging. From the Windows Program Manager, select File, Run, type SYSEDIT, and press the Enter key. First choose the AUTOEXEC.BAT window and make sure that the H value matches the D value. It if doesn't, make it match.

Next, select the SYSTEM.INI window. Go to the section [SNDBLST.DRV] and find the line that starts HDMAChannel=. Make whatever comes after the = match whatever comes after the = on the DMAChannel= line. For example:

Before

```
DMAChannel=1
HDMAChannel=5
```

After

```
DMAChannel=1
HDMAChannel=1
```

Okay, now select the CONFIG.SYS window and find the line

```
DEVICE=C:\SB16\CTSB16.SYS
```

so that the H parameter matches the D parameter. For example:

Before

```
DEVICE=C:\SB16\CTSB16.SYS /Unit=0/Blaster=A:220 I:5 D:1 H:5
```

After

```
DEVICE=C:\SB16\CTSB16.SYS /Unit=0/Blaster=A:220 I:5 D:1 H:1
```

Save your changes to all the files and exit. Exit Windows, and restart your computer. Everything should work now.

"Stuttering" Sounds

Problem: You hear stuttering sounds when you play sounds on your Sound Blaster 16.

Solution: Your computer probably doesn't handle 16-bit DMA. What's probably actually happening is that you're trying to play a compressed audio clip from a program like Microsoft *Dinosaurs*. You're going to have to tell your Sound Blaster *not to use 16-bit DMA*. Lucky you. Here's what you've got to do in a nutshell: run SBCONFIG from DOS and disable 16-bit DMA, then from Windows Control Panel, tell your Sound Blaster driver not to use 16-bit DMA. Here's the step-by-step.

From DOS, go to the SB16 directory and run SBCONFIG:

```
C:\>CD SB16
C:\SB16>SBCONFIG
```

Now let it go through all its various steps (just select Autoscan for everything but 16-bit DMA), but when it asks you if you want to test for 16-bit DMA, tell it to use 8-bit DMA instead.

Alternately, if you feel macho, you can skip running SBCONFIG and edit your AUTOEXEC.BAT file by hand (located in C:\) and modify the line that says SET BLASTER so that the parameter after H matches the parameter after D, like this

Before

```
SET BLASTER=A240 I5 D1 H5 P330 T6
```

After

```
SET BLASTER=A240 I5 D1 H1 P330 T6
```

Now go into Windows and run the Control Panel, and double-click on the Drivers icon. Select Sound Blaster 16 Wave/MIDI driver, and click on Setup. Under the HDMA setting, set it to DMA. Choose OK, then choose Restart Windows Now. Everything should be fine.

If you click on Setup and you find that you can't modify HDMA, you have a later version of the Sound Blaster 16 driver set and are going to have to do a little manual digging. From the Windows Program Manager, select File, Run, type SYSEDIT, and press the Enter key. First choose the AUTOEXEC.BAT window and make sure that the H value matches the D value. It if doesn't, make it match.

Next, select the SYSTEM.INI window. Go to the section [SNDBLST.DRV] and find the line that starts HDMA-Channel=. Make whatever comes after the = match whatever comes after the = on the DMAChannel= line. For example:

Before

```
DMAChannel=1
HDMAChannel=5
```

After

```
DMAChannel=1
HDMAChannel=1
```

Okay, now select the `CONFIG.SYS` window and find the line

```
DEVICE=C:\SB16\CTSB16.SYS
```

so that the `H` parameter matches the `D` parameter. For example:

Before

```
DEVICE=C:\SB16\CTSB16.SYS /Unit=0/Blaster=A:220 I:5 D:1 H:5
```

After

```
DEVICE=C:\SB16\CTSB16.SYS /Unit=0/Blaster=A:220 I:5 D:1 H:1
```

Save your changes to all the files and exit. Exit Windows, and restart your computer. Everything should work now.

Static

Problem: You hear static when you play sounds on your Sound Blaster 16.

Solution: Your computer probably doesn't handle 16-bit DMA. What's probably actually happening is that you're trying to play a compressed audio clip from a program like Microsoft *Dinosaurs*. You're going to have to tell your Sound Blaster *not to use 16-bit DMA*. Lucky you. Here's what you've got to do in a nutshell: Run `SBCONFIG` from DOS and disable 16-bit DMA, then from Windows Control Panel, tell your Sound Blaster driver not to use 16-bit DMA. Here's the step-by-step.

From DOS, go to the `SB16` directory and run `SBCONFIG`:

```
C:\>CD SB16
C:\SB16>SBCONFIG
```

Now let it go through all its various steps (just select Autoscan for everything but 16-bit DMA), but when it asks you if you want to test for 16-bit DMA, tell it to use 8-bit DMA instead.

Alternately, if you feel macho, you can skip running `SBCONFIG` and edit your `AUTOEXEC.BAT` file by hand (located in `C:\`) and modify the line that says `SET BLASTER` so that the parameter after `H` matches the parameter after `D`, like this

Before

```
SET BLASTER=A240 I5 D1 H5 P330 T6
```

After

```
SET BLASTER=A240 I5 D1 H1 P330 T6
```

Now go into Windows and run the Control Panel, and double-click on the Drivers icon. Select Sound Blaster 16 Wave/MIDI driver, and click on Setup. Under the HDMA setting, set it to DMA. Choose OK, then choose Restart Windows Now. Everything should be fine.

If you click on Setup and you find that you can't modify HDMA, you have a later version of the Sound Blaster 16 driver set and are going to have to do a little manual digging. From the Windows Program Manager, select File, Run, type `SYSEDIT`, and press the Enter key. First choose the `AUTOEXEC.BAT` window and make sure that the `H` value matches the `D` value. It if doesn't, make it match.

Next, select the `SYSTEM.INI` window. Go to the section `[SNDBLST.DRV]` and find the line that starts `HDMAChannel=`. Make whatever comes after the = match whatever comes after the = on the `DMAChannel=` line. For example:

Before

```
DMAChannel=1
HDMAChannel=5
```

After

```
DMAChannel=1
HDMAChannel=1
```

Okay, now select the `CONFIG.SYS` window and find the line

```
DEVICE=C:\SB16\CTSB16.SYS
```

so that the `H` parameter matches the `D` parameter. For example:

Before

```
DEVICE=C:\SB16\CTSB16.SYS /Unit=0/Blaster=A:220 I:5 D:1 H:5
```

After

```
DEVICE=C:\SB16\CTSB16.SYS /Unit=0/Blaster=A:220 I:5 D:1 H:1
```

Save your changes to all the files and exit. Exit Windows and restart your computer. Everything should work now.

No Sound at All

Problem: You don't hear *anything* when you play sounds on your Sound Blaster 16.

Solution: Your computer probably doesn't handle 16-bit DMA. What's probably actually happening is that you're trying to play a compressed audio clip from a program like Microsoft *Dinosaurs*. You're going to have to tell your Sound Blaster *not to use 16-bit DMA*. Lucky you. Here's what you've got to do in a nutshell: Run `SBCONFIG` from DOS and disable 16-bit DMA, then from Windows Control Panel, tell your Sound Blaster driver not to use 16-bit DMA. Here's the step-by-step.

From DOS, go to the `SB16` directory and run `SBCONFIG`:

```
C:\>CD SB16
C:\SB16>SBCONFIG
```

Now let it go through all its various steps (just select Autoscan for everything but 16-bit DMA), but when it asks you if you want to test for 16-bit DMA, tell it to use 8-bit DMA instead.

Alternately, if you feel macho, you can skip running SBCONFIG and edit your AUTOEXEC.BAT file by hand (located in C:\) and modify the line that says SET BLASTER so that the parameter after H matches the parameter after D, like this

Before

```
SET BLASTER=A240 I5 D1 H5 P330 T6
```

After

```
SET BLASTER=A240 I5 D1 H1 P330 T6
```

Now go into Windows and run the Control Panel, and double-click on the Drivers icon. Select Sound Blaster 16 Wave/MIDI driver, and click on Setup. Under the HDMA setting, set it to DMA. Choose OK, then choose Restart Windows Now. Everything should be fine.

If you click on Setup and you find that you can't modify HDMA, you have a later version of the Sound Blaster 16 driver set and are going to have to do a little manual digging. From the Windows Program Manager, select File, Run, type SYSEDIT, and press the Enter key. First choose the AUTOEXEC.BAT window and make sure that the H value matches the D value. It if doesn't, make it match.

Next, select the SYSTEM.INI window. Go to the section [SNDBLST.DRV] and find the line that starts HDMAChannel=. Make whatever comes after the = match whatever comes after the = on the DMAChannel= line. For example:

Before

```
DMAChannel=1
HDMAChannel=5
```

After

```
DMAChannel=1
HDMAChannel=1
```

Okay, now select the `CONFIG.SYS` window and find the line

```
DEVICE=C:\SB16\CTSB16.SYS
```

so that the H parameter matches the D parameter. For example:

Before

```
DEVICE=C:\SB16\CTSB16.SYS /Unit=0/Blaster=A:220 I:5 D:1 H:5
```

After

```
DEVICE=C:\SB16\CTSB16.SYS /Unit=0/Blaster=A:220 I:5 D:1 H:1
```

Save your changes to all the files and exit. Exit Windows, and restart your computer. Everything should work now.

Computer Hangs

Problem: Your computer hangs when you play sounds on your Sound Blaster 16.

Solution: Your computer probably doesn't handle 16-bit DMA. What's probably actually happening is that you're trying to play a compressed audio clip from a program like Microsoft *Dinosaurs*. You're going to have to tell your Sound Blaster *not to use 16-bit DMA*. Lucky you. Here's what you've got to do in a nutshell: run `SBCONFIG` from DOS and disable 16-bit DMA, then from Windows Control Panel, tell your Sound Blaster driver not to use 16-bit DMA. Here's the step-by-step.

From DOS, go to the `SB16` directory and run `SBCONFIG`:

```
C:\>CD SB16
C:\SB16>SBCONFIG
```

Now let it go through all its various steps (just select Autoscan for everything but 16-bit DMA), but when it asks you if you want to test for 16-bit DMA, tell it to use 8-bit DMA instead.

Alternately, if you feel macho, you can skip running `SBCONFIG` and edit your `AUTOEXEC.BAT` file by hand (located in `C:\`) and modify the line that says `SET BLASTER` so that the parameter after `H` matches the parameter after `D`, like this

Before

```
SET BLASTER=A240 I5 D1 H5 P330 T6
```

After

```
SET BLASTER=A240 I5 D1 H1 P330 T6
```

Now go into Windows and run the Control Panel, and double-click on the Drivers icon. Select Sound Blaster 16 Wave/MIDI driver, and click on Setup. Under the HDMA setting, set it to DMA. Choose OK, then choose Restart Windows Now. Everything should be fine.

If you click on Setup and you find that you can't modify HDMA, you have a later version of the Sound Blaster 16 driver set and are going to have to do a little manual digging. From the Windows Program Manager, select File, Run, type `SYSEDIT`, and press the Enter key. First choose the `AUTOEXEC.BAT` window and make sure that the `H` value matches the `D` value. It if doesn't, make it match.

Next, select the `SYSTEM.INI` window. Go to the section `[SNDBLST.DRV]` and find the line that starts `HDMAChannel=`. Make whatever comes after the = match whatever comes after the = on the `DMAChannel=` line. For example:

Before

```
DMAChannel=1
HDMAChannel=5
```

After

```
DMAChannel=1
HDMAChannel=1
```

Okay, now select the `CONFIG.SYS` window and find the line

```
DEVICE=C:\SB16\CTSB16.SYS
```

so that the H parameter matches the D parameter. For example:

Before

```
DEVICE=C:\SB16\CTSB16.SYS /Unit=0/Blaster=A:220 I:5 D:1 H:5
```

After

```
DEVICE=C:\SB16\CTSB16.SYS /Unit=0/Blaster=A:220 I:5 D:1 H:1
```

Save your changes to all the files and exit. Exit Windows, and restart your computer. Everything should work now.

Exit Windows, Return to DOS Problem

Problem: Your computer exits Windows and returns to DOS when you try to play sounds on your Sound Blaster 16.

Solution: Your computer probably doesn't handle 16-bit DMA. What's probably actually happening is that you're trying to play a compressed audio clip from a program like

Microsoft *Dinosaurs*. You're going to have to tell your Sound
Blaster *not to use 16-bit DMA*. Lucky you. Here's what
you've got to do in a nutshell: run SBCONFIG from DOS and
disable 16-bit DMA, then from Windows Control Panel, tell
your Sound Blaster driver not to use 16-bit DMA. Here's the
step-by-step.

From DOS, go to the SB16 directory and run SBCONFIG:

```
C:\>CD SB16
C:\SB16>SBCONFIG
```

Now let it go through all its various steps (just select
Autoscan for everything but 16-bit DMA), but when it asks
you if you want to test for 16-bit DMA, tell it to use 8-bit
DMA instead.

Alternately, if you feel macho, you can skip running
SBCONFIG and edit your AUTOEXEC.BAT file by hand (located in C:\) and modify the line that says SET BLASTER so
that the parameter after H matches the parameter after D,
like this

Before

```
SET BLASTER=A240 I5 D1 H5 P330 T6
```

After

```
SET BLASTER=A240 I5 D1 H1 P330 T6
```

Now go into Windows and run the Control Panel, and double-
click on the Drivers icon. Select Sound Blaster 16 Wave/ MIDI
driver, and click on Setup. Under the HDMA setting, set it
to DMA. Choose OK, then choose Restart Windows Now.
Everything should be fine.

If you click on Setup and you find that you can't modify
HDMA, you have a later version of the Sound Blaster 16
driver set and are going to have to do a little manual digging. From the Windows Program Manager, select File,

Run, type SYSEDIT, and press the Enter key. First choose the AUTOEXEC.BAT window and make sure that the H value matches the D value. It if doesn't, make it match.

Next select the SYSTEM.INI window. Go to the section [SNDBLST.DRV] and find the line that starts HDMAChannel=. Make whatever comes after the = match whatever comes after the = on the DMAChannel= line. For example:

Before

```
DMAChannel=1
HDMAChannel=5
```

After

```
DMAChannel=1
HDMAChannel=1
```

Okay, now select the CONFIG.SYS window and find the line

```
DEVICE=C:\SB16\CTSB16.SYS
```

so that the H parameter matches the D parameter. For example:

Before

```
DEVICE=C:\SB16\CTSB16.SYS /Unit=0/Blaster=A:220 I:5 D:1 H:5
```

After

```
DEVICE=C:\SB16\CTSB16.SYS /Unit=0/Blaster=A:220 I:5 D:1 H:1
```

Save your changes to all the files and exit. Exit Windows, and restart your computer. Everything should work now.

"Configuration or Hardware Problem" Entering Windows

Problem: You have a Sound Blaster and receive the following error message when you start Windows: "A configuration or hardware problem has occurred. Use driver option in Control Panel to reconfigure the Sound Blaster driver."

Solution: Assuming that your Sound Blaster is still in your computer (removing it will result in this error sometimes), you probably have some kind of configuration problem.

Go out to DOS and run your Sound Blaster's test program. This will be called either `\SB\TEST-SBC.EXE` (for the standard Sound Blaster), `\SBP\TEST-SBP.EXE` (for the Sound Blaster Pro), or `\SB16\TESTSB16.EXE` (for the Sound Blaster 16). Select Autotest for all the options (remember to leave 16-bit DMA disabled if you've had problems with it in the past) and mark down the configuration information for the card.

Now go into Windows, and run the Control Panel (from the Main group). Double-click on Drivers, then select the WAV/MIDI driver for your card. Click on Setup. Make sure the settings match those found by the test program.

If they do, you may have either a corrupted `SNDBLST.DRV` or `SNDBLST2.DRV`, or even a corrupted `SYSTEM.INI`. The first of these two files live in the `\WINDOWS\SYSTEM` directory. Replace the one you find there with the one from the Sound Blaster's `WINDRV` directory. If the problem persists, open `SYSTEM.INI` in a text editor such as Notepad (from Windows Program Manager select File, Run, type `NOTEPAD`, press the Enter key, then select File, Open and type `\WINDOWS\SYSTEM.INI`) and see if you get an error message. If you do, delete the file and restore it from backup. If you don't have a backup, you may have to reinstall Windows.

Monaural Sound

Problem: Your Sound Blaster isn't producing sounds in stereo.

Solution: That's just the way life is. The only part of the Sound Blaster that is fully stereo is the creative music synthesizer. The rest of the card is monaural.

JukeBox and Sound Blaster

Problem: After you set up the JukeBox program that came with your Sound Blaster I card, you receive this error message: "The Sound Blaster cannot be installed. Please check your WIN.INI settings."

Solution: The Sound Blaster I JukeBox isn't compatible with Windows. According to Microsoft, "This version of JukeBox does not use the Multimedia Extensions. It uses a custom DLL file called SNDBLST.DLL and assumes that it has complete control over the Ad Lib synthesizer. This causes problems with the Microsoft Multimedia Ad Lib driver."

You're going to have to dial into the Creative Labs bulletin board at (405) 742-6660 (8 bits, one stop bit, no parity), or contact technical support at (405) 742-6622.

Mixer and Sound Blaster Pro

Problem: You have a Sound Blaster Pro, and your system hangs under Windows when you run its mixer program.

Solution: You may have an old version of the mixer program. Locate `SBMIXER.EXE` and `SNDBLST.DLL` (the former should be in `\SBP\WINAPPL`, the latter in `\WINDOWS`) and check their file sizes. If `SBMIXER` is 25,792 bytes and `SNDBLST` is 23,776, then you need to upgrade.

You're going to have to dial into the Creative Labs bulletin board at (405) 742-6660 (8 bits, one stop bit, no parity), or contact technical support at (405) 742-6622.

Popping or Clicking Noises

Problem: While playing sounds under Windows in Enhanced mode, your Sound Blaster makes periodic popping or clicking noises.

Solution: There isn't really one. Here's what's happening. You probably have a Sound Blaster with version 1.x of its Digital Signal Processor (DSP). That click is caused by what's called an interrupt latency. That means the Sound Blaster's interrupts aren't being processed by your CPU fast enough. This causes the Sound Blaster to generate an interrupt when its DMA buffer becomes empty. During the time it takes for the Sound Blaster to generate the interrupt and the time it takes for the Sound Blaster driver to process it, you hear a click.

Version 2.0 of the DSP solves the problem by keeping two DMA buffers and filling one while the other empties.

"MIDI Device Not Installed" Error

Problem: You're playing a MIDI file (a file with a .MID extension) on a Sound Blaster, but you hear nothing. You may see the error message "The current MIDI setup references a MIDI device which is not installed on your system. Do you want to continue?"

Solution: Your MIDI Mapper is configured to use a MIDI device that's not installed in your PC. What *have* you been doing? If you don't get the error message, but sound doesn't play, check to see if your MIDI Mapper is configured with a port name of "Creative Labs Sound Blaster 1.0" or "Creative Labs Sound Blaster 1.5" and is trying to send instructions to an external synthesizer. Check by running Windows Control Panel (found in the Main program group) and double-clicking on the Devices icon. Click on the MIDI Mapper entry and click on Setup. See what it says.

To solve the problem, select Adlib or Adlib general in the MIDI Mapper. Save the settings and restart Windows.

Media Vision Pro Audio Spectrum Questions

The second most common sound card.

Windows Hangs on Wave Files

Problem: You have a Media Vision Pro Audio Spectrum 16 card, you're trying to run a DOS application in Windows 3.1, and your computer hangs when you try to play a .WAV file in a Windows application.

Solution: You have a version of the Windows driver earlier than 1.42. You need to get the upgrade from Media Vision. Here's what's happening. The Pro Audio Spectrum (PAS) can have separate DMA and IRQ settings for Windows and DOS. (The benefit of this is that Windows applications can take advantage of 16-bit DMA channels even if DOS can't.) Anyway, the PAS needs to reset itself when it switches back and forth between Windows and DOS. What's happening is that, by having Windows and DOS up at the same time, the PAS is getting confused and resetting at the wrong time, leading to a DMA buffer overflow, which hangs Windows.

A sometimes-workaround is to open your SYSTEM.INI file and increase the DMABufferSize line higher than the default 16. To do this, from Program Manager select File, Run, type SYSEDIT, then press the Enter key. Select the SYSTEM.INI window and go to the [386Enh] section of the file. Find the DMABufferSize= line and set the number after the = to at least 64. Save and exit, then restart Windows and see if the problem persists. If it does, contact Media Vision technical support at (800) 638-2807, or try their bulletin board at (510) 770-0527.

Distorted Wave Files

Problem: You're (or a game is) playing .WAV files under Windows and they're distorted when using a Media Vision Pro Audio Spectrum 16 or Creative Labs Sound Blaster 16 driver on a 486 EISA or ISA bus computer.

Solution: Your DMA setting for the driver probably needs to be changed. Run the Control Panel (in the Main group) and double-click on the Drivers icon. Select either the Media Vision Pro Audio wave form driver or the Sound Blaster 16 wave form driver (depending on your card) and click on Setup. Change the DMA channel to 7 or 5. Exit and restart Windows.

Errors During Installation

Problem: During the installation of your Media Vision Pro Audio Spectrum Multimedia drivers for Windows, you receive the following error message: "Cannot load the Pro Audio Spectrum Stereo Wave Form Driver. The driver file may be missing. Try installing the driver again, or contact your system administrator." Or you may install everything, but the Pro Audio Spectrum Wave Form Driver doesn't appear in the list of installed drivers in the Control Panel's Driver applet.

Solution: You need a new bunch of drivers from Media Vision. You can reach Media Vision either at their own bulletin board service at (510) 770-0968, on CompuServe by typing GO MEDIAVISION, or by calling tech support at (800) 638-2807.

Miscellaneous

When all else fails . . .

Packard-Bell MMP16 and Windows Sound System

Problem: You want to use the Packard-Bell MMP16 sound card with the Microsoft Windows Sound System.

Solution: Here's how to do it. Just type these commands:

```
C:\>CD \MMP16P\UTILITY
C:\MMP16P\UTILITY\> SETMODE/MSS
```

MemMaker and Turtle Beach Sound Card

Problem: You just ran MemMaker (or another memory configuration utility) and your Turtle Beach sound card isn't working right anymore.

Solution: The problem is the MemMaker didn't detect the memory range that the sound card's ROM (read-only memory) chip uses. Here's how to work around the problem.

First, edit your CONFIG.SYS file using a utility such as DOS 5's (and later versions') EDIT and find the line that looks like this:

```
device=c:\dos\emm386.exe noems highscan
```

Change it to look like this:

```
device=c:\dos\emm386.exe noems highscan x=d000-d1ff x=d600-d7ff
```

Adding the X= parameters causes EMM386 to exclude the memory area your sound card uses. You may have to reread your hardware manuals to find out exactly which areas your card uses, but these should work.

Now rerun MemMaker and choose Custom Setup instead of the default. When it asks you if you want to keep current EMM386 memory exclusions and inclusions, say Yes. Then just do what MemMaker asks.

Reveal and Creative Writer

Problem: You have a Reveal sound card and the application Creative Writer doesn't work if it's the first application that tries to use sound during your Windows session.

Solution: Well, this isn't so much a solution as a workaround. You've got to make Windows startup event play a .WAV file (which it should do by default). So go into Windows and run the Control Panel (found in the Main group). Double-click on the Sound icon. Under Events, select Windows Start. Under sounds, select any available sound (Ta-da is the default). Click on OK, then restart Windows.

Sound Blaster MCV Doesn't Work Under Windows

Problem: You just purchased a Sound Blaster MCV and it works under DOS but not under Windows.

Solution: Get rid of your Micro Channel Architecture PC! Sorry, but using Windows won't work with this card.

IBM M-Audio Won't Play MIDI

Problem: You have the IBM M-Audio sound card, and it works fine playing .WAV files through the PC speaker but won't play MIDI files through it.

Solution: The M-Audio card is pretty clever: it can play sounds through the internal PC speaker even though most sound cards can't. Unfortunately, the PC speaker isn't set up by default to play MIDI sounds—only .WAV files. You need to make a quick modification. Run the Control Panel (found in the Main group) and double-click on Drivers. Select IBM M-Audio Sound Driver and click on Setup. You should see an option for playing MIDI sounds through the PC speaker.

Advanced Gravis UltraSound Hangs Microsoft Arcade

Problem: You have an Advanced Gravis 16-bit UltraSound card and you're playing Microsoft *Arcade.* It hangs. What do you do?

Solution: You have two alternatives. First, you can punt. From Program Manager, select File, Run, type NOTEPAD, and press the Enter key. Now select File, Open, and type C:\WINDOWS\WAVEMIX.INI. Go to the bottom of the file and type the following:

```
[UltraSound Waveform Output]
Remix=2
GoodWavePos=0
WaveBlocks=3
SamplesPerSec=11
```

Save and exit. Now restart Windows and it should work, although there may be a slight delay in playing sounds.

Alternately, you can just log into the Advanced Gravis bulletin board service at (604) 431-5927 and download GU20035.ZIP. You'll need PKUNZIP to get to the files in this compressed archive. If worse comes to worse, call Advanced Gravis tech support at (604) 431-1807.

Wave File Sounds Get Repeated

Problem: You're playing .WAV files on a Sound Blaster 2.0 (or compatible such as Media Concepts' card) and sounds get repeated. Repeated.

Solution: You'll love this: the problem is probably the fault of a defective parallel port card. Never would have guessed, would you? If the problem occurs after you've used your parallel port several times (printing, probably), what's happening is that the parallel port is locking the IRQ lines and blocking the Sound Blaster out. The only solution is to buy a new parallel port card. They aren't very expensive (like $50 for a typical one).

System Hangs with Roland Micro Channel MPU IMC

Problem: You're installing a Roland Micro Channel MPU IMC sound card, and your system hangs when you try to install the Windows Roland MPU-401 driver just after you tell it which IRQ to use.

Solution: This card doesn't work with the driver included with Windows 3.1. Call Roland tech support to get one that does.

Zoltrix 16 Card Doesn't Support Compressed Audio

Problem: You're using a Zoltrix 16 sound card and you need it to support compressed audio (used by most Microsoft applications).

Solution: Use the Sound Blaster driver on this card. Here's how. There's a driver disk that comes with the Zoltrix card that includes a file called SNDBLST2.DRV. Find the disk and copy the file to C:\WINDOWS\SYSTEM.

Go into Windows. From the Program Manager, select File, Run, type SYSEDIT and press the Enter key. From the resulting application, select the SYSTEM.INI window. For our purposes, we'll assume that your IRQ is 7, your DMA channel is 1, and your base memory address is 220. Okay, now find the section called [Drivers]. It should look something like this:

```
[Drivers]
timer=timer.drv
MIDI=apdev.drv
Wave=apdev.drv
MIDI1=apmus.drv
VIDC.MSVC=msvidc.drv
VIDC.RT21=indeo.drv
WaveMapper=msacm.drv
VIDC.CVID=iccvid.drv
MidiMapper=midimap.drv
```

Change it to look like this (I've boldfaced the changes):

```
[Drivers]
timer=timer.drv
;MIDI=apdev.drv
;Wave=apdev.drv
;MIDI1=apmus.drv
VIDC.MSVC=msvidc.drv
VIDC.RT21=indeo.drv
WaveMapper=msacm.drv
VIDC.CVID=iccvid.drv
MidiMapper=midimap.drv
Wave1=sndblst2.drv
MIDI2=sndblst2.drv
```

The semicolons comment out lines, by the way. Now locate the section called [apdev.drv]. It should look like this:

```
[apdev.drv]
port=220
int=7
dmachannel=1
```

Change it to look like this:

```
;[apdev.drv]
;port=220
;int=7
;dmachannel=1
```

Now locate the section called [apmus.drv]. It should look like this:

```
[apmus.drv]
port=220
```

Change it to look like this:

```
;[apmus.drv]
;port=220
```

Finally, add two new sections that look like these:

```
[sndblst2.drv]
port=220
int=7
[MSACM]
Install=msadpcm.acm
```

Save, exit, and restart Windows. If you have problems, contact Zoltrix technical support at (510) 657-5737.

"The Hardware Is Not Responding" Error

Problem: You start Windows and receive the error that
your "hardware is not responding. Use the drivers applet to
reconfigure."

Solution: This usually happens to me when I have removed
a sound card and not disabled its drivers from Windows. It
can also happen because the Windows sound driver for your
card isn't configured to match the hardware settings on
your card (for example, the base memory addresses don't
match). The easiest thing to do is click on OK, then, once
you're in Windows, to run the Control Panel, then double-
click on the Drivers applet.

Find the driver for your sound card. It'll probably have a name that includes the words "Wave and MIDI." Click on Setup and make sure that any settings match what your card is actually configured for.

CD-ROM Clicks or Sticks Out Its Caddy

Problem: When you turn your computer on, your CD-ROM drive starts acting funny by sticking out its disk caddy at you or making clicking noises.

Solution: You probably have the ribbon cable from the sound card to the CD-ROM drive reversed at one end. In other words, what you plugged in as pin 1 at the sound card end isn't pin 1 at the CD-ROM drive end. The solution is to turn your computer off, open it (if it isn't already), and un-plug one end of this ribbon cable and reverse it.

SCSI Host Adapter Won't Recognize CD-ROM Drive

Problem: Your SCSI host adapter won't recognize your CD-ROM drive when you power on your computer.

Solution: There are a few possible solutions to this problem. The most common is that the CD-ROM drive is set to the same SCSI ID as another device. Every device on the SCSI bus must have a unique SCSI ID number. There are eight possible numbers, with the number 7 reserved for your SCSI host adapter itself. Dig out the manual for your CD-ROM drive and set its jumpers to use another ID.

If that doesn't work, you may have a more subtle problem. When I was installing a Texel CD-ROM drive into a computer with an Adaptec AHA-2842, the Adaptec host adapter wouldn't see the Texel CD-ROM drive. The SCSI IDs were set correctly. As it turned out, I needed to go into the host adapter's BIOS (which you get at by pressing Ctrl+A as you boot the computer) and reset some of the configuration for the CD-ROM drive. Specifically, I needed to configure the device so that it didn't use synchronous data transfers, and I had to lock its speed at 5 MB per second. Synchronous SCSI is a way that you can get greater speed out of a SCSI device—it means that the device can send and receive data at the same time. In order to find out if the devices support synchronous SCSI, the host adapter queries them. The Texel CD-ROM drive didn't support the host adapter's query, so it locked up and wouldn't even be recognized.

After that, the SCSI host adapter would see the CD-ROM drive, but the whole SCSI bus would periodically lock up. It seemed that the Texel CD-ROM didn't support what are called SCSI disconnects. (Disconnects are another way to boost performance.) So basically, I had to turn off all the advanced features on my host adapter.

Here's another possible solution: are your SCSI terminators fully in place? Poor SCSI termination (loose terminators or resistors that have blown) can cause similar problems. If the previous solution doesn't work, try tightening your SCSI terminators, then try replacing them.

"CD-ROM Drive Isn't Ready" Error

Problem: As your computer boots, it tells you that the CD-ROM controller or host adapter or CD-ROM drive isn't ready and would you like to abort or retry.

Solution: Here we have an interesting problem. Generally, I see this error when I've been "soft" rebooting a computer a lot by pressing Ctrl+Alt+Del. On a soft or warm reboot, some system BIOSes don't reset what's called the ROM area of memory. This causes some devices not to get reset resulting in this error. If you turn your computer all the way off, wait a few seconds, then power it back on, it should work.

That is, of course, assuming that everything else is working right. Other possible causes are that the ribbon cable from sound card to CD-ROM drive is loose or that the CD-ROM drive isn't getting electrical power. Check all the cable connections into the CD-ROM drive.

"Device Driver Not Found" Error

Problem: As you boot your computer, you see the error message "Device driver not found . . . No valid CDROM device drivers selected." (Except in place of the ellipsis [. . .] there's a bunch of numbers and capital letters.)

Solution: This message comes from the line in your AUTOEXEC.BAT that loads MSCDEX.EXE, the Microsoft CD-ROM extensions for DOS. It's telling you that it couldn't find the space in memory that it's looking for your CD-ROM driver in. For some reason, your CONFIG.SYS isn't loading the device driver for your CD-ROM drive. There should be a line in it like one of these:

```
DEVICE=C:\MOZART\SLCD.SYS /D:SONY_OAK /V /B:360 /M:P /C /2
```

or

```
DEVICE=C:\SB16\DRV\SBCD.SYS /D:MSCD001 /P:240
```

These lines load the CD-ROM device driver. If there isn't a line that looks at all like this, you probably aren't loading your driver. You'll need to rerun your CD-ROM drive's installation program. Otherwise, you should look for a CD-ROM device driver (hint: their names usually end in CD.SYS) and put a line like one of those above into your CONFIG.SYS.

"No Drives Are Attached" Error

Problem: You get an error message like this: "No drives are attached, drives are powered down, or communication failed. The device driver is not installed."

Solution: Simple, actually. You're being told that the wrong base memory address is specified on the line in your CONFIG.SYS that loads your CD-ROM device driver. You need to determine what base memory address your CD-ROM drive is using (check the manual that came with your CD-ROM drive controller or your sound card). Once you've done that, edit your CONFIG.SYS using a text editor such as DOS 5's and DOS 6's EDIT and put that number onto a line that should look a bit like one of the following:

```
DEVICE=C:\MOZART\SLCD.SYS /D:SONY_OAK /V /B:360 /M:P /C /2
```

or

```
DEVICE=C:\SB16\DRV\SBCD.SYS /D:MSCD001 /P:240
```

Save and exit. Next restart your computer.

"Device Not Found" Error Playing Music from Windows

Problem: You're trying to play a .WAV of MIDI file and you receive the error "Device not found" from Windows.

Solution: You may be missing some stuff from your SYSTEM.INI. To find out, open SYSTEM.INI in a text editor such as SYSEDIT (to run SYSEDIT, go to Program Manager, choose File, Run, type SYSEDIT, and press the Enter key). Select the SYSTEM.INI window and look for a section called [mci]. It should look like this:

```
[mci]
WaveAudio = mciwave.drv
Sequencer = mciseq.drv
CDAudio  =  mcicda.drv ;this is only for owners of
CD-ROM drives
```

If you're missing something, quit SYSEDIT, run the Control Panel, double-click on the Drivers applet, and click on Add. Click on Creative Labs Sound Blaster 1.5 and click on OK. Then follow the prompts. Don't just add the lines to your SYSTEM.INI—a proper installation also copies files into your WINDOWS\SYSTEM directory.

Poor Sound Playback from Windows

Problem: Sound playback from Windows sounds broken and irregular.

Solution: This is usually the fault of poor system performance. There's not much you can do about most aspects of system performance except buy a faster computer. If you have a 486 or Pentium, you shouldn't be having these problems, however. So here are some system performance tuning tricks.

From Windows, open the Control Panel (it's in the Main group) and double-click on the 386 Enhanced icon. Click on Virtual Memory, then on Change. Under New Swapfile Settings, select None as the Type, then click on OK. And yes, you do want to make changes to the virtual memory settings of your computer. Now exit Windows.

If you have DOS 6 or later, you have a utility called DEFRAG. Run it. You want to defragment drive C and perform a full optimization. This may take a while. (If you get an error message about lost allocation units, go back to the DOS prompt and run either CHKDSK /F or SCANDISK /AUTOFIX /NOSUMMARY /NOSAVE if you have DOS 6 or later, then rerun DEFRAG.) When the defragmentation is done, restart Windows, go into the Control Panel, double-click on 386 Enhanced, click on Virtual Memory, click on Change, and under Type, select Permanent. Click on OK and Yes, you do want to make changes to your virtual memory settings, and restart Windows.

Try again. Performance should improve overall.

Unwanted Noise During Recording

Problem: During the playback of something you recorded, you hear unwanted noise.

Solution: You may be picking up ambient noise from other sources. Run the mixer application that came with your sound card and adjust the recording volume for your input source to close to maximum. Turn all other input source volumes to zero. Now try rerecording your sound.

Hissing During Playback

Problem: You hear hissing when playing music or some applications.

Solution: You might be the victim of a sound that was recorded in 8 bits. Most 16-bit sound cards will play an 8-bit sound as though it were a 16-bit sound, which is rather like looking at a piece of wood under a microscope: it may look smooth to the naked eye, but under magnification you see every imperfection. Eight-bit sounds are considerably less detailed than 16-bit sounds, so when you play them back with a 16-bit sound card, you're magnifying the imperfections.

The solution is to turn the treble way down with your sound card's mixer controls. You can reduce the hissing, but you won't get all the high frequencies, either.

Poor Performance During Wave Playback

Problem: Your computer seems slow when you play back some .WAV files.

Solution: Some .WAV files are compressed, and decompressing them takes a lot of your computer's power. The only solution is to buy a faster computer.

Skips in Wave Playback

Problem: You're playing a .WAV sound, but there are skips in the sound.

Solution: Are you doing something else with your computer? Chances are that you are. The problem is that your computer's really busy decoding and decompressing the .WAV file. When you try to do something else, it gets distracted. The solution is to do nothing else when playing this .WAV file.

Duplicate Icons in Sound Blaster 16 Group

Problem: Your Sound Blaster 16 group in Windows Program Manager has duplicate icons in it.

Solution: This isn't a serious problem—somehow you ran WINSETUP twice. Just delete the icons you don't want by selecting the icon(s) you don't want and pressing the Delete key.

Skips or Crashes with DoubleSpace

Problem: You're recording or playing back a .WAV file from a disk compressed with DoubleSpace (or another disk compression utility), and there are skips or your program crashes.

Solution: Compressing a disk slows it down. It's a fact of life. Unfortunately, you've slowed it down so much that your program can't read or write the information it needs from disk. If this is consistently a problem, you're going to have to set aside an uncompressed partition or disk drive or uncompress your whole drive.

With DOS 6.2 and later, you can type DOUBLESPACE /UN-COMPRESS to decompress your DoubleSpace-compressed disk (provided you have enough room). If you can't do that, you can either purchase a new disk drive and install it (which is probably the easier of the solutions) or repartition your disk drive using FDISK (destroying all data on it) and setting up two partitions, one to be compressed, one to be left alone. With disk drive prices plummeting to around $.50 per MB, it's probably best to spend $250 on a 500MB hard drive (or larger) and add a second drive to your system. See your computer owner's manual for how to do that.

Audio CDs Won't Play from Windows

Problem: You're trying to play an audio CD from Windows, but it won't work.

Solution: You're probably missing the Windows MCI CD Audio driver. From the Main group, run the Control Panel, and double-click on the Drivers applet. Click on Add, then on [MCI] CD Audio, then click on OK. Just follow the instructions (you'll be prompted to insert your original Windows distribution diskettes).

Video and Sound Aren't Synchronized

Problem: You're playing a video clip and it skips or the sound isn't synchronized with the video.

Solution: For some reason, your computer isn't fast enough. It could be that all you need to do is follow the instructions in Chapter 6 to get more performance out of your computer. Or your PC may just not be fast enough. You'll need at least a 33MHz 486DX with 8MB of RAM, some kind of fast video, and a fast hard disk to make video look really smooth.

Continual Hissing and Popping from Speakers

Problem: You hear hissing, crackling, or popping all the time from your speakers.

Solution: You may have installed your sound card too close to the power supply or to another card that's generating a lot of radio interference. Power down your computer and move the sound card so that it's a few slots from anything else.

6
Better
Performance

Optimism, said Candide, is a mania for maintaining that
all is well when things are going badly.

—FRANÇOIS MARIE AROUET
(VOLTAIRE), *Candide,* 1759

By this time you've gotten your multimedia PC working perfectly. Everything plays with everything else. But are you getting the most out of your computer? Not just with multimedia, but in general? Maybe we could do a little tune-up and eke out a bit more raw speed.

Tools for Measuring Performance

There are lies, damn lies, and benchmarks. So goes the saying, anyway. The basic idea behind any benchmark is to create a task of some kind that you can repeat to measure one system's performance against another. We call these beasts benchmarks, because one system becomes the benchmark for another.[1]

There are many benchmarks, these days. *PC Magazine*, a Ziff-Davis publication, really popularized benchmarks in the PC consumer market by developing a series of benchmarks, including PCBench, WinBench, and WinStone. These benchmarks pump out a variety of numbers, like DOSMarks,

---

1. The term "benchmark" probably comes from carpentry—you make a mark on a bench and hold pieces of wood up to it to see if they're too long, too short, or just right.

WinMarks, DiskMarks, CPUMarks, and MarcAnthonys. Just kidding on the last one. Other magazines, such as *PC World* (from IDG) and *Byte* (McGraw-Hill) also have their own benchmarks. There are also benchmarks put together by consortia, such as the System Performance Evaluation Cooperative (SPEC) with the (you guessed) SPECmark.

For what they are, they're all fine measures of performance. But they aren't very much. The problem is that none of these benchmarks measure what *you* do. They measure what their creators imagine a "typical" person would do. I'm not trying to condemn any benchmarks (although it would be very easy to go through their source code line by line and nitpick until blue in the face). I'm just trying to give you a heads-up. So even if a billion benchmarks say your system is fast, if you think it's slow, then it's slow.

Bottlenecks

Why is a system slow? Usually, there's one component in it that's holding everything back. You can increase your CPU's speed a thousand times, but if your disk drive is slow, you won't notice much of an improvement.[2] The disk drive is the **bottleneck** that's keeping your system from flying. (In case you didn't guess, the term "bottleneck" comes from the neck of a bottle, which is usually narrower than the rest of the bottle.)

You can use a benchmark such as PCBench to find bottle-necks. Get a copy (pick up any issue of *PC Magazine* for information on where to find it) and run it. Then go through the results of each test and see how your system compares with their baseline system, which is a system the editors of

---

2. This is known as Amdahl's Law, which states that "the performance improve-ment to be gained from using some faster mode of execution is limited by the frac-tion of the time the faster mode can be used" (quoted from *Computer Architecture, A Quantitative Approach* by John Hennessy and Dave Patterson (San Mateo, Calif.: Morgan Kaufmann, 1990)—a great book if you want to design a computer). In plain English, that means that if writing a letter to Mom takes you two hours—fifteen minutes to figure out what you want to say and an hour and forty-five minutes to write it, speeding the thought process even infinitely (you don't think before you write), you'll still be left with only a 25 percent performance improve-ment. In other words: Speed up where it matters.

PC Magazine chose as solid and representative of how a typical system should perform. You'll probably find areas where your system is much faster than the baseline, and areas where it's much slower. Concentrate on areas that are slower. And what might those be?

Disk

Your hard disk drive is probably the number one bottleneck in your system. That's because, relative to virtually every other component, it's slow. Just locating a piece of data on a disk can take a whopping 10 milliseconds (ms). Okay, that sounds pretty fast (it is, after all, ten one-thousandths, or one one-hundredth, of a second) but relative to other components that operate in nanoseconds or billionths of a second, that's slow. Most PCs sold today have disk drives that are this fast, but with older PCs, the performance of disk drives is considerably slower. As much as ten times slower.

Why is it so slow? Because it's a mechanical device. Inside your disk drive are several round plates (called **platters**) stacked on top of each other like pancakes, but with a little space in between. The platters spin anywhere from 1,000 rpm to 10,000 rpm, depending on how new your disk drive is (faster drives spin their platters faster). The platters, which actually hold your data, have a thin layer of metal on them; the metal can be polarized like a magnet. The things that do the polarizing are the read/write heads—little fingers (one per platter) that stick out and onto the platters. Each head can move back and forth. This motion, combined with the platters' rotation, enables the read/write heads to reach any point on the surface of the disk drive.

So the drive has all these moving parts, spinning, flipping back and forth, and so on. All this motion takes time, and if a read/write head misses the place on your disk where a particular piece of information lies, it's going to have to wait one full revolution before it can get the data again. And lots of misses do occur.

Now consider how often your computer uses its disk drive. The disk drive is, after all, where all the data are stored.[3] So when you run a program, your computer fetches it from the disk, piece by piece. What with all the missed bits of data and so on, you can see how that can be pretty slow.

So what's the solution? Well, you can use special applications that **cache** (pronounced *cash)* your disk drive into memory. Memory, by which I mean **random access memory (RAM),** is very fast. By sticking information from your disk drive into memory, your computer can get at it much faster.

Memory

But memory, although fast, isn't perfect. Your computer can fetch information from memory about once every 60 to 80 nanoseconds (billionths of a second). That may seem fast, but for a variety of reasons, it's not as fast as it could be.

One reason is that the **bus,** which is the bridge between your CPU and your memory, is limited in how fast it can transfer information. Another is that the type of memory in your computer (probably called DRAM for dynamic RAM) must be continually refreshed. In other words, your computer must take time to rewrite each section of memory on a regular (and fast) basis. (The opposite is called SRAM for static RAM, and it can hold data without being refreshed; SRAM is much more expensive than DRAM and is rarely used on PC motherboards.)

There's not a lot you can do to improve your memory performance. Buying faster memory chips (usually called SIMMs for single in-line memory modules) might sound like it'll make memory faster, but it won't: your computer probably isn't designed to talk to them any faster. Memory is kind of the ultimate bottleneck: there's no easy way to solve it.

---

3. Did you know that the word "data" is actually plural? The singular is "datum." I figured I'd use it correctly just this once, then go back to how we're all used to hearing it.

Video

By video, I mean the transfer of graphical information from wherever it resides in your computer onto your screen. Usually this involves several components: your CPU, memory, possibly your disk drive, your system's expansion bus, your video card, and your monitor. Where are the likely bottlenecks in this circuit? Your video card and the bus.

There are many types of video cards (generally called graphics accelerators these days). At the low end are the "dumb" video cards that really don't know how to do much except take preprocessed information from your CPU and transfer it into electrical signals that will make a picture show up on your monitor. At the high end are graphics accelerators that can take raw data out of memory, figure out how to represent it, and pass the signals on to the monitor without involving any of the rest of the computer. The advantage of the latter is that they offload work from your computer. Part of what makes a graphics accelerator fast is that it has memory (usually something called VRAM or video RAM) that can write information out to the screen at the same time as it takes it in from the computer. Having RAM on the board again offloads the computer (particularly the bus) from having to do a lot of work all the time.

I've used graphics accelerators from Number Nine, Matrox, Diamond, and ATi. They've all been fast—much faster than the Trident cards that came by default in many of my systems.

But what really speeds up a computer is the addition of a faster graphics bus. Virtually every desktop PC today comes with an Industry Standard Architecture (ISA) bus. This bus is fine for transferring data to and from slow peripherals such as CD-ROM drives and even disk drives. But when it comes to transferring data to and from your video card, it's sorely lacking. The ISA bus is throttled back to a maximum transfer rate of about 8MB/second. Graphics data can come through as high as 300MB/second.

What's the solution? There are two. The first is called the VESA-Local bus. This architecture is clever, but limited. Somebody took a look at a typical 486 CPU and said, "Gee, the 486 has an internal bus that runs at 132MB/second. If I extended that bus outside the CPU, I'd have a great graphics bus." So somebody (actually a consortium) figured out how to do it. The VESA-Local bus hooks graphics directly into the heart of a 486 CPU, so it's darn fast. However, many of its advantages are limited to the 486.

What with Pentiums and other CPUs coming down the pike, there needed to be a more portable bus. So Intel created the PCI bus. This is *not* a local bus, despite what anyone may call it. What makes the VESA-Local bus local is that it's connected *directly into the heart of the CPU*. With PCI, there's a controller chip between the CPU and the bus. This gives PCI a portability advantage: any CPU can be coupled with a PCI controller to add the 132MB/second PCI bus to its computer.

The one problem with all these great buses is that you have to buy a new computer to get one if you don't already have one. They're not add-on components. Bummer.

CD-ROM

The path from your CD-ROM drive can be a bottleneck, too. In fact, the CD-ROM drive itself can be a bottleneck. Here's what I mean. A CD-ROM drive is like a hard disk with one platter and one read/write head. Except the platter spins much slower—down in the hundreds of rpms (the actual speed varies, unlike a disk drive)—and the read/write head moves back and forth more slowly. That means the read/write head gets fewer chances per second to catch a point on the drive. Overall, unlike the 10 millisecond seek times of a disk drive, CD-ROM drives can be as slow as 400ms. And rather than 5MB/second data transfer rates, CD-ROM drives will be about 150K/second. Slow.

Fortunately, somebody (at NEC Technologies, nearly as I can trace) figured out how to spin a CD twice as fast, then three times as fast, then four times as fast. These CD-ROM drives are known as double-, triple-, and quad-speed drives. Their data transfer rates are much better—300K/second, 450K/second, and 600K/second, respectively. Their seek times are even a little better—as fast as 150ms (which is still fifteen times slower than a disk drive, but they're improving).

All that is to say that if you still have a single-speed CD-ROM drive, dump it and buy the fastest CD-ROM drive and controller you can find.

CPU

Here's a component that isn't usually a bottleneck, but it can be. When? Well, the CPU does all your computer's calculations, so when you dump something on the CPU that requires a lot of calculations (like recalculating a 1,000-cell spreadsheet or decompressing a large archive), the CPU can become the bottleneck.

What do you do? Well, you can try a CPU upgrade. Intel makes OverDrive processors and upgrade processors, as do Buffalo, Cyrix, and AMD. Check a copy of your favorite computer magazine for ads that offer these CPU upgrades; they should cost only a few hundred dollars. These are chips that slide either into the pincushion where your existing CPU is, or into a special OverDrive socket. Do they work? Yes. Are they as good as buying a new computer? Sometimes, but usually not. However, they're much, much less expensive.

The Basic Improvements

Here are some simple steps you can take to gain performance from your system. I'm going to assume that you're running MS-DOS 6.0 or later. If you aren't, you can purchase utilities that will accomplish much the same thing as the utilities built into MS-DOS 6.0, but together they'll cost more than the upgrade, and I'm not convinced that the extra money is worth it.

Fix Your Disk

Before you do anything else, you must run either SCANDISK or CHKDSK. What's the difference? SCANDISK can do slightly more, and it's only available in MS-DOS 6.0 and later. If you're running MS-DOS 6.0 or later, do a full backup (just in case) then type the following:

```
C:\>SCANDISK/AUTOFIX/SURFACE
```

And watch SCANDISK do its thing. It will find lost allocation units, fix misallocated clusters, and do all sorts of things. If you're running a previous version of DOS, try this:

```
C:\>CHKDSK/F
```

If it asks you to convert lost allocation units to files, say No. You can't do anything with them anyway. Only a guru could.

Now run that command again. And again. Until there are no error messages. *If you get any irreparable errors, you may be in serious trouble. Back up any critical data and re-format the disk.* You'll have to reinstall your operating system and all your programs from scratch, but you're playing with fire as it is.

Defragment Your Disk

Now that your disk is fixed, defragment it. With MS-DOS 6, you only have to type

```
C:\>DEFRAG C:
```

and DEFRAG will gladly go through and analyze your disk. When it asks you what kind of optimization you want, select whatever it defaults to. That'll be enough. For now.

Note: If you have Windows installed on your system and you're using a permanent swapfile, get rid of it *before* you defragment your disk. Here's how. Go into Windows (type WIN) and open the Control Panel's 386 Enhanced applet. Click on Virtual Memory . . . then on Change>>. Under New

Swapfile Settings, pull down the Type list box and select None. Then click on OK, say Yes, you want to make changes to your virtual memory settings, and exit Windows. Only then should you defragment your hard disk. Once you're done, re-create your permanent swapfile by clicking on Permanent in the aforementioned drop-down list box.

Why? Because the permanent swapfile is a giant file on your hard disk and it can't be defragmented. That means that this section of your hard disk will remain fragmented for ever and ever. The only way to defragment it is to destroy it, defragment the whole disk, then re-create it.

Cache Your Disk

DOS has a variety of caches in it. The simplest is the old BUFFERS command that you (or some program) puts into your CONFIG.SYS. Beyond that, the primary cache (and most important to us) is SMARTDRV (also called Smart-Drive). Here's how both work and how to use them.

By default, you probably have a line in your CONFIG.SYS that says something like BUFFERS=10. This line tells MS-DOS to set aside ten 532-byte chunks of memory for caching your file system (the names of your files, directories) and some other stuff, like MS-DOS itself. Generally, this number is fine. Some programs, however, are tied to BUFFERS, and if they can't find them (that is, you run out), their performance will degrade. I recommend you set BUFFERS=30.

If you have SmartDrive, the BUFFERS help page in MS-DOS tells you not to use BUFFERS at all. I've found that to be a bad idea. I don't quite know why, but some programs (even Windows programs) feel slower or won't run unless that BUFFERS line is in CONFIG.SYS.

SmartDrive is the other cache. It's considerably more so-phisticated than BUFFERS. I say that because, under MS-DOS 6.2 and later it will cache CD-ROM drives. It appears as a line in your AUTOEXEC.BAT that probably looks like this:

```
C:\DOS\SMARTDRV /X 2048 1024
```

What does this mean? It means that SmartDrive has a 2MB cache (2048 bytes) under DOS, and that it will shrink to no less than 1MB (1024 bytes) under Windows. I've found that these are perfect general-purpose settings. They're also the settings recommended in the SMARTDRV help page under DOS.

The most important thing about SmartDrive is that it should appear on the first line of your AUTOEXEC.BAT. The only thing that should come before it is the command @ECHO OFF. Why? Because SmartDrive can't cache anything that loads after it. So if you load MSCDEX (the CD-ROM extensions) before SmartDrive in your AUTOEXEC.BAT, your CD-ROM drive won't be cached.

Optimize Your Memory

Now that the SmartDrive line is in your AUTOEXEC.BAT and your BUFFERS are set right, it's time to optimize your memory. There are two basic memory areas that DOS knows about as it's loading: high and low. Low memory goes from 0 to 640K, and it's the area that most DOS applications use by default. High memory goes from 640K to 1024K; the rest of the first megabyte of memory, which can go completely unused if you don't follow these instructions.

Wait, why is this important? Have you ever received the message that a program won't run because there's not enough memory? Then this is important. Beyond that, you can pick up some performance by freeing up the low memory where most applications like to run.

So run MemMaker, MS-DOS 6's automatic memory optimization utility. Just type MEMMAKER at the DOS prompt. Say that you want the Express customization. It'll also ask you if you use any programs that use Extended or Expanded memory. If you don't know, say no. MemMaker will reboot your system once to get a feel for it, then again to test the changes it's made. At the end it'll tell you how much memory you just freed up.

Create a Permanent Swapfile

If you run Windows, you should try to create a permanent swapfile. A swapfile is a place on your disk drive where Windows can dump the contents of RAM when it runs out of RAM. For example, say you're running a few applications then try to load a large document into your word processor. You'll run out of RAM to store all this stuff. So Windows swaps the contents of some memory (probably something that hasn't been used in a while) onto this giant file on the disk called the swapfile. Then it'll load your document. When you need whatever it swapped onto disk, it'll retrieve it and swap something else out onto disk.

Since disks are so much slower than memory, you can imagine that swapping slows things down a lot. It does, but the alternative is not to be able to run your applications at all. If you find yourself swapping a lot (or even if you don't), you'd do well to add RAM to your system. If you're running Windows, 16MB is probably a good amount, and it's not too very expensive (like $800).

The advantage of a permanent swapfile is that it's faster than what Windows creates by default—a temporary swapfile. Here's why. When Windows loads with a temporary swapfile, it'll pull together whatever space on the disk it can find and call that a swapfile. That swapfile might not be the optimal size for Windows, and, worse, it might be fragmented—all over the disk. That means that swapping will be even slower. When you use a permanent swapfile, however, Windows allocates one contiguous string of disk space and uses it time and time again. The disadvantage is that you lose that disk space when you're using DOS without Windows—it's taken in the form of a giant file that's always there.

Okay, enough history, here's how to do it: Go into Windows, open the Control Panel (located in the Main group), and double-click on the 386 Enhanced icon. Click once on Virtual Memory . . . , then on Change>>. Under the Type pull-down, select Permanent. Let Windows decide automatically how large to make it. Click on OK, say Yes, you do want to alter your virtual memory settings, then restart Windows.

If you run into problems, you may have to keep using a temporary swapfile. However, the main problem is that Windows can't find enough disk space to create a permanent swapfile. You can free up disk space by deleting files, then try again. Or you can change the default swapfile size (in the same place you change the Type from Temporary to Permanent) to match the space available on your disk.

Advanced Improvements

I didn't tell you everything. I told you the 95 percent solutions to everything. But there's more. By tweaking a few parameters, you can get some slightly better results. I emphasize *slightly better*. These are not results that will blow you away. They won't even work every time. But they can, and it's nice to get everything you can.

Disk Defragmenting II

When you defragmented your disk, it's as though you created organized piles. You put all the As together, all the Bs together, and so on. But they're not in order—the Ns are next to the Cs, and the Xs are way over in the other room. Let's optimize a little further and put everything into really neat piles.

From the MS-DOS prompt, type this:

```
C:\>DEFRAG C: /F /SD- /H
```

What does this do that the regular DEFRAG doesn't? The /F tells DEFRAG to leave no space between files. You're going to have a crunched disk when this is over. The /SD- tells DEFRAG to sort the files in chronological order, with the most recently accessed file first. The /H tells DEFRAG to optimize hidden files as well.

Memory Optimizing II

The first time you ran MemMaker, you took all the default actions. That's like typing MEMMAKER /BATCH. That's fine, but you may be able to do better. Type MEMMAKER. When it asks if you want an Express or Custom setup, press the space bar once to select Custom Setup. Answer the question about EMS, but if you don't know, say No.

Now you'll get a big screen asking you to specify what you want to optimize. Here are the questions with my recommended answers.

Specify which drivers and TSRs to include in optimization?

No. You don't want to be bothered trying to figure out what goes where—MemMaker will do a much better job.

Scan the upper memory area aggressively?

Yes, most definitely.

Optimize upper memory for use with Windows?

Yes or no, your choice. I've never seen a performance improvement from doing this, however.

Use monochrome region (B000–B7FF) for running programs?

Yes.

Keep current EMM386 memory exclusions and inclusions?

No, unless you've done some hand tweaking and know that what MemMaker does by default won't work.

Move extended BIOS Data Area from conventional to upper memory?

Yes.

Again, MemMaker will reboot your system twice. After that, you'll find you've gained some extra memory. Or your system won't work at all, in which case you can tell MemMaker to restore its backups.

32-bit Disk Access

In Windows, certain disk drives and controllers can get a performance boost by running in 32-bit "protected" mode (as opposed to 16-bit "real" mode). This enables Windows to reduce something called mode switching, which can bog it down. By default, Windows leaves it turned off because not all disk drives and controllers support it. You can easily find out if yours does by trying, however, and no harm will be done. Here's how.

In Windows, open the Control Panel's 386 Enhanced applet, click on Virtual Memory . . . and click on Change>>. At the bottom of the screen, you'll see a check box for 32-bit Disk Access. Click it on, click on OK, say Yes, and restart Windows. If something's wrong, Windows will give you an error message that says basically that Windows couldn't figure out how to support your disk drive and controller in 32-bit disk access mode. Windows will still start (albeit in 16-bit disk access mode), and you should go into the Control Panel and reverse the click of that check box.

32-bit File Access

If you have Windows for Workgroups 3.11, you also have something called 32-bit file access, which is a disk cache (like SmartDrive) that runs under Windows protected mode (SmartDrive is in what's called real mode). You don't need to know the technical reasons this is better, but Windows can get at it faster, and it's more stable. To enable it, follow these steps.

In Windows, open the Control Panel's 386 Enhanced applet, click on Virtual Memory . . . and click on Change>>. At the bottom of the screen, you'll see a check box for 32-bit File Access. Click it on and create a cache that's at least 1,024 bytes and at most 2,048 bytes. (These are the boundaries for getting the most performance out of your system while sacrificing the least memory.) Click on OK, say Yes, and restart Windows. You should have no problems; unlike 32-bit disk access, 32-bit file access isn't hardware-dependent.

Appendix A: Tech Support

A woman with a terribly advanced case of rheumatoid arthritis once told me this story. She had just gotten a new doctor and was in his office. He asked her to take a simple test to determine how bad her arthritis was. He asked her questions like "Do you have any problem writing?" And "Any trouble opening jars?" She said she had no problem with any of these things. The doctor looked at her clawlike hands and exclaimed, "I can't believe you have no trouble opening jars with those." She replied, "Oh. You mean do *I* have any trouble. Usually I just ask someone." There comes a time in everyone's life when they just can't do any more without a little help.

Acer America

2641 Orchard Pkwy.
San Jose, CA 95134

(800) 733-2237; (408) 432-6200
Direct sales: (800) 239-2237 (Acer Direct)
FAX: (408) 922-2965
Tech support: (800) 637-7000
Tech support BBS: (408) 428-0140

ACS Computer

398-400 Convention Way
Redwood City, CA 94063

(800) 282-5747; (415) 780-9988
FAX: (415) 780-0222
Tech support: Use toll-free number.

Actix Systems

3350 Scott Blvd., Bldg. 9
Santa Clara, CA 95054

(800) 927-5557; (408) 986-1625
FAX: (408) 986-1646
Tech support: Use main number.
Tech support BBS: (408) 970-3719

Addtech Research

41348 Christy St.
Fremont, CA 94538

(510) 623-7583
FAX: (510) 623-7538
Tech support: (510) 623-0602

Advanced Gravis

3750 N. Fraser Way, Ste. 101
Burnaby, BC, CD V5J 5E9

(800) 663-8558; (604) 431-5020
FAX: (604) 431-5155
Tech support: (604) 431-1807
Tech support BBS: (604) 431-5927

AITech International

47971 Fremont Blvd.
Fremont, CA 94538

(800) 882-8184; (510) 226-8960
FAX: (510) 226-8996
Tech support: (510) 226-8267

Alpha Systems Lab

2361 McGaw Ave.
Irvine, CA 92714

(800) 576-4ASL; (714) 622-0688
FAX: (714) 252-0887
Tech support: (714) 252-9200
Tech support BBS: (714) 252-0624

Antex Electronics

16100 S. Figueroa St.
Gardena, CA 90248

(800) 338-4231; (310) 532-3092
FAX: (310) 532-8509
Tech support: Use toll-free number.

Aztech Labs

46707 Fremont Blvd.
Fremont, CA 94538

(800) 886-8829; (510) 623-8988
FAX: (510) 623-8989
Tech support: Use main number.

Best Data Products

21800 Nordhoff St.
Chatsworth, CA 91311

(800) 632-BEST; (818) 773-9600
FAX: (818) 773-9619
Tech support: Use main number.
Tech support BBS: (818) 773-9627

Calypso Micro Products

160-A Albright Way
Los Gatos, CA 95030

(800) 822-5977; (408) 379-9494
FAX: (408) 379-8998

Cardinal Technologies

1827 Freedom Rd.
Lancaster, PA 17601

(717) 293-3000
Direct sales: (717) 293-3049
FAX: (717) 293-3055
Tech support: (717) 293-3124
Tech support BBS: (717) 293-3074

Creative Labs

1901 McCarthy Blvd.
Milpitas, CA 95035

(800) 998-1000; (408) 428-6600
Direct sales: (800) 998-5227
FAX: (408) 428-6611
Tech support: (405) 742-6622
Tech support BBS: (405) 742-6660

Criterion Computer

9425 N. MacArthur Blvd.
Irving, TX 75063

(800) 782-1818; (214) 401-2100
FAX: (214) 401-0600

Diamond Computer Systems

949 W. Spring Creek Pkwy.
Plano, TX 75023-4431

(214) 676-2998
Tech support: Use main number.

DSP Solutions

2464 Embarcadero Way
Palo Alto, CA 94303

(415) 494-8086
FAX: (415) 494-8114
Tech support: (415) 494-8088

Echo Speech

6460 Via Real
Carpinteria, CA 93013

(800) DSP-ECHO; (805) 684-4593
FAX: (805) 684-6628

Focus Information Systems

46713 Fremont Blvd.
Fremont, CA 94538

(800) 925-2378; (510) 657-2845
FAX: (510) 657-4158
Tech support: (510) 657-4586
Tech support BBS: (510) 657-9451

Genoa Systems

75 E. Trimble Rd.
San Jose, CA 95131

(800) 934-3662; (408) 432-9090
Direct sales: (408) 432-9123
FAX: (408) 434-0997
Tech support: (408) 432-8324
Tech support BBS: (408) 943-1231

IBM

3039 Cornwallis Rd., Bldg. 203
Research Triangle Park, NC 27709

(800) 426-7938
Tech support BBS: (919) 517-0001 (ValuePoint)

ImagiMedia

1991 Hartog Dr.
San Jose, CA 95131

(408) 453-9911
FAX: (408) 453-9912
Tech support: Use main number.

Jovian Logic

47929 Fremont Blvd.
Fremont, CA 94538

(510) 651-4823
FAX: (510) 651-1343
Tech support BBS: (510) 651-6989

KYE International

2605 E. Cedar St.
Ontario, CA 91761-8511

(800) 456-7593; (909) 923-3510
FAX: (909) 923-1469
Tech support: (909) 923-2417

Logitech

6505 Kaiser Dr.
Fremont, CA 94555

(800) 231-7717; (510) 795-8500
Direct sales: (800) 732-2990
FAX: (510) 792-8901
Tech support: (510) 795-8100
Tech support BBS: (510) 795-0408

Media Innovations

2109 O'Toole Ave.
San Jose, CA 95131

(408) 954-0611
FAX: (408) 954-8380

Media Vision

47300 Bayside Pkwy.
Fremont, CA 94538

(800) 348-7116; (510) 770-8600
Direct sales: (800) 845-5870
FAX: (510) 770-8648
Tech support: (800) 638-2807
Tech support BBS: (510) 770-0527

Mediatrix Peripherals

4229 Garlock
Sherbrooke, QC, CD J1L 2C8

(800) 820-8749; (819) 829-8749
FAX: (819) 829-5100

Microsoft

One Microsoft Way
Redmond, WA 98052-6399

(800) 426-9400; (206) 882-8080
Direct sales: (800) MSPRESS
FAX: (206) 883-8101
Tech support: (206) 454-2030; (206) 637-7098 (Windows)
Tech support BBS: (206) 936-6735

Midi Land

440 S. Lone Hill Ave.
San Dimas, CA 91773

(909) 592-1168
FAX: (909) 592-6159
Tech support: Use main number.

Multiwave Innovation

747 Camden Ave., Ste. D
Campbell, CA 95008

(408) 379-2900
FAX: (408) 379-3292
Tech support: (408) 379-2848
Tech support BBS: (408) 379-2927

New Media Corporation

One Technology Way, Bldg. A
Irvine, CA 92718

(800) 453-0550; (714) 453-0100
FAX: (714) 453-0114
Tech support: Use main number.
Tech support BBS: (714) 453-0214

Omni Labs

785 Market St., Ste. 1100
San Francisco, CA 94103

(415) 512-2638
Direct sales: (800) 70MEDIA
FAX: (415) 512-2636
Tech support: Use main number.

Orchid Technology

45365 Northport Loop West
Fremont, CA 94538

(800) 767-2443; (510) 683-0300
FAX: (510) 490-9312
Tech support: (510) 683-0323
Tech support BBS: (510) 683-0327

Reveal Computer Products

6045 Variel Ave.
Woodland Hills, CA 91367

(800) 669-3559; (818) 704-6300
FAX: (818) 340-3671
Tech support: Use main number.

Roland

7200 Dominion Circle
Los Angeles, CA 90040-3696

(213) 685-5141
FAX: (213) 722-0911
Tech support: Use main number.

Sigma Designs

46501 Landing Pkwy.
Fremont, CA 94538

(800) 845-8086; (510) 770-0100
FAX: (510) 770-2640
Tech support: Use main number.
Tech support BBS: (510) 770-0111

Sound Minds Technology

1600 Dell Ave., Ste. S
Campbell, CA 95008

(408) 374-7070
FAX: (408) 374-7193
Tech support: Use main number.

Toptek Technology

14140 Live Oak Ave., Unit C
Baldwin Park, CA 91706

(800) 416-8889; (818) 960-9211
FAX: (818) 960-0703
Tech support: Use toll-free number.
Tech support BBS: (818) 962-2851

Turtle Beach Systems

52 Grumbacher Rd.
York, PA 17402

(800) 645-5640; (717) 767-0200
FAX: (717) 767-6033
Tech support: (717) 764-5265
Tech support BBS: (717) 767-0250

Vision Enhancements

29 W. Thomas, Ste. F
Phoenix, AZ 85013

(602) 265-5665
FAX: (602) 265-5813
Tech support: Use main number.

Wearnes Technology

1015 E. Brokaw Rd.
San Jose, CA 95131

(408) 456-8838
FAX: (408) 456-8846

Appendix B:
Sound Card Specs

In case you haven't yet bought one of these wondrous devices, here's a list, including phone numbers and all the specifications, for all the major sound cards (and a lot of the minor ones, too) on the market. Feel free to browse. Although I've listed lots of cards here, if I were buying a card, I'd be looking for a fully 16-bit fully stereo card that supported a SCSI CD-ROM and had wave table synthesis. But that's just me.

Acer America

Model: Acer PAC Magic
Phone: (408) 432-6200
    Warranty: 1 Year
    Computer Interface: 16-bit ISA (AT) only
    IRQs Above 7 Supported: Yes
    DMA Channels Above 3 Supported: No
    Max Sample Rate—Recording in kHz: 48
    Max Sample Rate—Mono Playback in kHz: 48
    Max Sample Rate—Stereo Playback in kHz: 48
    DSP Included: No
    ADPCM Data Compression Supported: Yes
    Synthesizer Type: FM4, Optional Wave table
    Synthesizer Chip Set: OPL3
    MIDI Interface Included: Yes
    Adlib Compatible: Yes
    Sound Blaster Compatible Via: FM Chip
    Via MPU-401 Emulation: No
    Onboard Mixer: Yes
    CD-ROM Interface: Proprietary

ACS Computer

Model: Futura 16
Phone: (415) 875-6633
   Warranty: 1 Year
   Computer Interface: 16-bit ISA (AT) only
   IRQs Above 7 Supported: Yes
   DMA Channels Above 3 Supported: No
   Max Sample Rate—Recording in kHz: 48
   Max Sample Rate—Mono Playback in kHz: 48
   Max Sample Rate—Stereo Playback in kHz: 48
   DSP Included: No
   ADPCM Data Compression Supported: Yes
   Synthesizer Type: FM4, Optional Wave table
   Synthesizer Chip Set: OPL3
   MIDI Interface Included: Yes
   Adlib Compatible: Yes
   Sound Blaster Compatible Via: FM Chip
   Via MPU-401 Emulation: UART
   Onboard Mixer: Yes
   CD-ROM Interface: Proprietary or optional SCSI

Actix Systems

Model: Lark
Phone: (408) 986-1625
   Warranty: 1 Year
   Computer Interface: Any ISA
   IRQs Above 7 Supported: Yes
   DMA Channels Above 3 Supported: No
   Max Sample Rate—Recording in kHz: 44
   Max Sample Rate—Mono Playback in kHz: 44
   Max Sample Rate—Stereo Playback in kHz: 44
   DSP Included: No
   ADPCM Data Compression Supported: Yes
   Synthesizer Type: FM4
   Synthesizer Chip Set: OPL3
   MIDI Interface Included: Yes
   Adlib Compatible: Yes
   Sound Blaster Compatible Via: FM Chip
   Via MPU-401 Emulation: No
   Onboard Mixer: Yes
   CD-ROM Interface: SCSI w/ ASPI

Ad Lib Multimedia Inc.

Model: Ad Lib Gold 1000
Phone: (418) 656-8742

Warranty: 1 Year
Computer Interface: Any ISA
IRQs Above 7 Supported: Information not available
DMA Channels Above 3 Supported: Information not available
Max Sample Rate—Recording in kHz: 44
Max Sample Rate—Mono Playback in kHz: 44
Max Sample Rate—Stereo Playback in kHz: 44
DSP Included: No
ADPCM Data Compression Supported: Information not available
Synthesizer Type: FM
Synthesizer Chip Set: OPL3 YMF262
MIDI Interface Included: Yes
Adlib Compatible: Yes
Sound Blaster Compatible Via: Information not available
Via MPU-401 Emulation: Information not available
Onboard Mixer: Information not available
CD-ROM Interface: SCSI Optional

Addtech Research

Model: Sound Pro II
Phone: (510) 623-7583
Warranty: 1 Year
Computer Interface: 16-bit ISA (AT) only
IRQs Above 7 Supported: Yes
DMA Channels Above 3 Supported: Yes
Max Sample Rate—Recording in kHz: 44
Max Sample Rate—Mono Playback in kHz: 44
Max Sample Rate—Stereo Playback in kHz: 44
DSP Included: Yes
ADPCM Data Compression Supported: Yes
Synthesizer Type: Wave table
Synthesizer Chip Set: Aria, TMS320 DSP
MIDI Interface Included: Yes
Adlib Compatible: Yes
Sound Blaster Compatible Via: SW Emul
Via MPU-401 Emulation: UART
Onboard Mixer: Yes
CD-ROM Interface: None

Advanced Gravis

Model: Ultrasound
Phone: (604) 431-5020
Warranty: 3 Years
Computer Interface: Any ISA
IRQs Above 7 Supported: Yes

Advanced Gravis (continued)

DMA Channels Above 3 Supported: Yes
Max Sample Rate—Recording in kHz: 44
Max Sample Rate—Mono Playback in kHz: 44
Max Sample Rate—Stereo Playback in kHz: 44
DSP Included: No
ADPCM Data Compression Supported: No
Synthesizer Type: Wave table
Synthesizer Chip Set: GFI
MIDI Interface Included: Yes
Adlib Compatible: Yes
Sound Blaster Compatible Via: SW Emul
Via MPU-401 Emulation: UART
Onboard Mixer: Yes
CD-ROM Interface: None

Model: Ultrasound Max
Phone: (604) 431-5020
Warranty: 3 Years
Computer Interface: Any ISA
IRQs Above 7 Supported: Yes
DMA Channels Above 3 Supported: Yes
Max Sample Rate—Recording in kHz: 48
Max Sample Rate—Mono Playback in kHz: 44
Max Sample Rate—Stereo Playback in kHz: 44
DSP Included: No
ADPCM Data Compression Supported: Yes
Synthesizer Type: Wave table
Synthesizer Chip Set: GFI
MIDI Interface Included: Yes
Adlib Compatible: Yes
Sound Blaster Compatible Via: SW Emul
Via MPU-401 Emulation: UART
Onboard Mixer: Yes
CD-ROM Interface: Proprietary and SCSI

AITech International

Model: Audio Show
Phone: (510) 226-8960
Warranty: 1 Year
Computer Interface: 16-bit ISA (AT) only
IRQs Above 7 Supported: Yes
DMA Channels Above 3 Supported: Yes
Max Sample Rate—Recording in kHz: 44
Max Sample Rate—Mono Playback in kHz: 44
Max Sample Rate—Stereo Playback in kHz: 44

DSP Included: No
ADPCM Data Compression Supported: Yes
Synthesizer Type: FM4
Synthesizer Chip Set: OPL3
MIDI Interface Included: Yes
Adlib Compatible: Yes
Sound Blaster Compatible Via: FM Chip
Via MPU-401 Emulation: No
Onboard Mixer: Yes
CD-ROM Interface: SCSI w/ASPI

Model: Audio/Video Blender
Phone: (510) 226-8960
Warranty: 1 Year
Computer Interface: 16-bit ISA (AT) only
IRQs Above 7 Supported: Yes
DMA Channels Above 3 Supported: No
Max Sample Rate—Recording in kHz: 44
Max Sample Rate—Mono Playback in kHz: 44
Max Sample Rate—Stereo Playback in kHz: 44
DSP Included: No
ADPCM Data Compression Supported: No
Synthesizer Type: FM4
Synthesizer Chip Set: OPL3
MIDI Interface Included: No
Adlib Compatible: Yes
Sound Blaster Compatible Via: FM Chip
Via MPU-401 Emulation: No
Onboard Mixer: Yes
CD-ROM Interface: Information not available

Alpha Systems Lab

Model: Cyber Audio Pro
Phone: (714) 252-0117
Warranty: 2 Years
Computer Interface: 16-bit ISA (AT) only
IRQs Above 7 Supported: Yes
DMA Channels Above 3 Supported: Yes
Max Sample Rate—Recording in kHz: 44
Max Sample Rate—Mono Playback in kHz: 44
Max Sample Rate—Stereo Playback in kHz: 44
DSP Included: Yes
ADPCM Data Compression Supported: Yes
Synthesizer Type: Wave table
Synthesizer Chip Set: Aria
MIDI Interface Included: Yes
Adlib Compatible: Yes

Alpha Systems Lab (continued)

Sound Blaster Compatible Via: HW Emul
Via MPU-401 Emulation: UART
Onboard Mixer: Yes
CD-ROM Interface: SCSI w/ASPI

Antex Electronics

Model: Z1
Phone: (310) 532-3092
Warranty: 1 Year
Computer Interface: Any ISA
IRQs Above 7 Supported: Yes
DMA Channels Above 3 Supported: No
Max Sample Rate—Recording in kHz: 50
Max Sample Rate—Mono Playback in kHz: 50
Max Sample Rate—Stereo Playback in kHz: 50
DSP Included: Yes
ADPCM Data Compression Supported: Yes
Synthesizer Type: FM4, Optional Wave table
Synthesizer Chip Set: OPL3
MIDI Interface Included: Yes
Adlib Compatible: Yes
Sound Blaster Compatible Via: FM Chip
Via MPU-401 Emulation: No
Onboard Mixer: Yes
CD-ROM Interface: SCSI w/ASPI

Model: Z1e
Phone: (310) 532-3092
Warranty: 1 Year
Computer Interface: Any ISA
IRQs Above 7 Supported: Yes
DMA Channels Above 3 Supported: No
Max Sample Rate—Recording in kHz: 50
Max Sample Rate—Mono Playback in kHz: 50
Max Sample Rate—Stereo Playback in kHz: 50
DSP Included: Yes
ADPCM Data Compression Supported: Yes
Synthesizer Type: FM4, Optional Wave table
Synthesizer Chip Set: OPL3
MIDI Interface Included: Yes
Adlib Compatible: Yes
Sound Blaster Compatible Via: FM Chip
Via MPU-401 Emulation: No
Onboard Mixer: Yes
CD-ROM Interface: SCSI w/ASPI

Aztech Labs

Model: Sound Galaxy Basic 16
Phone: (510) 623-8988
    Warranty: 1 Year
    Computer Interface: 16-bit ISA (AT) only
    IRQs Above 7 Supported: Yes
    DMA Channels Above 3 Supported: Yes
    Max Sample Rate—Recording in kHz: 44
    Max Sample Rate—Mono Playback in kHz: 44
    Max Sample Rate—Stereo Playback in kHz: 44
    DSP Included: Yes
    ADPCM Data Compression Supported: Yes
    Synthesizer Type: FM4, Optional Wave table
    Synthesizer Chip Set: OPL3
    MIDI Interface Included: Yes
    Adlib Compatible: Yes
    Sound Blaster Compatible Via: FM Chip
    Via MPU-401 Emulation: No
    Onboard Mixer: Yes
    CD-ROM Interface: Proprietary or optional SCSI

Best Data Products

Model: ACE 5000
Phone: (818) 773-9600
    Warranty: 2 Years
    Computer Interface: 16-bit ISA (AT) only
    IRQs Above 7 Supported: Yes
    DMA Channels Above 3 Supported: Yes
    Max Sample Rate—Recording in kHz: 44
    Max Sample Rate—Mono Playback in kHz: 44
    Max Sample Rate—Stereo Playback in kHz: 44
    DSP Included: Yes
    ADPCM Data Compression Supported: Yes
    Synthesizer Type: FM4, Optional Wave table
    Synthesizer Chip Set: Mwave DSP Crystal Codec
    MIDI Interface Included: No
    Adlib Compatible: Yes
    Sound Blaster Compatible Via: SW Emul
    Via MPU-401 Emulation: No
    Onboard Mixer: No
    CD-ROM Interface: Information not available

Model: ACE 5000
Phone: (818) 773-9600
    Warranty: 2 Years
    Computer Interface: 16-bit ISA (AT) only

Best Data Products (continued)

IRQs Above 7 Supported: No
DMA Channels Above 3 Supported: No
Max Sample Rate—Recording in kHz: 44
Max Sample Rate—Mono Playback in kHz: 44
Max Sample Rate—Stereo Playback in kHz: 44
DSP Included: Yes
ADPCM Data Compression Supported: No
Synthesizer Type: Optional Wave table
Synthesizer Chip Set: Ensoniq
MIDI Interface Included: Yes
Adlib Compatible: Yes
Sound Blaster Compatible Via: HW Emul
Via MPU-401 Emulation: UART
Onboard Mixer: Yes
CD-ROM Interface: Proprietary

Calypso Micro Products

Model: Audio Magician
Phone: (408) 379-9494
Warranty: 1 Year
Computer Interface: Any ISA
IRQs Above 7 Supported: No
DMA Channels Above 3 Supported: No
Max Sample Rate—Recording in kHz: 22
Max Sample Rate—Mono Playback in kHz: 22
Max Sample Rate—Stereo Playback in kHz: 22
DSP Included: No
ADPCM Data Compression Supported: Yes
Synthesizer Type: FM2
Synthesizer Chip Set: OPL2
MIDI Interface Included: Yes
Adlib Compatible: Yes
Sound Blaster Compatible Via: FM Chip
Via MPU-401 Emulation: No
Onboard Mixer: Yes
CD-ROM Interface: SCSI

Model: Audio Magician 3D
Phone: (408) 379-9494
Warranty: 1 Year
Computer Interface: 16-bit ISA (AT) only
IRQs Above 7 Supported: Yes
DMA Channels Above 3 Supported: Yes
Max Sample Rate—Recording in kHz: 44
Max Sample Rate—Mono Playback in kHz: 44

Max Sample Rate—Stereo Playback in kHz: 44
DSP Included: No
ADPCM Data Compression Supported: Yes
Synthesizer Type: FM4
Synthesizer Chip Set: OPL3
MIDI Interface Included: Yes
Adlib Compatible: Yes
Sound Blaster Compatible Via: FM Chip
Via MPU-401 Emulation: No
Onboard Mixer: No
CD-ROM Interface: Information not available

Cardinal Technologies

Model: Digital Sound Pro 16
Phone: (717) 293-3000
Warranty: 3 Years
Computer Interface: 16-bit ISA (AT) only
IRQs Above 7 Supported: Yes
DMA Channels Above 3 Supported: Yes
Max Sample Rate—Recording in kHz: 48
Max Sample Rate—Mono Playback in kHz: 48
Max Sample Rate—Stereo Playback in kHz: 48
DSP Included: Yes
ADPCM Data Compression Supported: Yes
Synthesizer Type: FM4, Optional Wave table
Synthesizer Chip Set: Echo ESC624, Analog Dev. DSP
MIDI Interface Included: Yes
Adlib Compatible: Yes
Sound Blaster Compatible Via: HW Emul
Via MPU-401 Emulation: UART and Smart
Onboard Mixer: Yes
CD-ROM Interface: Proprietary

Model: Digital Sound Pro 16 Plus
Phone: (717) 293-3000
Warranty: 3 Years
Computer Interface: 16-bit ISA (AT) only
IRQs Above 7 Supported: Yes
DMA Channels Above 3 Supported: Yes
Max Sample Rate—Recording in kHz: 48
Max Sample Rate—Mono Playback in kHz: 48
Max Sample Rate—Stereo Playback in kHz: 48
DSP Included: Yes
ADPCM Data Compression Supported: Yes
Synthesizer Type: FM4, Optional Wave table
Synthesizer Chip Set: Echo ESC624, Analog Dev. DSP
MIDI Interface Included: Yes

Cardinal Technologies (continued)

Adlib Compatible: Yes
Sound Blaster Compatible Via: HW Emul
Via MPU-401 Emulation: UART and Smart
Onboard Mixer: Yes
CD-ROM Interface: SCSI w/ ASPI

Creative Labs

Model: Sound Blaster 16 Basic Edition
Phone: (408) 428-6600

Warranty: 1 Year
Computer Interface: Any ISA
IRQs Above 7 Supported: Yes
DMA Channels Above 3 Supported: Yes
Max Sample Rate—Recording in kHz: 44
Max Sample Rate—Mono Playback in kHz: 44
Max Sample Rate—Stereo Playback in kHz: 44
DSP Included: No
ADPCM Data Compression Supported: Yes
Synthesizer Type: FM4, Optional Wave Blaster
Synthesizer Chip Set: OPL3
MIDI Interface Included: Yes
Adlib Compatible: Yes
Sound Blaster Compatible Via: FM Chip
Via MPU-401 Emulation: No
Onboard Mixer: Yes
CD-ROM Interface: Proprietary

Model: Sound Blaster 16 MultiCD
Phone: (408) 428-6600

Warranty: 1 Year
Computer Interface: Any ISA
IRQs Above 7 Supported: Yes
DMA Channels Above 3 Supported: Yes
Max Sample Rate—Recording in kHz: 44
Max Sample Rate—Mono Playback in kHz: 44
Max Sample Rate—Stereo Playback in kHz: 44
DSP Included: Optional
ADPCM Data Compression Supported: Yes
Synthesizer Type: FM4, Optional Wave Blaster
Synthesizer Chip Set: OPL3
MIDI Interface Included: Yes
Adlib Compatible: Yes
Sound Blaster Compatible Via: FM Chip
Via MPU-401 Emulation: No
Onboard Mixer: Yes
CD-ROM Interface: Proprietary

Model: Sound Blaster 16 SCSI-2
Phone: (408) 428-6600
    Warranty: 1 Year
    Computer Interface: Any ISA
    IRQs Above 7 Supported: Yes
    DMA Channels Above 3 Supported: Yes
    Max Sample Rate—Recording in kHz: 44
    Max Sample Rate—Mono Playback in kHz: 44
    Max Sample Rate—Stereo Playback in kHz: 44
    DSP Included: Optional
    ADPCM Data Compression Supported: Yes
    Synthesizer Type: FM4, Optional Wave Blaster
    Synthesizer Chip Set: OPL3
    MIDI Interface Included: Yes
    Adlib Compatible: Yes
    Sound Blaster Compatible Via: FM Chip
    Via MPU-401 Emulation: No
    Onboard Mixer: Yes
    CD-ROM Interface: SCSI

Criterion Computer

Model: Sound Genie
Phone: (510) 657-3898
    Warranty: Life
    Computer Interface: 16-bit ISA (AT) only
    IRQs Above 7 Supported: Yes
    DMA Channels Above 3 Supported: Yes
    Max Sample Rate—Recording in kHz: 44
    Max Sample Rate—Mono Playback in kHz: 44
    Max Sample Rate—Stereo Playback in kHz: 44
    DSP Included: Yes
    ADPCM Data Compression Supported: Yes
    Synthesizer Type: Wave table
    Synthesizer Chip Set: Aria
    MIDI Interface Included: Yes
    Adlib Compatible: Yes
    Sound Blaster Compatible Via: SW Emul
    Via MPU-401 Emulation: UART and Smart
    Onboard Mixer: Yes
    CD-ROM Interface: Proprietary

Model: Sound Genie Pro
Phone: (510) 657-3898
    Warranty: Life
    Computer Interface: 16-bit ISA (AT) only
    IRQs Above 7 Supported: Yes
    DMA Channels Above 3 Supported: Yes

Criterion Computer (continued)

Max Sample Rate—Recording in kHz: 44
Max Sample Rate—Mono Playback in kHz: 44
Max Sample Rate—Stereo Playback in kHz: 44
DSP Included: No
ADPCM Data Compression Supported: No
Synthesizer Type: Wave table
Synthesizer Chip Set: Ensoniq
MIDI Interface Included: Yes
Adlib Compatible: Yes
Sound Blaster Compatible Via: SW Emul
Via MPU-401 Emulation: UART and Smart
Onboard Mixer: Yes
CD-ROM Interface: Proprietary

Diamond Computer Systems

Model: SonicSound
Phone: (408) 736-2000
Warranty: 2 Years
Computer Interface: 16-bit ISA (AT) only
IRQs Above 7 Supported: Yes
DMA Channels Above 3 Supported: No
Max Sample Rate—Recording in kHz: 44
Max Sample Rate—Mono Playback in kHz: 44
Max Sample Rate—Stereo Playback in kHz: 44
DSP Included: No
ADPCM Data Compression Supported: No
Synthesizer Type: FM4, Optional Wave table
Synthesizer Chip Set: OPL3
MIDI Interface Included: Yes
Adlib Compatible: Yes
Sound Blaster Compatible Via: FM Chip
Via MPU-401 Emulation: No
Onboard Mixer: Yes
CD-ROM Interface: Proprietary

Model: SonicSound
Phone: (408) 736-2000
Warranty: 2 Years
Computer Interface: 16-bit ISA (AT) only
IRQs Above 7 Supported: Yes
DMA Channels Above 3 Supported: Yes
Max Sample Rate—Recording in kHz: 44
Max Sample Rate—Mono Playback in kHz: 44
Max Sample Rate—Stereo Playback in kHz: 44
DSP Included: Yes
ADPCM Data Compression Supported: Yes

Synthesizer Type: Wave table
Synthesizer Chip Set: Aria
MIDI Interface Included: Yes
Adlib Compatible: Yes
Sound Blaster Compatible Via: HW Emul
Via MPU-401 Emulation: UART
Onboard Mixer: Yes
CD-ROM Interface: SCSI

DSP Solutions

Model: Port-Able Sound Plus
Phone: (415) 494-8086
   Warranty: 90 days
   Computer Interface: Parallel Port
   IRQs Above 7 Supported: N/A
   DMA Channels Above 3 Supported: N/A
   Max Sample Rate—Recording in kHz: 44
   Max Sample Rate—Mono Playback in kHz: 44
   Max Sample Rate—Stereo Playback in kHz: 44
   DSP Included: Yes
   ADPCM Data Compression Supported: Yes
   Synthesizer Type: FM (in software)
   Synthesizer Chip Set: TI TMS320
   MIDI Interface Included: No
   Adlib Compatible: Yes
   Sound Blaster Compatible Via: SW Emul
   Via MPU-401 Emulation: No
   Onboard Mixer: Yes
   CD-ROM Interface: Information not available

Echo Speech

Model: Echo DSP
Phone: (805) 684-4593
   Warranty: 5 Years
   Computer Interface: 16-bit ISA (AT) only
   IRQs Above 7 Supported: Yes
   DMA Channels Above 3 Supported: Yes
   Max Sample Rate—Recording in kHz: 48
   Max Sample Rate—Mono Playback in kHz: 48
   Max Sample Rate—Stereo Playback in kHz: 48
   DSP Included: Yes
   ADPCM Data Compression Supported: Yes
   Synthesizer Type: FM4, Optional Wave table
   Synthesizer Chip Set: Echo ESC624, Analog Dev. DSP
   MIDI Interface Included: Yes
   Adlib Compatible: Yes

Echo Speech (continued)

Sound Blaster Compatible Via: HW Emul
Via MPU-401 Emulation: UART and Smart
Onboard Mixer: Yes
CD-ROM Interface: Proprietary

Focus Information Systems

Model: 2-the-Max Music Maker
Phone: (510) 657-2845
Warranty: 2 Years
Computer Interface: 16-bit ISA (AT) only
IRQs Above 7 Supported: Yes
DMA Channels Above 3 Supported: Yes
Max Sample Rate—Recording in kHz: 48
Max Sample Rate—Mono Playback in kHz: 48
Max Sample Rate—Stereo Playback in kHz: 48
DSP Included: No
ADPCM Data Compression Supported: No
Synthesizer Type: FM4
Synthesizer Chip Set: OPL3
MIDI Interface Included: Yes
Adlib Compatible: Yes
Sound Blaster Compatible Via: FM Chip
Via MPU-401 Emulation: No
Onboard Mixer: Yes
CD-ROM Interface: Proprietary

Model: 2-the-Max Music Maker Pro
Phone: (510) 657-2845
Warranty: 2 Years
Computer Interface: 16-bit ISA (AT) only
IRQs Above 7 Supported: Yes
DMA Channels Above 3 Supported: No
Max Sample Rate—Recording in kHz: 48
Max Sample Rate—Mono Playback in kHz: 48
Max Sample Rate—Stereo Playback in kHz: 48
DSP Included: Yes
ADPCM Data Compression Supported: No
Synthesizer Type: FM4, Optional Wave table
Synthesizer Chip Set: Euphonics
MIDI Interface Included: Optional
Adlib Compatible: Yes
Sound Blaster Compatible Via: FM Chip
Via MPU-401 Emulation: No
Onboard Mixer: Yes
CD-ROM Interface: Proprietary or optional SCSI

Genoa Systems

Model: Audioblitz Stereo 16+ Mo. A3300
Phone: (408) 432-9090
   Warranty: 2 Years
   Computer Interface: 16-bit ISA (AT) only
   IRQs Above 7 Supported: Yes
   DMA Channels Above 3 Supported: Yes
   Max Sample Rate—Recording in kHz: 44
   Max Sample Rate—Mono Playback in kHz: 44
   Max Sample Rate—Stereo Playback in kHz: 44
   DSP Included: No
   ADPCM Data Compression Supported: Yes
   Synthesizer Type: FM4, Optional Wave table
   Synthesizer Chip Set: OPL3
   MIDI Interface Included: Yes
   Adlib Compatible: Yes
   Sound Blaster Compatible Via: FM Chip
   Via MPU-401 Emulation: No
   Onboard Mixer: Yes
   CD-ROM Interface: Proprietary

Model: Audioblitz Stereo 16+ Mo. A3400
Phone: (408) 432-9090
   Warranty: 2 Years
   Computer Interface: 16-bit ISA (AT) only
   IRQs Above 7 Supported: Yes
   DMA Channels Above 3 Supported: Yes
   Max Sample Rate—Recording in kHz: 44
   Max Sample Rate—Mono Playback in kHz: 44
   Max Sample Rate—Stereo Playback in kHz: 44
   DSP Included: Yes
   ADPCM Data Compression Supported: Yes
   Synthesizer Type: FM4, Optional Wave table
   Synthesizer Chip Set: OPL4
   MIDI Interface Included: Yes
   Adlib Compatible: Yes
   Sound Blaster Compatible Via: FM Chip
   Via MPU-401 Emulation: No
   Onboard Mixer: Yes
   CD-ROM Interface: Proprietary

IBM

Model: M-Audio
Phone: (800) 887-7771
   Warranty: N/A
   Computer Interface: Any ISA

IBM (continued)

IRQs Above 7 Supported: No
DMA Channels Above 3 Supported: No
Max Sample Rate—Recording in kHz: 88
Max Sample Rate—Mono Playback in kHz: 88
Max Sample Rate—Stereo Playback in kHz: 44
DSP Included: Yes
ADPCM Data Compression Supported: Yes
Synthesizer Type: FM (in software)
Synthesizer Chip Set: TI TMS320
MIDI Interface Included: No
Adlib Compatible: No
Sound Blaster Compatible Via: Information not available
Via MPU-401 Emulation: Information not available
Onboard Mixer: Information not available
CD-ROM Interface: Information not available

ImagiMedia

Model: Audio Image 16
Phone: (408) 453-9911
Warranty: 1 Year
Computer Interface: 16-bit ISA (AT) only
IRQs Above 7 Supported: Yes
DMA Channels Above 3 Supported: No
Max Sample Rate—Recording in kHz: 44
Max Sample Rate—Mono Playback in kHz: 44
Max Sample Rate—Stereo Playback in kHz: 44
DSP Included: No
ADPCM Data Compression Supported: No
Synthesizer Type: FM2, Wave table
Synthesizer Chip Set: BREVE
MIDI Interface Included: Yes
Adlib Compatible: Yes
Sound Blaster Compatible Via: FM Chip
Via MPU-401 Emulation: UART
Onboard Mixer: Yes
CD-ROM Interface: SCSI

Jovian Logic

Model: Sonia
Phone: (510) 651-4823
Warranty: 1 Year
Computer Interface: 16-bit ISA (AT) only
IRQs Above 7 Supported: Yes
DMA Channels Above 3 Supported: No

Max Sample Rate—Recording in kHz: 48
Max Sample Rate—Mono Playback in kHz: 48
Max Sample Rate—Stereo Playback in kHz: 48
DSP Included: Yes
ADPCM Data Compression Supported: Yes
Synthesizer Type: FM4
Synthesizer Chip Set: OPL3
MIDI Interface Included: Yes
Adlib Compatible: Yes
Sound Blaster Compatible Via: FM Chip
Via MPU-401 Emulation: No
Onboard Mixer: Yes
CD-ROM Interface: Information not available

KYE International

Model: SoundMaker 16
Phone: (909) 923-3510
Warranty: N/A
Computer Interface: 16-bit ISA (AT) only
IRQs Above 7 Supported: Yes
DMA Channels Above 3 Supported: Yes
Max Sample Rate—Recording in kHz: 44
Max Sample Rate—Mono Playback in kHz: 44
Max Sample Rate—Stereo Playback in kHz: 44
DSP Included: No
ADPCM Data Compression Supported: No
Synthesizer Type: FM4
Synthesizer Chip Set: OPL3
MIDI Interface Included: Yes
Adlib Compatible: Yes
Sound Blaster Compatible Via: FM Chip
Via MPU-401 Emulation: UART
Onboard Mixer: Yes
CD-ROM Interface: Proprietary

Logitech

Model: SoundMan 16
Phone: (510) 795-8500
Warranty: 3 Years
Computer Interface: Any ISA
IRQs Above 7 Supported: Yes
DMA Channels Above 3 Supported: Yes
Max Sample Rate—Recording in kHz: 44
Max Sample Rate—Mono Playback in kHz: 44
Max Sample Rate—Stereo Playback in kHz: 44

Logitech (continued)

DSP Included: No
ADPCM Data Compression Supported: No
Synthesizer Type: FM4
Synthesizer Chip Set: OPL3
MIDI Interface Included: Yes
Adlib Compatible: Yes
Sound Blaster Compatible Via: FM Chip
Via MPU-401 Emulation: UART
Onboard Mixer: Yes
CD-ROM Interface: Information not available

Model: SoundMan Wave
Phone: (510) 795-8500
Warranty: 3 Years
Computer Interface: Any ISA
IRQs Above 7 Supported: No
DMA Channels Above 3 Supported: Yes
Max Sample Rate—Recording in kHz: 44
Max Sample Rate—Mono Playback in kHz: 44
Max Sample Rate—Stereo Playback in kHz: 44
DSP Included: Optional
ADPCM Data Compression Supported: Yes
Synthesizer Type: FM4, Optional Wave table
Synthesizer Chip Set: OPL4
MIDI Interface Included: Yes
Adlib Compatible: Yes
Sound Blaster Compatible Via: FM Chip
Via MPU-401 Emulation: UART
Onboard Mixer: Yes
CD-ROM Interface: SCSI

Media Innovations

Model: Powermedia
Phone: (408) 954-0611
Warranty: 1 Year
Computer Interface: 16-bit ISA (AT) only
IRQs Above 7 Supported: No
DMA Channels Above 3 Supported: No
Max Sample Rate—Recording in kHz: 44
Max Sample Rate—Mono Playback in kHz: 44
Max Sample Rate—Stereo Playback in kHz: 44
DSP Included: Yes
ADPCM Data Compression Supported: Yes
Synthesizer Type: FM4
Synthesizer Chip Set: OPL3

MIDI Interface Included: Yes
Adlib Compatible: Yes
Sound Blaster Compatible Via: FM Chip
Via MPU-401 Emulation: UART
Onboard Mixer: Yes
CD-ROM Interface: Information not available

Media Magic

Model: DSP 16
Phone: (512) 339-3500
Warranty: 1 Year
Computer Interface: 16-bit ISA (AT) only
IRQs Above 7 Supported: Yes
DMA Channels Above 3 Supported: No
Max Sample Rate—Recording in kHz: 48
Max Sample Rate—Mono Playback in kHz: 48
Max Sample Rate—Stereo Playback in kHz: 48
DSP Included: Yes
ADPCM Data Compression Supported: No
Synthesizer Type: FM (in software)
Synthesizer Chip Set: OPL2
MIDI Interface Included: Yes
Adlib Compatible: Yes
Sound Blaster Compatible Via: FM Chip
Via MPU-401 Emulation: UART
Onboard Mixer: Yes
CD-ROM Interface: Proprietary or optional SCSI

Model: DSP 16 Plus
Phone: (512) 339-3500
Warranty: 1 Year
Computer Interface: 16-bit ISA (AT) only
IRQs Above 7 Supported: Yes
DMA Channels Above 3 Supported: No
Max Sample Rate—Recording in kHz: 48
Max Sample Rate—Mono Playback in kHz: 48
Max Sample Rate—Stereo Playback in kHz: 48
DSP Included: Yes
ADPCM Data Compression Supported: No
Synthesizer Type: Wave table
Synthesizer Chip Set: Pro Sound
MIDI Interface Included: Yes
Adlib Compatible: Yes
Sound Blaster Compatible Via: SW Emul
Via MPU-401 Emulation: UART
Onboard Mixer: Yes
CD-ROM Interface: Proprietary w/ASPI

Media Magic (continued)

Model: ISP 16
Phone: (512) 339-3500
    Warranty: 1 Year
    Computer Interface: 16-bit ISA (AT) only
    IRQs Above 7 Supported: Yes
    DMA Channels Above 3 Supported: No
    Max Sample Rate—Recording in kHz: 48
    Max Sample Rate—Mono Playback in kHz: 48
    Max Sample Rate—Stereo Playback in kHz: 48
    DSP Included: Yes
    ADPCM Data Compression Supported: No
    Synthesizer Type: FM (in software)
    Synthesizer Chip Set: OPL2
    MIDI Interface Included: Yes
    Adlib Compatible: Yes
    Sound Blaster Compatible Via: FM Chip
    Via MPU-401 Emulation: Information not available
    Onboard Mixer: Yes
    CD-ROM Interface: Proprietary

Media Vision

Model: Pro Audio 16 Basic
Phone: (510) 770-8600
    Warranty: 3 Years
    Computer Interface: 16-bit ISA (AT) only
    IRQs Above 7 Supported: Yes
    DMA Channels Above 3 Supported: Yes
    Max Sample Rate—Recording in kHz: 44
    Max Sample Rate—Mono Playback in kHz: 44
    Max Sample Rate—Stereo Playback in kHz: 44
    DSP Included: No
    ADPCM Data Compression Supported: Yes
    Synthesizer Type: FM4
    Synthesizer Chip Set: OPL3
    MIDI Interface Included: Optional
    Adlib Compatible: Yes
    Sound Blaster Compatible Via: HW Emul
    Via MPU-401 Emulation: UART
    Onboard Mixer: Yes
    CD-ROM Interface: Information not available

Model: Pro Audio Spectrum 16
Phone: (510) 770-8600
    Warranty: 3 Years
    Computer Interface: 16-bit ISA (AT) only

IRQs Above 7 Supported: Yes
DMA Channels Above 3 Supported: Yes
Max Sample Rate—Recording in kHz: 44
Max Sample Rate—Mono Playback in kHz: 44
Max Sample Rate—Stereo Playback in kHz: 44
DSP Included: No
ADPCM Data Compression Supported: Yes
Synthesizer Type: FM4
Synthesizer Chip Set: OPL3
MIDI Interface Included: Optional
Adlib Compatible: Yes
Sound Blaster Compatible Via: HW Emul
Via MPU-401 Emulation: UART
Onboard Mixer: Yes
CD-ROM Interface: SCSI w/ASPI

Model: Pro Audio Studio 16
Phone: (510) 770-8600
Warranty: 3 Years
Computer Interface: 16-bit ISA (AT) only
IRQs Above 7 Supported: Yes
DMA Channels Above 3 Supported: Yes
Max Sample Rate—Recording in kHz: 44
Max Sample Rate—Mono Playback in kHz: 44
Max Sample Rate—Stereo Playback in kHz: 44
DSP Included: No
ADPCM Data Compression Supported: Yes
Synthesizer Type: FM4
Synthesizer Chip Set: OPL3
MIDI Interface Included: Optional
Adlib Compatible: Yes
Sound Blaster Compatible Via: HW Emul
Via MPU-401 Emulation: UART
Onboard Mixer: Yes
CD-ROM Interface: SCSI

Mediatrix Peripherals

Model: Audiotrix Pro
Phone: (819) 563-6722
Warranty: 1 Year
Computer Interface: Any ISA
IRQs Above 7 Supported: Yes
DMA Channels Above 3 Supported: Yes
Max Sample Rate—Recording in kHz: 44
Max Sample Rate—Mono Playback in kHz: 44
Max Sample Rate—Stereo Playback in kHz: 44

Mediatrix Peripherals (continued)

DSP Included: No
ADPCM Data Compression Supported: Yes
Synthesizer Type: FM4, Wave table
Synthesizer Chip Set: OPL4
MIDI Interface Included: Yes
Adlib Compatible: Yes
Sound Blaster Compatible Via: FM Chip
Via MPU-401 Emulation: UART
Onboard Mixer: Yes
CD-ROM Interface: Optional w/ASPI

Microsoft

Model: Windows Sound System
Phone: (206) 882-8086
Warranty: Life
Computer Interface: Any ISA
IRQs Above 7 Supported: No
DMA Channels Above 3 Supported: No
Max Sample Rate—Recording in kHz: 44
Max Sample Rate—Mono Playback in kHz: 44
Max Sample Rate—Stereo Playback in kHz: 44
DSP Included: No
ADPCM Data Compression Supported: Yes
Synthesizer Type: FM4
Synthesizer Chip Set: OPL3
MIDI Interface Included: Yes
Adlib Compatible: Yes
Sound Blaster Compatible Via: FM Chip
Via MPU-401 Emulation: No
Onboard Mixer: Yes
CD-ROM Interface: Information not available

Midi Land

Model: Concurrent Sound Card
Phone: (909) 595-0708
Warranty: 1 Year
Computer Interface: 16-bit ISA (AT) only
IRQs Above 7 Supported: Yes
DMA Channels Above 3 Supported: No
Max Sample Rate—Recording in kHz: 44
Max Sample Rate—Mono Playback in kHz: 44
Max Sample Rate—Stereo Playback in kHz: 44
DSP Included: Yes
ADPCM Data Compression Supported: Yes
Synthesizer Type: FM4, Wave table
Synthesizer Chip Set: OPL3 Proprietary

MIDI Interface Included: Yes
Adlib Compatible: Yes
Sound Blaster Compatible Via: FM Chip
Via MPU-401 Emulation: UART
Onboard Mixer: Yes
CD-ROM Interface: Proprietary

Model: MidiWin
Phone: (909) 595-0708
   Warranty: 1 Year
   Computer Interface: 16-bit ISA (AT) only
   IRQs Above 7 Supported: Yes
   DMA Channels Above 3 Supported: No
   Max Sample Rate—Recording in kHz: 44
   Max Sample Rate—Mono Playback in kHz: 44
   Max Sample Rate—Stereo Playback in kHz: 44
   DSP Included: Yes
   ADPCM Data Compression Supported: Yes
   Synthesizer Type: FM4, Wave table
   Synthesizer Chip Set: OPL3
   MIDI Interface Included: Optional
   Adlib Compatible: Yes
   Sound Blaster Compatible Via: FM Chip
   Via MPU-401 Emulation: UART
   Onboard Mixer: Yes
   CD-ROM Interface: Proprietary

Multiwave Innovation

Model: Audiowave Platinum 16
Phone: (408) 379-2900
   Warranty: 1 Year
   Computer Interface: 16-bit ISA (AT) only
   IRQs Above 7 Supported: Yes
   DMA Channels Above 3 Supported: No
   Max Sample Rate—Recording in kHz: 48
   Max Sample Rate—Mono Playback in kHz: 48
   Max Sample Rate—Stereo Playback in kHz: 48
   DSP Included: No
   ADPCM Data Compression Supported: Yes
   Synthesizer Type: FM4, Wave table
   Synthesizer Chip Set: OPL3
   MIDI Interface Included: Yes
   Adlib Compatible: Yes
   Sound Blaster Compatible Via: FM Chip
   Via MPU-401 Emulation: UART
   Onboard Mixer: Yes
   CD-ROM Interface: Proprietary or Optional SCSI

New Media Corporation

Model: .Wavjammer
Phone: (714) 453-0100
    Warranty: Life
    Computer Interface: PCMCIA
    IRQs Above 7 Supported: Yes
    DMA Channels Above 3 Supported: N/A
    Max Sample Rate—Recording in kHz: 44
    Max Sample Rate—Mono Playback in kHz: 44
    Max Sample Rate—Stereo Playback in kHz: 44
    DSP Included: No
    ADPCM Data Compression Supported: No
    Synthesizer Type: FM4
    Synthesizer Chip Set: OPL3
    MIDI Interface Included: No
    Adlib Compatible: Yes
    Sound Blaster Compatible Via: FM Chip
    Via MPU-401 Emulation: No
    Onboard Mixer: Yes
    CD-ROM Interface: Information not available

Omni Labs

Model: Audio Master
Phone: (415) 788-1345
    Warranty: 1 Year
    Computer Interface: 16-bit ISA (AT) only
    IRQs Above 7 Supported: Yes
    DMA Channels Above 3 Supported: No
    Max Sample Rate—Recording in kHz: 44
    Max Sample Rate—Mono Playback in kHz: 44
    Max Sample Rate—Stereo Playback in kHz: 44
    DSP Included: Yes
    ADPCM Data Compression Supported: No
    Synthesizer Type: Wave table
    Synthesizer Chip Set: Ensoniq
    MIDI Interface Included: Yes
    Adlib Compatible: Optional
    Sound Blaster Compatible Via: Optional FM Chip
    Via MPU-401 Emulation: Information not available
    Onboard Mixer: Optional
    CD-ROM Interface: Optional SCSI with ASPI

Orchid Technology

Model: GameWave 32
Phone: (510) 683-0300

Warranty: 4 Years
Computer Interface: Any ISA
IRQs Above 7 Supported: Yes
DMA Channels Above 3 Supported: No
Max Sample Rate—Recording in kHz: N/A
Max Sample Rate—Mono Playback in kHz: 44
Max Sample Rate—Stereo Playback in kHz: 44
DSP Included: Yes
ADPCM Data Compression Supported: Yes
Synthesizer Type: FM4, Wave table
Synthesizer Chip Set: Analog Dec. DSP
MIDI Interface Included: Yes
Adlib Compatible: Yes
Sound Blaster Compatible Via: SW Emul
Via MPU-401 Emulation: UART
Onboard Mixer: No
CD-ROM Interface: Proprietary

Model: SoundWave 32
Phone: (510) 683-0300
Warranty: 4 Years
Computer Interface: Any ISA
IRQs Above 7 Supported: Yes
DMA Channels Above 3 Supported: Yes
Max Sample Rate—Recording in kHz: 48
Max Sample Rate—Mono Playback in kHz: 44
Max Sample Rate—Stereo Playback in kHz: 44
DSP Included: Yes
ADPCM Data Compression Supported: Yes
Synthesizer Type: FM4, Wave table
Synthesizer Chip Set: Analog Dec. DSP
MIDI Interface Included: Yes
Adlib Compatible: Yes
Sound Blaster Compatible Via: SW Emul
Via MPU-401 Emulation: UART
Onboard Mixer: Yes
CD-ROM Interface: Proprietary

Reveal Computer Products

Model: SC600
Phone: (800) 236-2222
Warranty: 1 Year
Computer Interface: 16-bit ISA (AT) only
IRQs Above 7 Supported: Yes
DMA Channels Above 3 Supported: Yes
Max Sample Rate—Recording in kHz: 44

Reveal Computer Products (continued)

Max Sample Rate—Mono Playback in kHz: 44
Max Sample Rate—Stereo Playback in kHz: 44
DSP Included: No
ADPCM Data Compression Supported: Yes
Synthesizer Type: Wave table
Synthesizer Chip Set: Ensoniq
MIDI Interface Included: Yes
Adlib Compatible: Yes
Sound Blaster Compatible Via: SW Emul
Via MPU-401 Emulation: UART and Smart
Onboard Mixer: Yes
CD-ROM Interface: Proprietary

Roland

Model: RAP-10/A+
Phone: (213) 685-5141
Warranty: 1 Year
Computer Interface: 16-bit ISA (AT) only
IRQs Above 7 Supported: Yes
DMA Channels Above 3 Supported: Yes
Max Sample Rate—Recording in kHz: 44
Max Sample Rate—Mono Playback in kHz: 44
Max Sample Rate—Stereo Playback in kHz: 44
DSP Included: Yes
ADPCM Data Compression Supported: No
Synthesizer Type: Wave table
Synthesizer Chip Set: Roland Sound Canvas
MIDI Interface Included: Optional
Adlib Compatible: No
Sound Blaster Compatible Via: SW Emul
Via MPU-401 Emulation: UART
Onboard Mixer: Yes
CD-ROM Interface: Information not available

Sigma Designs

Model: WinSound 16
Phone: (510) 770-0100
Warranty: 5 Years
Computer Interface: 16-bit ISA (AT) only
IRQs Above 7 Supported: Yes
DMA Channels Above 3 Supported: Yes
Max Sample Rate—Recording in kHz: 44
Max Sample Rate—Mono Playback in kHz: 44
Max Sample Rate—Stereo Playback in kHz: 44
DSP Included: No

ADPCM Data Compression Supported: No
Synthesizer Type: FM4
Synthesizer Chip Set: OPL3
MIDI Interface Included: Yes
Adlib Compatible: Yes
Sound Blaster Compatible Via: SW Emul
Via MPU-401 Emulation: UART
Onboard Mixer: Yes
CD-ROM Interface: SCSI

Sound Minds Technology

Model: ITL1600
Phone: (408) 374-7070
Warranty: 1 Year
Computer Interface: 16-bit ISA (AT) only
IRQs Above 7 Supported: Yes
DMA Channels Above 3 Supported: Yes
Max Sample Rate—Recording in kHz: 48
Max Sample Rate—Mono Playback in kHz: 48
Max Sample Rate—Stereo Playback in kHz: 48
DSP Included: No
ADPCM Data Compression Supported: No
Synthesizer Type: FM4
Synthesizer Chip Set: OPL3
MIDI Interface Included: Yes
Adlib Compatible: Yes
Sound Blaster Compatible Via: FM Chip
Via MPU-401 Emulation: UART
Onboard Mixer: Yes
CD-ROM Interface: Proprietary

Toptek Technology

Model: Golden Sound Pro 16
Phone: (818) 960-9211
Warranty: 1 Year
Computer Interface: 16-bit ISA (AT) only
IRQs Above 7 Supported: Yes
DMA Channels Above 3 Supported: Yes
Max Sample Rate—Recording in kHz: 48
Max Sample Rate—Mono Playback in kHz: 48
Max Sample Rate—Stereo Playback in kHz: 48
DSP Included: Yes
ADPCM Data Compression Supported: Yes
Synthesizer Type: FM4, Wave table
Synthesizer Chip Set: OPL3

Toptek Technology (continued)

    MIDI Interface Included: Yes
    Adlib Compatible: Yes
    Sound Blaster Compatible Via: FM Chip
    Via MPU-401 Emulation: UART
    Onboard Mixer: Yes
    CD-ROM Interface: Proprietary

Model: Golden Sound Pro 16 Plus
Phone: (818) 960-9211
    Warranty: 1 Year
    Computer Interface: 16-bit ISA (AT) only
    IRQs Above 7 Supported: Yes
    DMA Channels Above 3 Supported: Yes
    Max Sample Rate—Recording in kHz: 48
    Max Sample Rate—Mono Playback in kHz: 48
    Max Sample Rate—Stereo Playback in kHz: 48
    DSP Included: Yes
    ADPCM Data Compression Supported: Yes
    Synthesizer Type: FM4, Wave table
    Synthesizer Chip Set: OPL4
    MIDI Interface Included: Yes
    Adlib Compatible: Yes
    Sound Blaster Compatible Via: FM Chip
    Via MPU-401 Emulation: UART
    Onboard Mixer: Yes
    CD-ROM Interface: SCSI

Turtle Beach Systems

Model: Multisound Monterey
Phone: (717) 767-0200
    Warranty: 1 Year
    Computer Interface: 16-bit ISA (AT) only
    IRQs Above 7 Supported: Yes
    DMA Channels Above 3 Supported: No
    Max Sample Rate—Recording in kHz: 44
    Max Sample Rate—Mono Playback in kHz: 44
    Max Sample Rate—Stereo Playback in kHz: 44
    DSP Included: Yes
    ADPCM Data Compression Supported: Yes
    Synthesizer Type: Wave table
    Synthesizer Chip Set: TurtleBeach/ICS
    MIDI Interface Included: Yes
    Adlib Compatible: No
    Sound Blaster Compatible Via: None
    Via MPU-401 Emulation: UART Windows only
    Onboard Mixer: Yes
    CD-ROM Interface: Information not available

Vision Enhancements

Model: Vision Sound Solution
Phone: (602) 265-5665
    Warranty: 3 Years
    Computer Interface: 16-bit ISA (AT) only
    IRQs Above 7 Supported: Yes
    DMA Channels Above 3 Supported: Yes
    Max Sample Rate—Recording in kHz: 48
    Max Sample Rate—Mono Playback in kHz: 48
    Max Sample Rate—Stereo Playback in kHz: 48
    DSP Included: Yes
    ADPCM Data Compression Supported: Yes
    Synthesizer Type: Wave table
    Synthesizer Chip Set: Oak Mozart
    MIDI Interface Included: Yes
    Adlib Compatible: Yes
    Sound Blaster Compatible Via: SW Emul
    Via MPU-401 Emulation: Information not available
    Onboard Mixer: Yes
    CD-ROM Interface: Proprietary

Wearnes Technology

Model: Beethoven ADSP-16
Phone: (408) 456-8838
    Warranty: 1 Year
    Computer Interface: 16-bit ISA (AT) only
    IRQs Above 7 Supported: Yes
    DMA Channels Above 3 Supported: Yes
    Max Sample Rate—Recording in kHz: 48
    Max Sample Rate—Mono Playback in kHz: 48
    Max Sample Rate—Stereo Playback in kHz: 48
    DSP Included: Yes
    ADPCM Data Compression Supported: No
    Synthesizer Type: Wave table
    Synthesizer Chip Set: ADI
    MIDI Interface Included: Yes
    Adlib Compatible: Yes
    Sound Blaster Compatible Via: HW Emul
    Via MPU-401 Emulation: UART
    Onboard Mixer: Yes
    CD-ROM Interface: Proprietary

Appendix C: How Sound Works

Mr. Watson, come here, I want you.

—ALEXANDER GRAHAM BELL,
March 10, 1876

At this moment, there's a plumber in my bathroom working on our house's sewer system. He's using a snake. I can hear it quite clearly, making a variety of noises: the *rrrrrr* of the motor, the *scree* of metal on metal, the *splish* of water. I can even hear the *ka-ching* of money going down the drain. Anyway, this is the perfect time to be talking about how incredible sound is and how it gets from the bathroom next door into my computer.

An Analog World

Sound starts life as vibrations. When these vibrations travel to our ear, we perceive them as sound. A tuning fork is the classic example: strike it and it vibrates. You can feel it vibrate, sometimes you can even see it vibrate. You can definitely hear it vibrate. The speed at which it vibrates is called its **frequency,** and it's measured in Hertz (abbreviated as Hz), sometimes called cycles per second. We perceive frequency as pitch—the "highness" and "lowness" of a sound.

Sound has another attribute, called **amplitude** by physicists and volume by everybody else. Amplitude is generally measured in decibels (db for short). Getting the hang of decibels is pretty hard because decibels are logarithmic, like the Richter earthquake scale. That means the difference between 1 and 2 decibels is actually smaller than the difference between 99 and 100 decibels. In any event, I think we'll all agree that 120 decibels is really loud (it's like standing on top of a jackhammer) and that 10 decibels is pretty soft (like a whisper).

So sound has two properties: frequency and amplitude. That means it's a perfect candidate for expressing on a graph. You'll see this done often, so let's get it out of the way by showing you a sine wave like the one in Figure C.1.

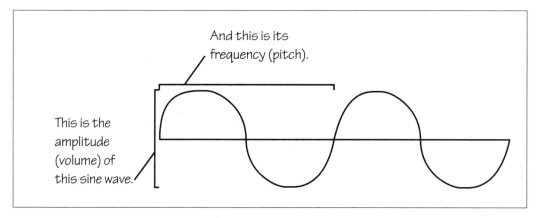

Figure C.1 A simple sine wave

The wave is the curly thing. I drew in a horizontal line to represent an axis. You figure frequency on how many times the sine wave crosses the axis, divided by two. In other words, in order to be a complete sound, the sine wave must cross the axis twice: once going up, and once going down. It sounds more complicated than it is.

The bones and skin in our ears register this nice continuous line by vibrating—little parts bang together very quickly, and our brain interprets the frequency at which they're

banged as the frequency of the sound. Something to notice
about this sine wave (aside from how horribly drawn it is) is
that it's continuous. A nice smooth line. That continuity is
referred to as an analog signal. Our ears hear that nice,
smooth line pretty well, from about 20Hz up to about
20,000Hz (or 20kHz). Beyond these two extremes, most of us
simply can't hear sounds. We may "feel" lower sounds in our
bodies, or get a headache from higher sounds, but we can't
really perceive them and identify them.

A Digital Computer

Computers (mostly) aren't analog. They're digital. That
means that computers perceive things as on or off. As we all
know, the world is seldom so unambiguous. So how does an
analog sound get into a digital computer? Two words: sample and digitize.

It works a bit like this: You say something into the microphone on your sound card. The sound card samples it (takes
periodic readings of frequency and amplitude) then digitizes
those samples. When most physics books sketch these samples, they come out looking like rectangles hiding below the
curve of the sine wave. Kind of like what's in Figure C.2.

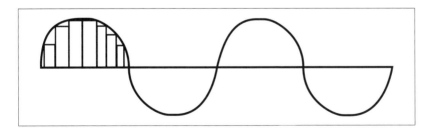

Figure C.2 Sampling a sine wave

So each of these bars has a height, right? Forgetting that
they also have width (I can't draw lines that thin), you now
have a bunch of one-dimensional measures of the sine wave.
That's easy for a computer to understand. It knows that

when the height measure falls to zero, the sine wave is crossing the axis. It knows how often it's sampling, so it knows the frequency. And, of course, it knows the height of the bar, so it knows the amplitude.

Sound Quality

The quality of a digital signal depends on how often the sound card takes a sample and how much information is stored in that sample. These two attributes are called **sample rate** and **sample size.**

Sample rate is generally measured in kHz; it ranges from 11kHz (11,000 samples a second) to 44kHz. The more frequently you take samples, the better the resemblance of the sampled sound to the original. It works like this: imagine that you're going to create a cartoon. You know (or you are about to) that the human eye can't distinguish between 30 frames per second and reality. So in order to produce a cartoon that looks smooth, you'll have to have 30 cels flipping by every second. The human ear is far more sensitive—it can distinguish up to about 50,000 samples per second—so digital sound recording devices need to run much faster than video devices.

Sample size is measured in bits, with 8 bits being the smallest allowable (below that, sounds don't really sound like sounds) and 16 bits being what's commonly called "CD-quality audio." On most sound cards I've listened to, it isn't anywhere near CD-quality audio, but let's live the myth.

So why wouldn't you take 44,000 16-bit samples every second? Because of the file size that would create. Say you want to capture just 10 seconds of sound. With a mono (single channel—good enough for voice but not much else) 8-bit, 11kHz sampling rate, that file would be 110K. Not too big. Now look at a 16-bit, stereo sample at 44kHz: 1.76MB for those same 10 seconds.

Other Sound Tricks

In addition to the sample rate and size, some sound card manufacturers are employing "3D" sound. To explain 3D sound, let's take a (very truncated) look at recording history.

In the beginning of recording, recording engineers used one microphone. When recording a symphony orchestra, for example, this caused problems because the microphone was likely stationed slightly behind the conductor—dead center in front of the orchestra. Someone playing a solo had to run up to the microphone and play directly into it. This effect is known as monaural sound, or simply mono. When you play back such a record through a modern stereo while wearing a pair of headphones, the music you'll hear will seem to coalesce somewhere in the middle of your head. The middle of your head becomes the location where the microphone was placed, so you're hearing exactly what the microphone heard. Clearly, it's not what the members of the audience heard—they had two ears, which hear in stereo.

Stereo was the next advance for recording engineers. They stationed *two* microphones in front of the orchestra, so the cellos on the right sounded distinct from the violins on the left. A much better solution, but when you listen to early stereo recordings, the sound, although separated, is very flat. That's because of something called ambient (or 3D) sound—sound that's reflected and comes from a distance.

Today, recording engineers have gotten pretty good at creating ambient sound: They virtually cover the orchestra with microphones, all of which are fed into a giant mixing panel. Thanks to careful timing, the recording engineer can create very subtle effects, so when you listen to the orchestra the violins are on the left, cellos on the right, and the clarinets are clearly sitting behind the oboes. All this with only two channels in your stereo: left and right. But how?

Like the secret to telling a great joke, the answer is timing. Even with only two microphones, you can create 3D sound.

Imagine you're in a concert hall and have set up two microphones, one at center stage left, the other at center stage right. A harpist at back stage left plays a few notes. That music reaches the left microphone and a fraction of a second later reaches the right microphone. That's called **channel separation.** A good sound card can take that timing information, couple it with all the reflected occurrences of these notes (they do bounce off the walls), and place that harp spatially during playback. The creation of this 3D effect is quite interesting, but because it runs sounds through more electronics, it can degrade the quality. For most of us, however, playing MIDI files and wave files, it will only help.

So turn on your sound card's 3D imaging effects and get set. You can hear 3D sound best through headphones, but if you only have speakers, place them about 2 feet apart, facing out.

The Practical Information

So what does all this mean for you? Basically, match your sample size and rate to the sound being recorded. If all you're doing is recording a speaking voice, 8-bit mono samples at 11kHz are fine. If you want symphonic color and texture, record at 44kHz, 16-bit stereo. There are also gradations in between. The most noticeable are the first few steps away from 8-bit, 11kHz mono. For example, recording that voice at 16-bits with the same sampling rate would only create a 220K file (for ten seconds), and it would sound much better. Double the sample rate to 22kHz and that 440K file will sound terrific.

Appendix D:
Plug and Play

Although it's not quite here as I write this appendix, Microsoft's Windows 95 is promising to make some substantial changes in how we all interact with our computers. One of the most important ways it's going to do this is with Plug and Play.

Plug and Play is a series of standards involving many hardware and software vendors. The idea is to enable users (that's you and me) to plug peripheral devices into our computers without having to think about setting IRQs, DMAs, and base memory addresses. Ideally, the Plug and Play standard will make large parts of this book obsolete.[1] I say ideally because there's a lot more to a computer than configuration.

Unfortunately, Plug and Play (or PnP for short) is going to require some drastic changes in the way hardware and software are made. See, in order for PnP to work, you need three things: a Plug and Play operating system, a Plug and Play computer (specifically, a Plug and Play BIOS), and a Plug and Play peripheral. Microsoft is solving the software problem with Windows 95; many system vendors are solving part of the hardware problem with PnP computers; and several peripheral vendors are working on PnP peripherals. Here's how it all comes together.

1. You plug a Plug and Play board, let's say a sound card, into your Plug and Play computer.

---

1. Please buy this book anyway.

2. You turn the computer on. It queries all the devices that are plugged into it to see what's there. It senses that there's a new device and asks what IRQs, DMAs, and base memory addresses it supports, then juggles that information with the requirements of all the other components. It then passes all this information off to the Plug and Play operating system (in this case, Windows 95).

3. Windows 95 reads the information and determines what drivers it needs to load for all these devices and configures the drivers properly. Since you've installed a new board, Windows 95 will either try to find previously installed drivers that it can use or it asks you to tell it where to find drivers.

4. Your system boots, with your new board ready to use.

Now doesn't that sound easier than what you've been through? It is. PnP even has the capability to handle non-PnP peripherals, for example, an old sound card. The BIOS does this by checking to see what the sound card is set at, then configuring everything else to match.

Appendix E: Buying New

There comes a time when there's nothing more you can do with what you've got. I reach that point about once an hour. With computers, the solution you'll hear most often is "Buy a new one." To many, that sounds like a silly suggestion. After all, you don't buy a new dishwasher every six or twelve months; you don't replace your car every time the ashtrays fill. So why should you replace your PC just because it's slow?

Because dishwashers aren't doubling in speed once a year, that's why. Eighteen months ago, I purchased a Dell Dimension XPS 466V. It was a wonder system: the fastest we'd ever benchmarked, great add-ons, and a nice design, to boot. And it was only $3,500. I recently started shopping for a new computer, and I've decided on the Dell Dimension XPS P90. It's twice as fast, has more memory in its base configuration, a bigger hard disk, and more extras. And it's only $3,500.

I'm not saying that you should go out right now and drop over $3,000 on a new computer. I'm saying . . . well, I guess that I *am* saying you should drop $3,000 on a new computer. If your computer is over twelve months old, it's time to start to think about your next one. Here are the steps I take before I buy.

Research the Hardware

Read every PC magazine written to see what they think about all the "modern" systems. In particular, look at *PC*

Magazine, PC Computing, and *PC World.* I'll admit that I'm biased because I work for *PC Computing,* but these three magazines review the most systems with the best benchmarks and the most critical eyes.

Of course, magazine eyes aren't all that critical. See, magazines make money on advertising—even if you pay cover price for every issue, you're barely covering printing and paper costs. (I could quote you some numbers, but I'd then have to kill you.) No, the money is made by all those glossy ads you have to thumb past in order to read the articles. If you think that the articles sound soft-pedaled, wishy-washy, or not as hard-hitting as you'd like, you're probably right. They aren't. If magazines told the absolute, nasty truth about all the stuff they reviewed, nobody would advertise and they'd go under. Not to mention the lawsuits they'd be confronted with.

There are even more subtle forms of this than blatant wishy-washiness. Here's a great example: a magazine decides to review a bunch of new computers, say 100MHz Pentium systems. How do they go about selecting? Do they perform an all-out, complete research job to find every system vendor on the market? No. They call the vendors they already know— the IBMs, DECs, Dells, and Compaqs of the world. That means you aren't hearing about Joe's Corner Computer Store. The magazine's rationale is that you don't want to buy a computer from good ol' Joe because he may go out of business next month and who'd service the computer? Okay, I can see that argument, but what happens with middle-tier vendors like Quantex? They've been around awhile, aren't going under, but don't often get reviewed. Or Packard-Bell, a vendor that sells through what's called a "channel," meaning superstores. Packard-Bell doesn't often get invited to participate in computer roundup reviews. So this is discrimination by omission.

This is not to say that magazines are all on the sides of the vendors. In particular, *PC Magazine* makes an effort to round up *every* system in a class. It then runs some of the most stringent benchmarks on the systems and writes up the results of every system. You can see why they chose a particular system as number one. If I had to choose a single computer magazine, it'd be *Mag*.

But *Mag* (and many other magazines) assume you already know exactly what you want. But do you? Whether you think so or not, I'm going to make some suggestions that will help you in the long run.

#1 Get the fastest CPU available.

If you're going to buy a new system, go first class. True, in eighteen months, it'll be completely obsolete, but at least you'll have eighteen months of good performance. The main reason you want the fastest you can get is that there's little economic reason *not* to get the fastest. Right now, $3,500 will get you a superfast system. Sure, $2,000 will get you a pretty-fast system, but you're going to be using this for at least twelve months, and in twelve months new applications will have emerged that make this pretty-fast system look slow. At least with a superfast system, it'll only degrade to pretty-fast.

My Pick: Midwest Micro Elite P5-100 or Dell Dimension XPS P100

As I write this book, Intel is shipping a 100MHz Pentium, AMD is about to release its new Pentium killer (code-named K5), Cyrix is preparing its Pentium killer (code-named M1), and Intel is readying its next generation of CPU (code-named P6). Wait until systems based on these new processors are benchmarked and see if they're really faster than the Pentium (I can only guarantee that the P6 will be). Then, if you can get a faster processor, do it.

#2 Get as much RAM as you can afford.

Graphical applications like Windows, WordPerfect for Windows, and Encarta use a lot of memory. True, they're limited by some other technical thingamadoodles (called resource heaps in Windows parlance, but that's not a discussion for here), but they still like RAM. I think 16MB is an optimal balance between performance and price. If you can get 24MB, think about it, but don't make it a buy-stopper. Beyond that, you'll probably not see much of an advantage unless you're

My Pick: 16MB

running an application like Adobe Photoshop, which can really suck up memory like there was no tomorrow.

#3 Get the fastest, biggest disk you can.

My Pick: Western Digital Caviar 31000

Get a gigabyte, get it with an access time below 12 milliseconds or a seek time below 10 milliseconds. One gigabyte is 1,000 or 1,024 megabytes (depending on who's counting). You'll fill it up. Trust me. Applications and data files (especially multimedia data files) tend to have a way of eating up hard disks like Bill Clinton munches fries. The drive I've recommended is representative of a bunch of drives from Seagate, Hewlett-Packard, and IBM, among others, that meet my criteria for adequate performance.

Do you want IDE or SCSI? I say IDE or Enhanced IDE. It's fast becoming the standard for desktop disk drives, it's easy to install, and easy to replace. And it's built onto your motherboard, so you don't have to worry about installing a second controller.

#4 Get a 16-bit sound card with wave table synthesis.

My Pick: Creative Labs Sound Blaster AWE 32

Now for the multimedia part. If you want good sound, you want 16-bit sound and wave table synthesis. The Creative Labs Sound Blaster AWE 32 has both, and it's truly Sound Blaster compatible. Why do you care? Because the Sound Blaster is the most widely supported sound card: If an application makes sound, then it supports the Sound Blaster. There are a lot of sound cards that claim Sound Blaster compatibility, but I've found a lot of them don't do it quite right. The result is that you get no sound or distorted sound. It's simpler to avoid the whole issue.

#5 Get at least a dual-speed CD-ROM drive.

My Pick: Any quad-speed drive

There are three classes of CD-ROM drives I'd consider as I write this book: dual-speed, triple-speed, and quad-speed. The last of these can support data throughput at 600K per second and has an access time of about 180 milliseconds. Compared to a disk drive, that's terrible. Compared to the original, single-speed CD-ROM drives, that's pretty good. If all you can find is a dual-speed drive, go with it, but there are plenty of quad-speed drives to be had for only a little more money. Okay, why do I drop the name brands here? Because we've tested a bunch of these and mostly they perform about the same.

#6 Get the fastest local bus graphics accelerator you can.

The "fastest" graphics accelerator title changes hands monthly, so check *PC Magazine* or *PC Computing* to see who's won the latest roundup. This card will probably come with your system when you buy it, so make sure that your system vendor has the graphics card you want. Don't settle for less. Some other killer graphics accelerators come from Matrox, so if you can't get my pick from Number Nine, get a Matrox card.

My Pick: Number Nine Imagine 128

#7 Get at least a 17-inch monitor.

Put a 15-inch monitor next to a 17-inch monitor and you'll immediately see why the latter is better: you can see more at once. That's good. Whether you prefer the Trinitron tube in the 20-inch Nanao T2-20 or the flat-square tube in the NEC 6FG (don't get the 6FGe—it's not as good) is up to you. I have grown to prefer the Trinitron's look. If you can't afford the T2-20, try the 17-inch Nanao T2-17 or the NEC 5FG. But don't bother with a 15-inch monitor, and certainly not with a 14-inch monitor. They're just not useful for running multimedia.

My Pick: Nanao T2-20

#8 Get great speakers.

I like my sound to have some real kick, and the subwoofer gives it that by accentuating the booming bass line of my favorite games. Speakers from Altec-Lansing have subwoofers, as do some from Bose and ADR. They'll be a little more expensive than the cheapies that come with the sound card, but well worth the extra dough.

My Pick: Anything with a subwoofer

Research the Price

How much are you willing to spend? I've outlined a $4,500 system up there. Chances are you aren't willing to spend that much. So where are you willing to compromise? On graphics speed? On screen size? You're going to have to pick one, then settle for less.

Once you have a price point, start calling direct vendors. Dell at (800) 338-8239, Zeos at (800) 554-7172, and Insight at (800) 327-2007 are good places to start your telephone shopping. Explain what you want, get prices, but don't give anyone a credit card number. Make sure the salesperson knows from the start of your call that you're shopping around. Get them to list part numbers and prices for everything. Have them fax you the information if you can.

Get at least three bids.

Finally, *stand firm on your requirements.* Their salespeople may try to dissuade you, but if you've read your magazines, *you know more than they do.* It's a sad truth, but most people who sell computers don't know squat about them—they know what's in stock and what they're going to get as a bonus for selling you. That's right, salespeople live on commission, and certain parts (usually what the company has overstock on) give them larger commissions. This can be particularly true with computer stores as opposed to direct vendors. They have to get rid of what's in stock.

Haggle

This is the last step. When you have prices on all the parts you want, call back the vendor who gave you the best bid and ask for your original salesperson. (Unless you really didn't like him or her, in which case, ask for anybody *but*.) Then haul out all your research and confound them with your knowledge. If a different vendor offered you a better price on a hard drive, see if the current vendor will match it. Make it seem like the whole deal hangs on that one part.

In the end, you'll wind up with the best deal on the system you want.

Index